# An Introduction [illegible]
# History of Project [illegible]

## From the Earliest Times to A.D. 1900

# An Introduction to the History of Project Management

## From the Earliest Times to A.D. 1900

Y. C. Chiu

Eburon Delft
2010

ISBN 978-90-5972-437-2

Eburon Academic Publishers
P.O. Box
2601 CW Delft
The Netherlands
tel.: +31 (0)15-2131484 / fax: +31 (0)15-2146888
info@eburon.nl / www.eburon.nl

Cover design: Studio Hermkens, Amsterdam
Cover painting: Hendrick van Cleef (1525-1589), The building of the Tower of Babel (c. 1580), Collection Kröller-Müller Museum, Otterlo, The Netherlands
Graphic design: Textcetera, The Hague

To my dear wife, Wai Kuen, my best friend and inspiration in life

# Contents

# Preface

This book is an attempt to investigate the history of project management from the earliest times to AD 1900. Project management applies knowledge, skills, tools and techniques to project activities in order to achieve defined requirements. It is the very deliberate orchestration of the areas of expertise to complete a specific project. Investigating the history of project management is to reach a comprehensive view of the historical development of the areas of expertise and their application to project activities.

This research identifies six research topics, based on the areas of project management expertise, to guide data collection and the research process. In the contribution to architecture, the research regards "building construction and engineering structures" as the application area of project management. The research considers twelve periods of architectural history that represent a 5,000-year timeline from the earliest recorded time to AD 1900, just before the two forefathers of twentieth century project management, Henry Gantt and Henri Fayol, formulated their project management tools and the core elements of knowledge for contemporary project management. In addition, the research employs twenty architectural projects to demonstrate the application of the areas of expertise to project activities.

From an analysis of the literature retrieved during chapter 2, the research presents and analyses data and obtains the results outlined in chapter 3 by investigating the development through time of the following topics at different historical periods:

1. *Historical and Cultural Environment*
2. *Knowledge and Scientific Environment*
3. *General Management*
4. *Construction Technology*
5. *Master Builder Tradition*
6. *Twenty Building Projects*

Following analysis of the results described in chapter 3, the research synthesizes and discusses the relationship between the research topics and the chosen historical periods. In this way, it produces an understanding of how project management developed from the earliest times up to AD 1900. Project management in the following eras is examined individually and studied collectively in order to attain the significant findings outlined in chapter 4:

1. *History of Project Management from the Earliest Times to the Classical Antiquity*
2. *History of Project Management of Medieval Period*
3. *History of Project Management from the Renaissance to the Industrial Revolution*

At the end of the chapter, the findings are discussed and significant conclusions are drawn in chapter 5. In addition, recommendations are made for future research study. The work reviewed in this research study has indicated that project management is as old as humankind and that ancient history reflects the development of different expertise areas and their application to various project activities.

Project management has evolved over the ages in step with the evolution of the cultural and knowledge environments of a particular historical period. General management skills, project tools, and techniques have also evolved, along with the tradition of master builders and project activities in construction. A mature cultural environment gives rise to civilisation and leads to various project activities that reflect that civilisation. Likewise, a mature knowledge environment leads to efficient management skills and sophisticated construction techniques and tools. When mature management skills, construction techniques, and tools combine, it allows a professional tradition to emerge and develop. The application of these environments, knowledge, skills, tools, techniques, and traditions to project activities make project management possible.

The hypothesis of this research is that there are circumstances at different historical periods that affect the development of the areas of expertise and their application to project activities. The significance of this study is that it adds knowledge and insight to the existing body of knowledge concerning project management prior to AD 1900. It attempts to define a template for investigation into the history of project management. The study also contributes to the development of project management as a discipline. Furthermore, it increases understanding and appreciation of the profession of project management and situates it historically.

The author would like to express his gratitude to a number of individuals for their help during the preparation of this book.Throughout the entire course of the publication process, the support provided by Eburon Academic Publishers was excellent. The author wishes to express sincere thanks to M. Fraanje, the publisher and W. Jager, the executive director. It has been a real pleasure working with them. The author would also like to express his deepest appreciation to J.S. for his helpful comments and critical evaluations of the original manuscript. Special thanks go to S.L. and T.H. for their thoughtful suggestions, proofreading and editorial improvement. Finally, the author wishes to thank his wife for her support. She is a source of inspiration to him throughout the entire period of research and writing. Her loving support and encouragement held the author steady throughtout the realization of his research objectives.

Y. C. Chiu

# Chapter 1

# Introduction

## 1.0 Background of the Study

Travellers who seek to experience the cultural heritage of a particular place often visit historical monuments built hundreds or even thousands of years ago. These ancient structures frequently display a multifaceted grandeur that at times appears to exceed contemporary construction techniques. The pyramids of ancient Egypt, for example, still stand in well-preserved form and maintain their impressive attention to detail after centuries. When examining such historical structures, travellers may wonder how they were built without the use of modern construction planning and technology. Building edifices of such magnitude and complexity must have required knowledge of planning, organisation, and technology that allowed the builders to complete the project at hand. The process must have involved some effective implementation of organisation procedures. This process, whatever it may have been, along with all of the resources pertaining to drafting, designing, and overseeing the execution of such a structure, form the basis of project management.

"Project management" was not generally used as a term until the 1950s, although its concept and practise stretch far back into history (Cleland and Gareis 5). Since time immemorial, people have collaborated to create, design, and manage construction projects. The great architectural projects of the ancient world and other magnificent structural accomplishments throughout human history provide evidence pointing to earlier forms of project management (Heldman). Since ancient times, project managers have supervised schemes that enrich the cultural heritage of a city, state, or country. The ziggurats of Mesopotamia, the pyramids of Ancient Egypt, and the Roman Colosseum, for example, bear witness to the undertakings of these managers. The buildings they constructed appear to rely as much on aesthetics as on scientific ingenuity. Yet none could have been completed without skillful project management. Ideas of project management, however rudimentary, enabled leaders to plan bold projects on a large scale and to manage the labour, materials, and financial resources needed to build to the desired schedule. The accomplishments of these past project managers are all the more impressive because they took place without sophisticated modern techniques of project management (Meyer).

Consider the construction of Noah's Ark, which historians have estimated took 120 years. Significant effort and organisation were required for a team of people to bring together the materials required to create a boat with an internal volume of 1.5 million cubic feet, let alone the technology required for their endeavours to be successful (Cleland and Ireland 11). The pyramids of Egypt also testify to a considerable management achievement. Likewise, during the third millennium BC, project managers supervised workers as they secured stones together to construct the great pyramids of Cheops. In *Project Management for Business and Engineering: Principles and Practise*, John M. Nicholas asserts that even though much of the technology the ancient Egyptians used to build pyramids remains a mystery, the enormity and quality of the finished product cannot cease to amaze those who view such marvellous edifices. Nicholas notes:

> *Despite the lack of sophisticated machinery, [the Egyptians] were able to raise and fit some 2,300,000 stone blocks, weighing two to 70 tons apiece, into a structure the height of a modern 40-story building. Each facing stone was set against the next with an accuracy of 0.04 inch, and the base, which covers 13 acres, deviates less than 1 inch from level. Equally as staggering was the number of workers involved. To quarry the stones and transport them down the Nile, about 100,000 labourers were levied. In addition, 40,000 skilled masons in attendance were employed in preparing and laying the blocks and erecting or dismantling the ramps. Public works were essential to keep the working population employed in Fayette, and it is estimated that no less than 150,000 women and children also had to be housed and fed.* (2)

The sheer magnitude of this accomplishment signifies that the Egyptians must have used disciplined and scientific project management to achieve their building aims. It is possible to educe many other examples that show the impressive nature of ancient building practises.

Thus, ancient civilisations practised the "science" of project management. Although project management did not yet claim a technical definition during those ancient projects, in practise the ancient builders understood and carried out the principles of project management. This history of building practises progressed alongside the development of other professions like architecture, medicine, economics, mathematics, and theoretical science. All of these have their own well-documented histories.

Because the term "project management" is not prevalent in ancient texts, the field of project management has been more elusive than these other professions. It has been subject to less historical investigation than one would imagine. As a result, there is a perceived gap between previous and contemporary understandings of project management. The need to bridge the gap provides the background motivation for the current investigation.

Others have noted this lacuna in synthetic research. David Cleland and Roland Gareis in their *Global Project Management Handbook* allude to the need for further research in ancient project management:

*A study of projects of the past would include an assessment of the effectiveness in management of the projects – as well as development of an informal 'lessons to be learned' profile in the conceptualization and completion of the projects. As an inventory of these profiles is developed, our knowledge of what to do in managing contemporary projects, as well as what to avoid, adds to our understanding of how project management should be carried out in both the present and the future... Only through studying the past can we fully perceive how the world has been changed by projects. A study of these projects helps us to understand how institutions have emerged and survived using a form of project management. Having a knowledge and appreciation of the past projects binds us to the present and the future. If we do not learn from the past, we are condemned to make the same mistakes and pay for those mistakes again.* (5)

These authors are aware that much of contemporary project management theory and practise lacks an historically conscious foundation. It is unaware of the development of project management through history. As a result, it is susceptible to pitfalls that could be avoided through a deeper understanding of and appreciation for the history of project management.

The current study asserts that project management deserves and requires a relevant historical exploration to fill in this gap in knowledge. This study adds perspective to present project management practise by grounding it retrospectively in a trajectory that begins in ancient civilisation. This should help project management professionals understand the original concepts of project management practise and to comprehend how project management figured in the historical, cultural, and technological contexts. The current investigation takes its mission from the belief that it is crucial for the contemporary practise of project management to foster awareness of past practises.

Based on what is known about ancient construction management, contemporary project management does not seem to differ too significantly from methods used hund-reds or thousands of years ago. Kim Heldman contends in her book, *Project Management Jumpstart,* that even though project managers have access to many tools not available during ancient days, like computers and software planning programs, the core processes employed today resemble in fundamental ways those utilised in the past (Heldman). This points importantly to the slow progress of civilisation. It also directs attention to the gradual evolution of science and building techniques over time. The lack of computer simulations and mechanized equipment did not prevent the ancients from building impressive, sturdy, and beautiful structures. A desire to know how they did this generates investigation of their methods and of the development of their social and mechanical technologies. Yet the technical application of project management has a more contemporary history that must be grasped. It is from this contemporary context of project management that this study takes its relevance.

## 1.1 The Forefathers of Project Management

In general, projects before the 1900s were led by architects and engineers assigned to the profession of master builder. There was not a separately recognized profession of project management. Common sense, determination, and hard work were the functional forces involved in construction. The work was designed and managed by a knowledgeable builder who had practical experience of building and understood the theoretical principles of design. Not until the 1900s did industrial engineers and behavioural scientists begin to investigate how work was undertaken in practise and to suggest organisational theories advocating widespread changes in procedure (Harrison and Lock 66–78). These procedural changes led to the disappearance of the master builder tradition through separation of the roles of architect and engineering project contractor.

In the early 1900s, Henri Fayol (1841–1925) and Henry Gantt (1861–1919) became the forefathers of twentieth century project management. Henri Fayol's major achievement was to delineate five primary management functions. Published in 1916 in the book *Administration Industrielle et Générale,* these were to constitute the basis of project management (Witzel 96–101). The five primary functions of management that he specified are planning, organizing, commanding, coordinating, and controlling. This theory effectively put contemporary project management on a more scientific footing.

Henry Gantt extended Fayol's theory. A significant originator of techniques for planning and control, Gantt created a project management tool called the Gantt Chart (Stevens xxii). The charts and diagrams he designed allowed processes to be charted and controlled. An example of their application occurred during the First World War in constructing ships for the U.S. Navy. Gantt documented and analysed the ship-building process step by step, which enabled him to assess and provide data about how the management functions outlined by Fayol interrelated. Gantt Charts have remained a significant aid in project management (Meyer). They have been used for major government projects, including in the construction of the Hoover Dam (1931–1936) and the U.S. interstate highway system (The Gantt Chart History). As a project management tool, their impact has been and continues to be immense.

Gantt and Fayol both drew inspiration from the theories that Frederick Winslow Taylor presented in his text *Scientific Management.* Taylor (1856–1915) anticipated current management concepts, including those of resource allocation and work breakdown. The Industrial Revolution led to worldwide expansion of business activities. The development of automation enabled more work to be undertaken more efficiently. Managing such activities successfully, including building projects, required the ability to manage resources, finances, and the workforce at different sites. Managers needed new ways of doing this faster and more effectively.

Taylor's scientific management was initially developed as a way of measuring the productivity of the workforce at a steel mill. He did not want them merely to work harder and for longer period of time, he wanted to instigate inovations in working procedures that enabled them to do their job more effectively (Meyer). He devised a method of worker incentives at the Bethlehem Steel Plant that was intended to accelerate work with cost-saving benefits. It succeeded partially and his example of scientific management entered history. Taylor spearheaded the advancement of management techniques and provided the groundwork for both Fayol's and Gantt's improvements.

Against the more modern advances in scientific project management, questions can be posed relating to the development of past projects that did not operate using a solid theory. If such scientific methods have only arisen after the Industrial Revolution, what were the methods and principles used to organize labour and to build more ancient structures? The Egyptian pyramids surely could not have been designed, and the workplace organized, without some form of effective management. The transportation of materials alone would have warranted a tremendous amount of rational organisation and technical skill, as would the erection of the massive stones. Could the Romans have built the wooden-beamed Rhine Bridge across a river 300 meters wide and 9 meters deep carrying the weight of 40,000 men, horses, and equipment in just ten days without project management? Could Gothic cathedrals have been constructed over decades out of just the right natural resources and utilising thousands of men in the absence of project management? Could Crystal Palace have been erected out of prefabricated cast-iron over a short period of only nine months without project management?

Here again lies the motivation for the present study. Given the inconceivability of such engineering and architectural feats in the past without some form of project management, the question becomes what those management principles and techniques were. Were they similar to or different from those that Taylor, Fayol, Gantt, and others influenced by the Industrial Revolution described and utilised? In other words, what body of knowledge and tools did ancient project managers access in their work without understanding the mechanics of contemporary project management?

This research project will attempt to answer such questions. Informed by an understanding of contemporary project management, it will delve into the history of project management from the earliest days. The investigation will attempt to make sense of the concepts and practises used prior to the modern scientific view of management. The intention of the research is to focus on the history of construction and management from the earliest times to the AD 1900. This study will encompass the time period up to and just before the time when the two forefathers of twentieth century project management, Henry Gantt and Henri Fayol, formulated their project management tools and the core elements of knowledge for contemporary project management. It will look at ancient projects that have left an inspiring legacy for architectural and engineering supervision without technology that is readily and inexpensively available today (Harrison and Lock, 66–78). As such, it will enable findings to be delineated and conclusions to be drawn about planning, design, leadership, materials, labour organisation, and construction technology prior to the development of the contemporary project management discipline.

## 1.2 Historical Background

Ancient civilisations developed on the banks of rivers. By 3,000 BC there were cultures settling in what is now the Middle East: in Mesopotamia, between the rivers Tigris and Euphrates (McNeil 15), and in Egypt along the banks of the river Nile (Grimal). From here, Western cultures spread. The scheme of Western history that will be followed here is commonly divided into four eras:

- *Antiquity* began with Mesopotamia and Egypt in the ancient Middle East and spread throughout the Mediterranean basin up to about the fifth century AD (Sasson).
- The *Middle Ages* constitute the time from the fifth through the fifteenth centuries AD (Fordham).
- The *Early Modern* period includes the European Renaissance and stretches from the fifteenth century to about the mid-eighteenth century AD (Rice).
- The *Late Modern* period moves from the Industrial Revolution, beginning about the mid-eighteenth century AD and extending into the present age.

These four time periods of Western history form the overarching temporal framework for this investigation. Within this broad timetable, many events took place that shaped the particular characteristics of the minor ages. For example, the fall of the Roman Empire around AD 476 marked the end of antiquity and the beginning of the European Middle Ages. Nevertheless, the continuance of the Byzantine Empire meant that knowledge of the ancient Western world was not entirely lost during the Middle Ages. In addition, such knowledge was significantly developed by the Arabs during the contemporaneous Islamic Golden Age (Lewis 3). Later, the Arabs brought ancient knowledge and new technology alike from the Middle East to the West, in what has been termed “one of the largest technology transfers in world history” (Middle Ages-Encyclopedia Britannica). In the mid-fifteenth century AD, Johannes Gutenberg invented modern printing that employed movable type. This revolutionized communication and helped to end the Middle Ages (Man). Out of this the European Renaissance (Burckhardt) and the Scientific Revolution (Grant) ushered in the modern era. By the eighteenth century AD, the accumulation of knowledge and technology in Europe had reached a critical mass, which brought about the Industrial Revolution (More).

This basic sketch will be filled out in much greater detail later in this study. Against this historical background, project management produced buildings and artefacts that were evidence of this wide cultural inheritance. Over 5,000 years after the development of civilisations by the banks of rivers, the growth of knowledge, techniques, tools, and skills accelerated. Leaders over the years in different cultural settings inspired the completion of various projects. These enhanced the human environment and in turn inspired the communities living there. These buildings and projects contribute greatly to world history. It is important for an understanding of human history to comprehend how construction produced cultural monuments over the centuries. Appreciating the history of construction technology and managem is a crucial field and task for history in general.

## 1.3 Project, Project Management, and Project Manager

Studying the history of project management requires a firm grasp of definitions. This study begins with the present world while casting light on the past. Therefore, the notions of project, project management, and project manager will be explained in the senses that they are typically understood to have today.

The origin of the word "project" is the Latin *projectum*, itself stemming from the Latin verb *proicere* meaning "to throw something forward." The prefix *pro-* indicates a behaviour or action that comes before something else. Preceding *iacere*, "to throw," "project" initially meant "something that comes before anything else happens" or something "thrown before." The word *management* is of more recent origin. It evolved from the Italian *maneggiare*, "to handle." This refers especially to the use of the hand, since it comes from the Latin *manus*, or "hand" (Oxford English Dictionary).

This study defines a project as a temporary activity with the aim of producing a unique physical product or service. Temporary means that the product or service has clearly defined starting and ending points. To be considered a project, the endeavour must be unique in the sense that it is definably different from comparable products or services. Examples of different projects include:

- Developing a new product or service,
- Effecting a change in the structure, staffing, or style of an organization,
- Developing or acquiring a new or modified information system,
- Constructing a building or infrastructure, or
- Implementing a new business process or procedure. (PMBOK Guide ch1)

Therefore, a project is an activity with the aim of producing a unique physical product or service and with defined starting and ending points. The objective of a project is typically to effect a desired change or to add value (Chartfield). Because a project is temporary, it can be contrasted to activities that are repeating, permanent, or ongoing in some respects. It can also be contrasted with activities whose prime function is to continually produce products or services. Although they may appear superficially to be similar, these two kinds of activities are managed in different ways and with different styles, requiring the utilisation of particular skills and techniques (Dinsmore 35).

Project management will be defined as in the *Project Management Body of Knowledge Guide* as the application of knowledge, skills, tools, and techniques to project activities in order to meet project requirements (PMBOK Guide ch1). This definition is general and can be applied to historical as well as current projects. It is not dependent on contemporary observation or on the definition of a particular project. The building projects of history all fall within this broad definition and are amenable to analysis as projects.

The *PMBOK Guide* recommends that project requirements are met through the application and integration of various process groups and knowledge areas. The project management process groups are initiating, planning, executing, monitoring and controlling, and closing (PMBOK Guide ch3). The project management knowledge areas are management of integration, scope, time, cost, quality, human resource, communication, risk, and procurement (PMBOK Guide ch4-12). From this perspective, project management involves:

- Identifying requirements;
- Addressing the various needs, concerns and expectations of the stakeholders as the project is planned and carried out; and
- Balancing the competing project constraints including, but not limited to, scope, quality, schedule, budget, resources and risk (PMBOK Guide ch1).

The primary challenge of project management is the achievement of all of the project's goals and objectives while remaining within project constraints (Philips 354), such as scope, time, and budget. Project management also incorporates allocation and integration of resources in the best way to meet the objectives that have been predefined (Chartfield).

It is important to clarify what project management is, since without such a notion, this study would operate outside of a well-defined terrain related directly to present-day management concepts. The historical research is guided by the assumption that past architectural projects can be valuably analysed through the lens of contemporary project management. This does not affect the interpretation of historical events except insofar as it places them within this framework of relevance.

Finally, a project manager can be defined as the person responsible for accomplishing the project objectives within the project constraints (PMBOK Guide ch1). He or she controls the assigned project resources and balances the constraints of scope, quality, schedule, budget, resources, and risk during the project to meet the project objectives in the most effective way. The project manager directs the project in response to uncertainty about what issues may arise. It is incumbent upon the project manager to understand the culture of the organisation undertaking the project. This ensures that project management is appreciated as a valuable activity and that sufficient accountability and authority are provided to enable the project to be achieved.

Although contemporary project management developed only recently as an academic discipline, and although it stems from different areas, including building, engineering, and military operations (Cleland and Gareis ch.1), it is not anachronistic to use it as a construct for analyzing the past. All concepts or analytical categories applied to history arise out of a contemporary standpoint. While the historical data must stand for themselves, the ideas used to organize them can appropriately come from present modes of understanding project management. Therefore, when looking at past building practises, the notion of project management can usefully serve as a guideline. Equally, the researcher must be sensitive to the fact that different cultures and projects in history may have had different understandings of project management than the contemporary one.

## 1.4 Areas of Expertise and History of Project Management

As just indicated, project management is the application of knowledge, skills, tools, and techniques to project activities to meet project requirements. The terms "knowledge, skills, tools and techniques" are well explained in the third edition of the *PMBOK Guide*:

> *Much of the knowledge and many of the tools and techniques for managing projects are unique to project management, such as work breakdown structures, critical path analysis, and earned value management. However, understanding and applying the knowledge, skills, tools, and techniques, which are generally recognized as good practise, are not sufficient alone for effective project management. Effective project management requires that the project management team understand and use knowledge and skills from at least five areas of expertise:*
> 1. *The Project Management Body of Knowledge*
> 2. *Project environments*
> 3. *General management skills*
> 4. *Interpersonal skills.*
> 5. *Knowledge of Application Area (ch1)*

### 1.4.1 Project Management Body of Knowledge

The Project Management Body of Knowledge outlines knowledge that is specific to the field of project management and that also occurs in other management disciplines. The *PMBOK Guide* describes knowledge in this context as consisting of:
- Project life cycle definition
- Five Project Management Process Groups
- Nine Knowledge Areas

### 1.4.2 Project Environments

Projects lead to consequences that are both intended and unintended, positive and negative, and are invariably conceived and undertaken within a particular context. The project team needs to understand the impact of the cultural, social, international, political, and physical environmental context on their project:
- *Cultural and social environment*
  Project activities are undertaken within various economic, demographic, educational, ethical, ethnic, and religious contexts, which need to be appreciated by the project team.
- *International and political environment*
  The team also needs to be aware of relevant international, national, regional, and local regulations and customs, as well as the political climate in which the project activities are performed.

- *Physical environment*
  The local ecology and physical geography may also have an impact that should not be ignored.

### 1.4.3 General Management Skills

General management can be defined as planning, organizing, staffing, executing, and controlling the operations of an organisation. Other functions are involved, such as finance, law, manufacturing, distribution, strategic and operational planning, and organisational development. Project management is a subset of general management, and project managers require a diversity of such skills at their disposal.

### 1.4.4 Interpersonal Skills

Project managers need to manage relationships, which involves the following:
- *Effective communication*
  Being able to exchange information effectively and in such a way that it is understood
- *Leadership*
  Constructing a vision and a strategy in which people are engaged and which they are motivated to achieve
- *Motivation*
  Empowering people to perform to the best of their ability and to overcome obstacles as they arise

### 1.4.5 Knowledge of Application Area

Projects can be divided among application areas, each of which represents a particular category that has various important common elements. Each application area follows particular standards and practises, often defined by regulation. Application areas may be relevant for:
- Functional departments and supporting disciplines, such as production logistics and marketing
- Technical elements, such as construction engineering
- Management specializations, such as new product development
- Industry groups, such as chemicals

Although these five areas of expertise are considered separately, they also coincide and cannot be taken in isolation. Effective project management involves their seamless integration. Project team members do not have to be expert in all five areas; indeed, such breadth of expertise would be unlikely. Nevertheless, the members of the team should be chosen to provide between them all the knowledge and skills required (PMBOK Guide 3rd Edition ch1).

It is important that the definition of project management is understood in order for its history to be considered, although they are distinct. In this study, the history of project management is seen as the history of the areas of expertise and their application to project activities in different historical periods.

## 1.5 Research Parameters

### 1.5.1 Research Topics

To investigate the history of project management, one needs to understand the historical development of the areas of expertise and their application to the activities of historical projects. The premise of this study derives from the notion of "areas of expertise and their application to project activities." It applies this concept to a particular field of history; namely, the history of construction from early times to AD 1900. This serves to guide the conduct of the historical research and questioning. Falling within these parameters are the following considerations:

1. Project Management Body of Knowledge (PMBOK)
   Since the historical development of the PMBOK is a twentieth-century event, it is not within the scope of this research study.
2. Project Environments
   The research focuses mainly on the following topics:
   - Historical and cultural environment
   - Knowledge and scientific environment
3. General Management
   The research combines general management and interpersonal skills as one topic.
4. Interpersonal Skills *(Refer to item 3)*
5. Knowledge of the Application Area
   In the contribution to architecture, the research regards *building construction and engineering structures* as the application area. In particular, the research focuses mainly on knowledge of the following topics:
   - Construction technology
   - The master builder tradition
6. Application of the Expertise Areas to the Project Activities
   The research employs building examples to demonstrate this topic.

### 1.5.2 Research Timeline

The study is conducted in the significant historical periods represented by the four main eras of the Western history (antiquity, middle ages, early modern, and late modern). In addition, early forms of project management are investigated in different geographical regions for each of the main eras (Mesopotamia, Greece, etc.). The study nuances these four main eras based on the history of architecture, following the timeline of the 12 periods of *architectural history* from the earliest time to AD 1900. These historical periods are:

1. *Mesopotamia (30th to 5th century BC)*
2. *Ancient Egypt (30th to 7th century BC)*
3. *Ancient Greece (7th century BC to 2nd century BC)*
4. *Roman Empire (1st century BC to 5th century AD)*
5. *Byzantine Empire (4th to 15th century)*
6. *Islamic Golden Age (8th to 13th century)*
7. *Crusades (11th to 13th century)*
8. *Romanesque (11th to 13th century)*
9. *Gothic (13th to 15th century)*
10. *Renaissance (15th to 17th century)*
11. *Baroque (17th to 18th century)*
12. *Industrial Revolution (18th to 19th century)*

### 1.5.3 Project Activities

The research employs the following ancient buildings to demonstrate the application of the areas of expertise to the project activities of the 12 historical periods of architectural history:

1. *Great Ziggurat of Ur (2100 BC)*
2. *Tower of Babylon (around 600 BC)*
3. *Hanging Gardens (around 600 BC)*
4. *Giza Pyramid in Ancient Egypt (2580–2560 BC)*
5. *Parthenon in Ancient Greece (477–438 BC)*
6. *Caesar's Rhine Bridge (55 BC)*
7. *Colosseum of Roman Empire (70–82 AD)*
8. *Pantheon of Roman Empire (118–126 AD)*
9. *Hagia Sophia of Byzantine Empire (532–537 AD)*
10. *Grand Mosque of Damascus (706–715 AD)*
11. *Krak des Chevaliers, Syria (1144–1250 AD)*
12. *Pisa Cathedral (1063–1180 AD)*
13. *Notre Dame de Paris (1163–1345 AD)*
14. *Dome of Florence Cathedral (1420–1436 AD)*
15. *Santa Maria Novella (1456–1470 AD)*
16. *St Peter's Basilica (1506–1626 AD)*
17. *St Paul's Cathedral (1668–1697 AD)*
18. *Menai Straits Suspension Bridge (1819–1826 AD)*
19. *Crystal Palace (June 1850–May 1851 AD)*
20. *Eiffel Tower (1887–1889 AD)*

These twenty buildings have been selected as key representatives of the major architectural periods within which they were built. They are only a sample from among many possible choices. From this sample empirical evidence of building practises and management techniques will be used to make the study's argument. These buildings are taken as emblematic and pivotal since each contributed significantly to the development of architectural and engineering practise.

## 1.6 Research Questions and Hypothesis

The premise of the study is that a history of project management requires exposition up to the nineteenth century. Such a broad exposition requires historical support which, while it cannot be extensive, must be significant and indicative enough to ground the research solidly in historical conditions. The hypothesis of the research is that there are circumstances at different historical periods that affect the development of the areas of expertise and their application to project activities. These circumstances include social and cultural movements, the development of scientific and technical knowledge within an historical period, the organisation of labour and management, and the development of technology, tools, materials, and skills. Using the division of history and the twenty specific buildings selected as representative of significant developments in project management, the research poses a number of specific questions that attempt to confirm or deny this hypothesis. These questions serve to guide the process of data gathering and provide the lens through which the data are analysed and interpreted.

The constellation of questions that drives this historical investigation is the following:

*What was the historical development in the following six areas during each specific historical period selected for analysis?*

1. *Historical and Cultural Environment*
2. *Knowledge and Scientific Environment*
3. *General Management and Interpersonal Skills*
4. *Construction Technology*
5. *The Master Builder Tradition*
6. *The Twenty Building Projects*

This constellation of questions may be further elaborated as follows. For each period in which the projects were performed:

- The historical and cultural environment represents the *cultural environment* in which the project activities are performed;
- The knowledge and scientific environment represents the *knowledge environment* that facilitated problem solving, decision making, and the development of the right skills and tools to get the projects done;
- General management represents the organisational and interpersonal *skills* to complete the projects;

- Construction technology represents the *techniques and tools* used to execute the project;
- The master builder tradition represents the *professional tradition* employed to manage the projects;
- The twenty building projects represent supporting examples and empirical historical evidence of *project activities.*

In the quest for credible answers to the research questions, the history of project management prior to AD 1900 will be traced and detailed using these six topics as directives. It is the application of these environments, knowledge, skills, techniques, tools, and traditions in project management, development, and execution that make project management possible. It is anticipated that significant findings will be uncovered in support of the above hypothesis. To understand the historical development of the areas of expertise and their application to project activities, the history of project management as it has unfolded offers crucial and hitherto undetected insights into the progression of management and the technologies used in architectural construction.

## 1.7 Data Collection and Analytic Method

### 1.7.1 Data Collection

The data used for this study is largely qualitative, not quantitative. The reason for this is that the ancient history of building methods is accessible primarily through qualitative investigation. Qualitative research is interpretive in nature. It is a type of documentary research that is well-suited to this type of study, since it is in essence an interpretive historical review. This historical review was conducted by means of an extensive survey of the literature pertaining to construction and management in the historical areas outlined for the study. The historical review covered many areas of background that are important for understanding the development and evolution of building practises. As a result, it will venture briefly into the general cultural background of each era, including such aspects as scientific knowledge and political management theories. Although based in architecture, the research also focused on the implications of literary and historical data for the project management of construction and engineering.

Information and data was collected through a review of the literature rather than through practical archaeology of buildings. Sources included scholarly and professional journals, books, periodicals, and other reports on historical project management prior to AD 1900. This study uses descriptive-normative research to record, describe, interpret, analyse, and compare the data collected. A literature review was conducted for the twelve significant historical-architectural periods given above, organized into the constellation of six primary topics of inquiry as listed.

Moreover, secondary data was also be utilised to provide more knowledge about the topic. Books about project management history and practises were employed as references and academic journals were also be consulted. The Internet proved to be of additional help in the information-gathering process. Other means of collecting secondary data were used as much as possible, with the proviso that these sources were reliable and helpful in the analysis of the topic. The sources of information/data the researcher accessed include:

- *Online Libraries: Questia, Highbeam*
- *Internet Search Engines: Google, Bing*
- *Web sites: Noted in Works Cited list*
- *Books and Journals - Noted in Works Cited list*

### 1.7.2 Obtaining Results

After analyzing the literature included in chapter 2, the researcher presents and analyses data and obtains results by conducting an investigation into the historical development of the following topics at different historical periods:

1. *Historical and Cultural Environment*
2. *Knowledge and Scientific Environment*
3. *General Management*
4. *Construction Technology*
5. *Master Builder Tradition*
6. *Twenty Building Projects*

The research topics related to the areas of expertise and their application to the project activities were previously identified in this chapter as the above six topics. In practise, these items are closely interrelated and interact to form project management as a whole; they are separated here and throughout chapter 4 only for ease of presentation. Through a careful study of events and practises related to these research topics, the researcher is able to trace circumstances at different historical periods that affect the development of the areas of expertise and their application to project activities. Through an understanding the historical development of the areas of expertise and their application to project activities, the history of project management can be detailed and unfolded.

### 1.7.3 Obtaining Findings

By analyzing the results obtained in chapter 3, the researcher discusses and evaluates the different eras and historical periods in an attempt to gain an understanding of how project management developed from the earliest times up to AD 1900. The following eras will be examined individually and studied as a group to produce the significant findings of chapter 4.

1. *The History of Project Management from the Earliest Times to the Classical Antiquity*
2. *The History of Project Management of the Medieval Periods*
3. *The History of Project Management from the Renaissance to the Industrial Revolution*

In the quest for credible answers to the research questions and in order to arrive at significant findings, the history of project management prior to AD 1900 is traced and detailed in three distinct periods.

### 1.7.4 Drawing Conclusions

Based on analysis of the evidence obtained in chapter 4, the researcher studies and summarizes the findings and draws significant conclusions in chapter 5, as well as makes recommendations for future research on the history of project management.

The hypothesis of the research is that there are circumstances at different historical periods that affect the development of the areas of expertise and their application to project activities. Through an understanding of the historical development of the areas of expertise and their application to project activities, the history of project management can be portrayed.

The above defines the scope of this research study. It may be summarized as the investigation of the history of project management throughout the significant turning points in Western architectural history. Because of its ambitious scope, this research will include interdisciplinary studies of history, architecture, construction technology, engineering, management, and science where it is deemed necessary for a full understanding of the context and practise of project management.

## 1.8 Objective and Significance of the Study

The research in this study takes an investigative journey through the history of project management from the earliest times to the turn of the twentieth century. It stops just before the two forefathers of twentieth century project management, Gantt and Fayol, formulated the core elements of project management. The objective of the research is to gain insights into the more ancient project management areas of expertise that were utilised by earlier civilisations to carry out their project activities efficiently. In other words, it aims to reveal pre-eighteenth century project methods through an historical examination. Such an investigation will place contemporary project management on a more solid historical footing.

The research fulfils the following three objectives:

*Objective 1*

- *Conduct an extensive review of the literature to address each of the aforementioned research questions.*
- *Present information retrieved for the literature review section in a thematic form.*

*Objective 2*

- *Analyse information retrieved during the literature review.*
- *Present results from the information analysed with a number of figures and tables.*

*Objective 3*

- *Present findings and determine the validity of the study's hypothesis.*
- *Present conclusions derived from the study and make recommendations for future study.*

Following these objectives through will contribute to answering the research questions posed in this study and to confirming the validity of the hypothesis.

The bulk of the research lies in the next chapter, which presents the historical data used for the analysis and discussion of later chapters. The significance of this research lies in the knowledge that will be added to the existing body of knowledge concerning project management prior to AD 1900. This study attempts to establish a template for investigation into the history of project management. In addition, the research contributes to the growth of project management as a discipline. It helps to increase knowledge about the profession of project management and its historical development.

## 3. Contribution to Western Civilisation

Mesopotamia boasted numerous developments that are not known to have previously existed. Among the most important were the invention of cuneiform writing and record keeping; basic architecture including city planning and the building of ziggurats; the establishment of domestication techniques for flora and fauna; the bases of religion, myth, and literature; the establishment of legislation with the Code of Hammurabi around eighteenth century BC; the formation of formal government with economic rules and regulations; technologies like copper working, glass making, water storage, and irrigation; and, finally, a formal medical system including written diagnosis and planning (Museum, 2009). All of these were significant for future civilisation. For example, the invention of writing changed economic practises by making possible record keeping and a documented financial system (Buccellati 35–47). This system of writing led to further advances in literature and religion, since it provided a way to pass down cultural activities and traditions through the generations in addition to oral transmission (Woods). In terms of civilisation, therefore, the Mesopotamians contributed much that was valuable.

### 2.1.2 Knowledge and Scientific Environment

The Mesopotamian people possessed a thirst for knowledge. From their beginnings around 3500 BC, they kept thorough and detailed observations of the world with numerical data. For instance, a concrete tablet that gives Pythagoras' law has been dated to as early as the eighteenth century BC (Hoffman 18). Clearly, they valued mathematical and astronomical information.

The Mesopotamians did not stick solely to mathematical advances. They were responsible for many notable inventions that are used even to this day. For example, they invented the wheel in 3500 BC, possibly the most important technological advance of all time (*Ancient Mesopotamia: Science & Inventions*). The wheel revolutionized transportation. According to the same source, the Mesopotamians also created the seeder plough, which reinvented agriculture by making possible both seeding and ploughing at the same time. They were also innovators in such diverse fields as copper working, water storage, irrigation, textile weaving, and glass making (Faiella 8–31). Moreover, they "discovered that by observing the movements of celestial bodies they could measure time, which was key for planting crops and for holding religious festivals" (Ancient Mesopotamia: Science & Inventions). According to Scofield, Mesopotamian astronomy permitted agricultural society to develop a calendar. As a result, crop growing and harvesting were optimized. Their technological achievements were prolific.

The astute astronomical observations of the Mesopotamians are still used today by scientists. Moreover, they influenced Western concepts of a seven-day week, a lunar month, and a solar year, in addition to the names of the planets (Scofield). There was no separation between astronomy and astrology at that time. The stars were studied for omens. Some 1,500 years later, Al-Batani used the collected horoscope and omen information to calculate the Earth's axis, citing it as being 54.5 arc-seconds per annum. The value currently estimated by scientists is 49.8 arc-seconds per annum. Clearly, then, the Mesopotamians' information was accurate. Babylonian astronomy influenced decisively all Greek, Indian, Islamic, and Western exact sciences (Aaboe 21–42).

Furthermore, the Mesopotamians devised the origins and rudiments of philosophy. Their wisdom incorporated such spheres as ethics, while their reasoning and rationality extended far beyond empirical observation (Buccellati 35–47). This philosophy laid the foundations for a revised approach to astronomy in the eighth and seventh centuries BC as astronomers began to study philosophy to gain an understanding of the universe. They combined their planetary system with an internal logic. In the philosophy of science, this Mesopotamian advance has been called the first scientific revolution by a number of scholars (Brown).

The Mesopotamians were also instrumental in medicine. In the medical field, they introduced procedures that remain part of modern-day treatment, such as prescriptions, diagnosis, physical examinations, and prognosis. Their most extensive medical text, the *Diagnostic Handbook*, explains therapeutic methods, disease aetiology, diagnostic symptoms of illness, and prognosis (Horstmanshoff, Stol and Tilburg 97–8).

Given all this, there can be no doubt that the Mesopotamians were people of vast intelligence, creating ideas and objects that not only helped them, but have remained in use over the millennia and continue to be an integral part of our societal structure.

### 2.1.3 General Management

Basic management techniques originated in the commercial system developed around 5000 BC, when Sumerian priests began to keep written records of business transactions. Writing allowed priests and farmers to keep inventories of their livestock, products, grain yields, land ownership, and temple tithes. Priests had to give formal accounts to the chief priest of all the transactions and payments of which they were in control, in a form of temple management rather than for religious purposes (George).

The Code of Hammurabi (eighteenth century BC) was the first important legal record of humans granting contracts, rights given to families and individuals, and primitive concepts of utilitarianism and the segregation of rights (Van De Mieroop). Hammurabi's law codified the underlying social structure, organisation, and managerial philosophy of Mesopotamia. Society was stratified into three distinct classes: nobles (government officials, priests, and warriors), freeman (merchants, artisans, professionals, wealthy farmers), and slaves. This code showed a commitment to justice, although the severity of criminal punishment was based on the class of the individual offended. The code regulated the duties of government officials. For instance, if a public official failed to catch a burglar, he was liable to replace the lost property. Builders were held responsible for their construction work. If the collapse of a house led to injury or death for its owner, the builder was executed. While certainly a patriarchal code determined by clearly segregated social classes (Kreis), the Code of Hammurabi was important as the first known legal instrument used in social management with relevance for building.

The Mesopotamian code established controls by documenting business activities and employing witnesses to provide evidence of activities or verbal agreements (George). It demonstrated a commitment to order that was crucial for the advancement of an agrarian society. Further, it allowed the progression of commerce through written methods used by merchants and craftspeople. Without writing, even if done on a perishable medium (Saggs 63), a stable commercial and agrarian economy would have been difficult to preserve.

### 2.1.4 Construction Technology

Out of developments in written communication and mathematics, Mesopotamian civilisation enabled the advance of construction technology. Its people built dwellings and temples, sometimes decorating them with geometric mosaics. The Babylonians developed approximations to algorithmic rules. This mathematics was important for building projects. In terms of materials for building, the Mesopotamians used what was available to them from the land. Another key factor for growth in construction efforts was the development of bronze and iron, which resulted in stronger tools and led to greater building opportunities.

### 1. Mud Brick

When the first permanent settlers inhabited the Tigris–Euphrates region, they built their dwellings out of marsh reeds bound together and layered on the outside with mud plastering. This changed with advancements in the manufacture of sun-dried mud bricks, which became the staple building material for Mesopotamian dwellings and temples (Bilkadi 2–9). Both the climate and the natural resources determined building styles and materials. Timber was not readily available in this environment. Therefore, mud bricks were used to construct arches, columns, domes, and walls. This was a natural choice. The industry that provided such bricks thrived alongside the developing size and scope of the first Bronze Age civilisations (Darby). The huge Babylonian temples are constructed out of bricks supported by buttresses and have drains which are sometimes made of lead. Pilasters and columns were early developments enables by the use of bricks, and frescoes and enamelled tiles were also employed. Sometimes walls were brightly coloured by painted tiles or plated with zinc or gold. Assyrian palaces and temples were also made of brick, even though stone was the northern country's material of choice.

With the introduction of agriculture, people required stable homes in a fixed location near the fields. This resulted in the foundation of towns, cities, laws, and government, which led to the proliferation of civic projects. As a result of this demand, building technology was an area of progressive knowledge. For example, geosynthetic reinforced soil developed out of mud brick building (Brown). Geosynthetic reinforcement refers to adding and/or layering reinforcement in the soil in order to stabilize it. Straw and bitumen were added to the clay as the reinforcement (International Finance Corporation of the World Bank Group). Bitumen is a naturally occurring organic substance, often referred to as tar. With this new material, the bricks changed from a loaf shape to a planoconvex shape and were baked in kilns. Another advance was made by using bitumen not only as an adhesive but for waterproofing in the layering of the bricks (Moorey 83–98). This increased the durability of the mud brick construction during rain and floods.

## 2. Barrel Vault and Reinforced Brick

The availability of bricks probably led to the development of tunnel vaulting, or barrel vaulting, in the construction of the Mesopotamian ziggurats. The paucity of wood led to the innovation of using bricks as a supporting mechanism for tunneling. The bricks were arranged along a given line in a circular or semi-circular shape (Roth). The concept of vaulting took on new dimensions during the construction of massive European cathedrals and public works (Faiella). Its origins lie in Mesopotamia.

## 3. Pump and Wheel

The Archimedes screw was the first water pump, and was employed by King Sennacherib of Assyria to irrigate the Hanging Gardens of Babylon in the seventh century BC. Archimedes provided a later description in the third century BC (Dalley and Oleson). The pump was important for water systems and for buildings such as gardens that required pumped-in water.

Mesopotamia was also the site of the invention of the wheel in the fifth millennium BC (Ubaid period). This archetypal invention was initially employed for a potter's wheel at Ur in Mesopotamia as far back as 3500 BC. It seems to have found an industrial application before being used on vehicles (Sax, Meeks and Collon 157–76), for example on Mesopotamian chariots around 3200 BC. The wheel can be considered as the most significant of all mechanical inventions and was of inestimable importance to human society. Nearly every machine developed since has involved a wheel. It is difficult to envisage achieving any mechanized activity without a wheel or the idea of circular motion (Yenne and Grosser). In the Industrial Revolution, the wheel became the fundamental element of mechanics (Wilson 1–32).

In summary, a confluence of factors ranging from agricultural settlement and city building to commerce and religion combined to produce the first platform on which building technology and project management could develop. Mesopotamia produced some crucial inventions, such as writing, legal organisation, the wheel, and the pump. These had an impact on work organisation and materials transportation. In terms of structures, the Mesopotamians used mud brick to build the first barrel vaults and irrigation systems employing the innovation of the water pump. As a result, ancient

Mesopotamia was a source of enduring construction technology with a legacy that is still influential in modern-day construction practises (Bilkadi 2–9). The example of the ziggurats and hanging gardens will clearly demonstrate the building prowess of the Mesopotamians.

### 2.1.5 Master Builder Tradition

Before the existence of master builders in design and construction, the Code of Hammurabi referred to building as a simple process. Produced approximately between 1792–1750 BC, this is the first known building code. Its rules and responsibilities and acceptable standards of workmanship were carved on stone tablets. Failure to adhere to these standards led to stiff and sometimes fatal penalties (Jackson 5).

The Code addressed the work of a master builder. It is interesting in that it viewed faulty design and improper construction as one unit (Beard, Loulakis and Wundrum 13). Five specific laws were geared towards the builder:
- If a builder builds a house for someone, does not construct it properly, and the house which he built falls in and kills its owner, then that builder shall be put to death;
- If it kills the son of the owner, the son of the builder shall be put to death;
- If it kills a slave of the owner, then he shall pay slave for slave to the owner of the house;
- If it ruins goods, he shall make compensation for all that has been ruined and inasmuch as he did not construct properly this house which he built and it fell, he shall re-erect for the house from his own means;
- If a builder builds a house for someone, even though he has not yet completed it; If then the walls seem toppling, the builder must make the walls solid from his own means. (Beard, Loulakis and Wundrum 15)

It is clear that some sort of established building tradition was referred to here, although it is not clear precisely what this tradition was. Nevertheless, it was demonstrably urban and comprised a form of social status. There was a rise in status for the most experienced of the builders and they would come later to be designated "master builders." The builders gained greater skill with the demands of urbanization and civic projects. Those cities with advanced opportunities for builders would become civilisations with construction at the center (Jackson 5).

### 2.1.6 Building Projects

#### 1. Great Ziggurat of Ur (ca 2100 BC)

The Great Ziggurat of Ur is the best preserved of the Mesopotamian tower-shrines. Its dimensions are 200 by 150 feet and its height is estimated at 70 feet (not including the temple shrine at the top, which no longer exists). McIntosh describes it as a -three-tiered, inwardly sloping structure with platforms at each stage and a triple staircase on one side going to the sanctuary on top (McIntosh 201–2). Supported by inscriptions from a later date, scholars believe this monument was built during the reign of Ur-Nammu (ca. 2114–2096 BC), who undertook an extensive restoration and building program (Klein and Klein 36).

In terms of construction, it was likely built in distinct graduated stages, with each platform providing the working area for the next. A stele depicts a busy construction scene, with workers on ladders carrying picks and mortar baskets, and the king himself carrying tools such as a measuring rod and line (Foster and Foster 62). This give some indication of how the building was constructed and that it was commissioned and overseen by the king.

What is impressive about the ziggurat in the history of architecture is the height it achieved. While the technology used to build ziggurats is a mystery, it must have involved intensive human labour and the use of ramps to build upward. The labour gangs were probably drawn from the peasantry and slaves, the same people who built roads, temples, and irrigation canals (McIntosh 83). Closely supervised temple tithes and palace taxes paid for the construction.

Like other ziggurats, the inner core was built of sun-dried bricks while the eight-foot outer layer was made of kiln-fired bricks of two kinds (Klein and Klein 34). This construction made it strong, durable, and time resistant. The priestly shrine on top was dedicated to the worship of the moon god Nanna-Sin, and was likely considered a portal for the gods to descend to earth.

Besides the building's immense size, it is important architecturally for its ingenious drainage system. The Chaldeans knew that bricks swelled in rain and could burst the walls of the ziggurat. Therefore, they pierced the walls with drainage ducts through which interior moisture could pass through. This innovation worked in conjunction with layers of reed matting at every seven courses of stone and with bitumen from pitch or crude petroleum used as mortar to waterproof the building (McIntosh 237). The structure was thus preserved from water damage. It was rebuilt by Nabonidus later, but must have deteriorated after the Persian defeat in 539 BC.

## 2. Tower of Babylon (ca 600 BC)

Scholars have come to view the Tower of Babel mentioned in Genesis 11 as the ziggurat of the temple of Marduk in Babylon (known as Etemenanki) (Foster and Foster 64). It was probably the most magnificent ziggurat of all. Scholars are uncertain who built the Temple of Marduk, but they are certain that Esarhaddon and Asshurbanipal refurbished it repeatedly, along with its ziggurat.

Any notion that the Tower of Babel is an example of a failure of project management and of communication breakdowns stems from the biblical text. There is evidence that the structure was finished, but this idea of project mismanagement is important in signalling the length of time the project took to come to fruition (over the reign of many kings), its constant rebuilding and renovation, and the labour force used to build it, which would have consisted largely of conquered slaves from various lands who would have spoken different languages. Thus, the project would have been difficult to manage because project managers may not have possessed the ability to communicate with those in the labour force who did not speak Babylonian. One can imagine the potential confusion on the worksite.

It was not until around 600 BC that this ziggurat received its definitive and most impressive expression – growing to either seven or eight tiers with a base and a height of 300 square feet – under the building program of Nebuchadnezzar that included the Ishtar Gate and Processional Way. According to McIntosh, "the Etemenanki, the precinct containing the 'Tower of Babel,' was also fortified" (McIntosh 109). Thus appears the notion of building defended religious structures. During this full-scale renovation project, the Tower was coloured. Stiebing writes, "Nebuchadnezzar embellished the eight-tiered ziggurat . . . with decorations and covered the temple at its top with blue glazed bricks" (Stiebing 283). Each tier of the building was probably painted a different colour. Nothing is known of what happened to the Tower of Babylon after the Assyrians sacked the city.

## 3. Hanging Gardens of Babylon (ca 600 BC)

The Hanging Gardens of Babylon were reputed to have been built in fifteen days under the orders of Nebuchadnezzar for his Median queen, Amytis. Recent scholarship places the site in Nineveh rather than Babylon (McIntosh 312). The earliest surviving mention of the gardens is around 270 BC in the work of a Babylonian author named Berossus. It was "an edifice resembling a mountain with stone terraces planted with trees" (McIntosh 311).

Later Greek descriptions fill out some details, indicating that the gardens were a tiered structure built on stone foundations with brickwork above and layers of reeds and bitumen – all standard features of Mesopotamian architecture. If accurate, this points to a building with thick lower walls, foundations, and vaulted chambers to support a tiered superstructure. In addition, it would have been close to a water source. If Snell's analysis of the social conditions of Babylonian society is correct, then the labour on the hanging gardens would have been carried out by peasants and slaves (Snell chs. 3 and 4). As with all ancient buildings, the designers are unknown, unless the king himself functioned in this capacity.

What makes the Hanging Gardens significant is their use of irrigation to create an artificial environment. Nebuchadnezzar was not the first to construct artificial pleasure gardens in a palace precinct that were stocked with exotic plants and animals. Foster and Foster attribute the founding of this tradition to the Assyrian king Sennacherib, who invented the water-raising machine known as the Archimedes screw (Foster and Foster 121) discussed above. Construction of an artificial habitat depended on a technology of this sort for capturing, raising, and distributing water. Greek descriptions mention a secret architectural mechanism embedded in the gardens for providing water to all the terraced plants. The Mesopotamians already used a device called a *shaduf*, which lifted water from canals for irrigation or into reservoirs (Snell 36). While the exact mechanism for supplying water to the gardens is not known exactly, the builders utilised some system of water-raising that was ingeniously hidden. The engineering technology was developed out of their expertise in irrigation systems. The tiered Hanging Gardens are the first known building that was constructed with such an engineered hydraulic system for water lifting.

## 2.2 Ancient Egypt

### 2.2.1 Historical and Cultural Environment

#### 1. Background

Archaeological evidence in rock carvings suggests that there were hunter-gatherer populations who roamed around the river Nile as early as 10,000 years ago (8000 BC). Around that time the climate began to change in the upper Sahara region and the early tribes relocated to the river Nile and its fertile basin, in which they centralised their society and developed an agricultural economy. The ancient Egyptian name for this country was *Kemet*, meaning black land, in recognition of the soil around the floodplain of the Nile. Ancient Egypt had fluid boundaries, depending on who was in political and military control. However, the country always maintained a strong base and relationship to the areas surrounding the sacred river (Bard).

#### 2. Relationship to Previous Period

The *Kemet* civilisation coalesced around 3150 BC when upper and lower Egypt were brought together under the first pharaoh (king). The political and economic unification was important because it allowed an actual country to exist with statecraft, political and social goals, and a sense of shared culture. In many ways, Egypt was the southern counterpart of Mesopotamia. There were many similarities in political and social development. However, Egyptian civilisation lasted longer (until about 31 BC when Rome formally annexed the land) and formed the basis of the great Mediterranean civilisations (Dodson). Ancient Egypt was successful partially because it was able to adapt to the varying conditions of the Nile Valley. It was important to establish predictability of flooding, planting times, and harvest times and to manage the storage of grain for lean years. All of this required an advanced political and social hierarchy, which engendered mathematics, writing, scribal administration, and labour stratification (James).

#### 3. Contribution to Western Civilisation

Because it lasted for a long time, Egyptian civilisation developed a sophisticated social and legal system. Writing advanced from cuneiform to hieroglyphics, which allowed for poetry, literature, and greater flexibility. Solar and lunar calendars developed based on agricultural needs. Advanced forms of architectural and artistic expression emerged that were able to create the pyramids. In addition, sophistication increased in shipbuilding, empirical anatomical and medical knowledge, astronomy, and geometry. The legacies of ancient Egypt passed to Greece and Rome through cultural exchange (Siliotto).

Religiously, Egypt experimented with monotheism. During Akhenaten's (Amenhotep IV) rule (roughly 1351–1334 BC), Egypt abandoned traditional polytheism for worship of Aten, a solar deity. After Akhenaten's death, however, traditional religious practises were restored (Aldred). Belief in an afterlife was a central tenet of Egyptian thought. Much time and effort was spent on the creation of a set of guidelines that would help the aristocracy enter their new life after death. Partially for this reason the society developed and maintained an elaborate set of burial customs, and, for the wealthy, mummification was the highest form of honour (Mummies and Mummification). The quest for eternal life led to construction of funerary monuments (Stierlin).

### 2.2.2 Knowledge and Scientific Environment

Like the Mesopotamians, the Egyptians made great strides in revolutionizing science in their time, with implications that have carried through to this day. Egyptian hieroglyphs are a notable example. Because they provided the basis of the Phoenician alphabet, they laid the foundations for languages such as Greek, Latin, Arabic, and Hebrew (Jensen 256). This has only become clear since the pictographic Proto-Sinaitic alphabet was discovered. The Phoenician language was the first widespread phonetic script. It spread rapidly around the world thanks to Phoenician merchant sailors who introduced the language to various parts of Europe and North Africa (Daniels 94–5). Historians have discovered Phoenician inscriptions around the world from Lebanon to Carthage, as well as indications of its use in Egypt (Wilford). Wilford notes that "the writing . . . with Egyptian influences, has been dated to somewhere between 1900 and 1800 BC, two or three centuries earlier than previously recognized uses of a nascent alphabet." Such a find has allowed scientists to trace the evolution of language from pictorial hieroglyphs to alphabetic writing formed by shorthand symbols. In addition, the method of writing on papyrus made it possible for texts to survive. Thus, any doubt about the influence of Egypt on developed language has been discarded.

The Egyptians also helped develop an understanding of physiology and medicine. One of the earliest extant medical documents is the Edwin Smith papyrus. According to the New York Academy of Medicine, the papyrus dates back to the sixteenth century BC and its contents predate that by 1,000 years (Wilkins 240–4). This document is the sole surviving copy of an ancient Egyptian textbook examining trauma surgery. It shows remarkable knowledge, demonstrating an understanding of major organs such as the heart, liver, kidneys, and bladder. It recognizes that the heart was connected to the circulatory system of blood vessels. Its attempt to describe and analyse the brain may be considered the origins of neuroscience. As in Mesopotamian medical texts, the papyrus utilises such concepts as examination, diagnosis, treatment, and prognosis, all of which are still standard components of medical practise today. Lloyd believes this Egyptian work plays a major part in the elaboration of scientific methodology (Lloyd). Thus, Egyptian civilisation not only played an enormous role in the development of language, it also furthered the field of medicine. Its influence is still felt today.

### 2.2.3 General Management

Ancient Egyptians encouraged the communication of information regarding the function of the government and religion, and the recording of information for posterity. The invention of written scripts with detailed hieroglyphics enabled them to record their stories and transactions. Ancient Egyptian government was based on a monarchical system of pharaohs (kings and queens), who made significant contributions to Egyptian society and many of whom were renowned for military leadership (Ruiz 177). The Old Testament provides a reference point for analyzing the pharaohs and Egypt as the first centralised government.

In his book *Management History: Text and Cases,* Morgan Witzel claims that *The Duties of the Vizier,* the first known text that outlines a set out the goals of management and the tasks of the manager, was written over 3,500 years ago during the eighteenth dynasty of ancient Egypt (Witzel 3). The vizier, the highest official in ancient Egypt, served the pharaoh. *The Duties of the Vizier* is an ancient Egyptian text found in Rekhmire's tomb at Thebes. It describes what the vizier did, how he was expected to behave, how he was appointed, and how his role related to that of other officials. According to the text certain traits and behaviours are required of a vizier:

- Act by the law
- Judge fairly
- Do not act wilfully or headstrong (Duties of the Vizier)

Priests were also among the most valued and revered leaders. Since religion was the cornerstone of society, the priesthood was an exclusive profession that garnered prestige from the people and the pharaohs.

A system of primary and secondary education developed in Egypt along with writing and literature. Social values were strong. The Egyptian approach to philosophy in its numerous texts provided examples of significant cries for social justice, monotheism, monogamy, and other moral virtues (Menu).

By 2500 BC, Egypt's fourth dynasty was in a golden age called the Old Kingdom. During this time the country enjoyed vibrant commerce, peace, and prosperity. In this dynasty and the ones that preceded and followed it, the massive pyramid tombs were built as lasting public monuments. For a society to have accomplished such an arduous task, the social values and project management must have demonstrated order, organisation, planning, and foresight. Written requests for materials were submitted in order for control to be maintained, and staff were consulted before decisions were made.

The task of constructing the pyramid of King Cheops, incorporating 2.3 million blocks of stone, is an example. The process was for each block to be quarried, cut to the right size and shape, left to harden in the sun, moved into place by a lengthy boat for journey and further transportation, given a number indicating its position, and then adjusted for a perfect fit. The organisation of labour for this enormous task must have been a significant endeavour. It is estimated that it took 20,000 workers at least twenty-three years to finish the pyramid. Quarrying and transportation of the stone alone required more than 8,000 workers and pack animals. A "quarry expedition" may have included 100 army officers, 50 government and religious officials, 200 courtiers as managers, 130 stone masons, 5,000 soldiers, 800 barbarians, and 2,000 bond servants to be used in transportation (Erman). Although the use of stone could be said to have created more work, Egyptian religious beliefs attracted the necessary workers since they also had a stake in the afterlife and the power of their god-king. Identification of the pharaohs as dieties brought about a closer relationship of the human to the divine. It was also thought that certain working and ruling classes, such as craftsmen and engineers, were endowed with a form of divinity (What Is Civil Engineering). A defined purpose or goal made construction like this more understandable to the average citizen at the time, who would have had fewer qualms about being organized as a result.

### 2.2.4 Construction Technology

The ancient Egyptians made many contributions to building technology. Politics and religion played important roles in the development and creation of building projects. Statues were a favorite commodity of the ruling class, bearing the likeness of the ruler, and funereal monuments were in great demand. This gave rise to a thriving class of craftsmen.

The historical record regarding ancient Egyptian engineering and construction technology is sparse. The main means for data gathering is through experimental archaeology. However, the field of experimental archaeology has not succeeded in answering all questions regarding how stone masonry was done and how the actual moving of large stones occurred. Furthermore, astrology was used to align stones in architectural design, but the precise methods employed are unknown. What is known is that the Egyptians' development of survey tools enabled the precise alignment and laying of stone works once the leveling and measurements had been established (Shaw).

#### 1. Surveyor Tools

Egyptian surveyors achieved incredible engineering feats using the tools available. Their achievements ranged from the construction of canals to the building of pyramids and other large-scale structures. They employed surveying equipment including plumb bobs, leveling devices, measuring ropes, and sighting instruments. Not much is known about the actual tools for long-distance measuring, but for short distances, two main tools were used, the water level tool and the A-frame level with a plumb bob suspended from the apex (Root). The Egyptians also understood the isosceles triangle, and used this concept to cut, chisel, set, and mortar square stones into place. The leveling tools and the high level of craftsmanship in ancient Egyptian masonry produced some of the world's most astounding building achievements that endure today (Patel 30–5).

## 2. Barrel Vault

The ancient Egyptians used the concept of vaulting known as barrel vaulting, a technique employed in Mesopotamia as well (Edwards). In addition, they developed the corbel vault, an architectural technique of creating an arch using "corbelling," where a piece of stone projecting from a wall supports an incumbent weight (such as the stone resting on it). The stones are keyed inside a wall to support the wall or arch the line (Lehner). The corbelling method used in pyramid construction can be considered a crucial development in stone building. In the evolution of engineering construction technology, it was important for the development of the arch and of tunnelling techniques.

## 3. Pyramid Construction, Stone Construction

Before the Old Kingdom dynasties, kings of the first and second dynasties used mud-brick as the basic substance for tomb construction. With the third dynasty, the archaeological record marks the beginning of stone utilization, primarily in the construction of private monuments on a grand scale. Imhotep is credited as being the first ruler to build with stone (Edwards). This shift away from mud-brick was historically novel. It enabled master builders to conceive the unimaginable. Coppens writes that the Great Pyramid of Giza remains one of the most accurately surveyed and built stone structures in the world, along with Zoser's Step Pyramid and Dashur's Red Pyramid. All of these buildings encountered challenges during their construction. One of the construction challenges was labour. Although many people worked on the first two pyramids, they either returned to work on the land or remained in Dashur, 40 miles away. Herodotus suggested that 100,000 men worked continually on the projects and were relieved by a fresh workforce every three months. By any measure, the organisation of such a labour force would have been fraught with difficulties (Coppens).

Some early theories argue that slave labour was used. More recent evidence suggests that there was an abundance of paid workers available in months when agricultural activity ceased due to the flooding of the river Nile. The need for payment would decrease the numbers employed to about 20,000. These 20,000 workers would have been divided into crews of 2,000 and then subdivided into gangs of 1,000, each of which in turn was divided into five *zaa*, or *phyloi* in ancient Greek – a tribe, group, or brotherhood. Each *phyle* consisted of about 200 men (Lehner 224). This gave those in charge greater ability to monitor activity and maintain control. Incredible effort and the use of paid labour rather than slaves would have made construction more efficient. Paid workers had more of a stake in the project, and as subjects of the pharaoh, they would have had a degree of pride in doing so (Merolla).

A second challenge was the plan. It has been erroneously argued that the plan for the Great Pyramid was changed at least twice. More recent theories suggest that rough on-site planning was conducted and implemented on real dimensions using "high-level estimates."

Construction materials were a third problem. The main component of the pyramids was limestone. Yet the ancient builders chose to use granite as well, especially for the King's Chamber in the Great Pyramid, which required 7,500 tons of granite. Granite was found in Aswan, 400 miles south of Giza. Transportation required barges with 400–500 people in attendance to move and manoeuvre the slabs. The building task for the chamber alone required eight years to complete. The choice of granite for the King's Chamber upset the timetable of fourteen years for the project. In addition to these challenges, there were problems associated with the economic impact of construction, insufficient or crude implements, and the lack of recognition, which were the key tasks. About 20 percent of the Egyptian population of 1.6 million had to be employed. This labour demand adversely affected the yearly harvest. Even with rotation of the workforce, problems of skill levels and training still surfaced (Coppens).

## 4. Linear and Spiral Ramps

One notable and major Egyptian contribution in terms of large and enduring construction technology is the development of the ramp. Archaeologists contend that in the construction of the pyramids it was necessary to use a system of ramps to move millions of blocks into position. Five different types of ramps have been suggested (Heizer 821–30). The most direct method was the linear ramp, which is likely to have been employed in the building of the pyramid of Sekhemkhet at Saqqara during the third dynasty. Nevertheless, the linear ramp was probably rarely used because it had to be of considerable width. Alternatively, a staircase ramp may have been used, narrow tall steps that run up one face of the pyramid. There are signs of such ramps at the Sinki, Meidum, Giza, Abu Ghurob, and Lisht pyramids (Shaw). The spiral ramp is another variation, although it would have covered the pyramid and it is therefore debatable what it would have rested on and how the pyramid could have been checked and modified (Nineteenth-Dynasty Papyrus Anastasi I). The reversing ramp consists of a zigzag up one face of a pyramid and was not likely used in constructing step pyramids. Finally, the remains of the pyramids of Sahura, Nyuserra and Neferirkara at Abusir, and of Pepi II at Saqqara, have revealed interior ramps (Heizer 821–30; Shaw).

Transportation of heavy stones (2.5 to 15 tons) into place during the construction of the Great Pyramid presented a number of issues. Some authorities assert that a ramp over a mile long was used, while others claim that an external spiral type of ramp was used. A recent theory suggests that an internal spiral ramp was constructed to leverage the stones, a method which avoided leaving the corners until last. What is significant is that despite the difficulty of knowing exactly what type of ramp was used, evidence for the different ramps exists.

In summary, the Egyptians contributed to building technology in similar ways to the Mesopotamians. They were able to manage a huge labour force effectively. They utilised the ramp for building vertically, but increased the number of ramp styles available. The Egyptians adopted the barrel vault as well but they added corbelling. Where they advanced beyond the Mesopotamians was in surveying with more geometrical precision, quarrying, levering, and transporting materials. Their tools were not vastly different than the Mesopotamians' but they worked with stone. This switch in material was important since stone was more durable than mud-brick.

### 2.2.5 Master Builder Tradition

The concept of master builder in Egypt encompassed the roles of architect, engineer, and builder. There was no distinction between the three roles and all were conducted by one person: the master builder. This concept lasted for some time until more complex structures and construction techniques led to the disciplines becoming separated (Jackson 5).

One such "master builder" was the Egyptian polymath Imhotep (2650–2600BC). He was an engineer, architect, and physician serving the third dynasty of King Djoser and is the first such whose name we know (Osler 12). He was one of the few commoners granted divine status after death. Imhotep designed and supervised the Step Pyramid of Djoser from 2630–2611 BC, thereby creating the largest structure ever built using only stone and one of the earliest uses of architectural columns (Kemp 159).

Imhotep was idealized as a creator of Egyptian culture, a view that endured into the time of Ptolemy. Manetho, an Egyptian historian, claimed that he developed a method of stone dressing a building, though stone had been used in construction before this time for walls, floors, lintels and door jambs.

### 2.2.6 Building Project

### 1. The Great Pyramid at Giza (2580–2560 BC)

Pyramids are principally royal tombs, not temple structures like the ziggurats. They exhibit different properties as a result. Their slope is more extreme, they have no platforms, and at the top they taper to a point. Any ritual would have been performed inside, not outside in open space due to the lack of an upper shrine or architectural climax. Furthermore, they were not equipped with stairs or ramps for climbing, as the ziggurats were.

The Giza Pyramid was built over three generations. Its walls, piers, and roofs are made of Aswan red granite and its passages and outer casing of polished Turah limestone. In a microgravimetric study of the pyramid's density, two French companies found that "the pyramid's macrostructure consists of thirty-four major 'blocks' with a low-density block near the top, and blocks of heterogeneous density below" (Lehner 67). It is uncertain whether the inner core is well cut or uniform, and the stones get smaller as they go upwards for increased precision. At the base, some casing stones weigh 15 tons, while the granite beams above the stress-relieved King's Chamber weigh 50 to 80 tons. An innovative arrangement was used above this chamber to distribute weight and stress by means of cantilevered stones forming a pent roof. The stones were held together by gypsum mortar poured into the interstices of the core (Lehner 109).

There are no extant Egyptian records giving the methods used. We do know that the land was first surveyed with measuring ropes of palm or flax fibre, and then levelled. It is still unclear whether the core was erected first with the use of earth ramps, or whether the casing stones were placed and bevelled to the incline angle and then the frame filled with core blocks (Kostof, Castillo and Tobias 77). The stones were quarried elsewhere with intensive labour that did not involve iron tools. Instead, the masons used dolerite hammers to split the rock and then drove copper or soaked wooden wedges into the trench to detach the blocks (Nuttgens 33). To cut the granite, they probably used copper saws to guide gypsum and sand, which had an abrasive effect (Lehner 215). Then they smoothed the casing with chisels and pounded out blocks with deep channels.

Transportation of stones weighing 2.5 to 15 tons into place during construction of the Great Pyramid presented a number of issues. The stones were loaded onto barges for transport down the Nile, sometimes hundreds of miles. The granite was unloaded from the barge by an earth embankment built around it (Lehner 202). Alternatively, the barge was brought into a narrow canal and cedar beams were placed beneath the load between supports as the barge slipped out, leaving the stones. Scholars believe that land transport of the stone was through the manual pulling of sledges (by humans or cattle) across timber-baulked hauling tracks lubricated with mud or water.

The greatest mystery is how such a massive structure was constructed without the use of cranes and pulleys. Egyptian technology knew only of levers to lift and pull stone (Nuttgens 33). Lehner's NOVA experiments show that levering and tumbling with wooden poles was possible, but only for side movements, final adjustments, and setting uppermost stones. He says that the most likely method was "some system involving a ramp or ramps" (Lehner 209). The ramps could have been either straight on, perpendicular, spiral at corners, or zigzag up one face, similar to the ramp styles discussed above. There is no scholarly consensus on the matter, but mud-brick ramps must have been built up as work progressed. The challenge is almost incomprehensible due to the steep gradient of the slope that would make building a ramp itself an incredible feat. The fact that the outside face was often staggered rather than flush, compounded by the reduced working space, suggests that for high levels the outer slope was cut into the blocks before they were set (Lehner 123).

The pharaohs employed a regular workforce of skilled masons and craftsmen that was "undoubtedly occupied full-time during the span of construction" (Kostof,

Castillo and Tobias 77)., probably augmented with peasant labour when flooding prevented farming from May to September. Lehner estimates a workforce of 20,000 stone haulers and setters on shift every three months (Lehner 224). The workshops would have used massive amounts of fuel from the countryside for forging copper tools, slaking gypsum to make mortar, and baking bread for workers.

Some of the earlier theories argued that slave labour was used. More recent evidence suggests that there was an abundance of workers available for pay due to cessation of agricultural activity due to the flooding of the river Nile. It appears that approximately 20,000 workers were required. These 20,000 workers would be divided into crews of 2,000 then subdivided into gangs of 1,000, which in turn was divided into five *zaa*. (Lehner 224). This gave those in charge greater ability to monitor activity and maintain control. Incredible effort and the use of paid labour would have combined more efficiently instead of theories that claim slaves must have been used. Clearly, paid workers had a great stake in the project and as subjects of the pharaoh they would have had a degree of pride in doing so. (Merolla)

As to the idea behind the construction, the pyramid was a tomb for the king's transport to the other world. Entrances were concealed and interior mazes built to protect royal wealth and ensure a safe translation into immortality. There is an obvious cosmological focus. The shafts in the king's tomb were aligned with the three stars of Orion. The geometry was precise, with perfect squares and sides of equilateral triangles. The abstractions had to do with sun worship.

## 2.3 Ancient Greece

### 2.3.1 Historical and Cultural Environment

#### 1. Background

The centre of Greek civilisation was the Ionian peninsula, a rocky and non-arable land just west of modern Turkey. With a burgeoning population, the early Greeks expanded their land by a factor of ten. Out of this expansion from 800 BC onwards, they produced an extremely viable civilisation that lasted through Roman times until the modern period. The Greeks lived near and around the Mediterranean Sea. Because of this proximity to water, they developed a seafaring culture that put them in contact with other Mediterranean civilisations such as Phoenicia, Egypt, and Babylon. This communication and interaction vitalized the Greek people. They borrowed a great deal of technology, science, and art from the older cultures they encountered and developed it in their own ways (Freeman). Their expansion went in all directions, eventually extending north to what is now the Ukraine, west into modern France, and east throughout the Turkish and southern Black Sea lands. Such colonization was a pivotal part of the dissemination and influence of the Greek language, culture, and politics through the Western world. Ancient Greece established long-distance trading networks which boosted its economy and made it easier for Rome later to subsume it into its territories (Hansen).

## 2. Relationship to Previous Period

The early civilisations based in and around the Mediterranean were part of the Iron and early Bronze Ages. The Minoans on the island of Crete, for instance, were primarily traders, whereas the Mycenaean Greeks (1600–1100 BC) advanced through warfare and conquest. Historians label the period between 1100 and 750 BC the Greek Dark Ages. During this time prior to the establishment of the Greek city-states, there was a great deal of trade and cultural influence between Greece, Egypt, and the Assyrian/Babylonian cultures. This cultural cross-fertilization catalysed important changes. It was the time in which the alphabetic script was brought to Greece. It formed the basis of the developing culture and technology of later Greek society. Because of the influence of the other major civilisations of the time, Greece was able to nurture its own civilisation. The Greek people took what they learned and rather quickly advanced into the Classical period of development (Hall). It was a combination of commerce, contact, and conquest that solidified into the early Greek culture in the eighth century BC (Castleden).

## 3. Contribution to Western Civilisation

Ancient Greece is still considered the fountain of modern European culture. Greece synthesised the best parts of the oriental civilisations it encountered. Out of this, it engendered its own philosophy, architecture, medicine, politics, literature, and education. These fields of knowledge and writing were transmitted via Roman adaptation and, by means of Latin, were disseminated through Western culture into modernity.

Politically and culturally, there was not one singular or monolithic "Greek culture" in ancient times. Instead, Greece consisted of several hundred city-states (*poleis*) engendered by and scattered around the unique geography of the Greek lands. These city-states were sovereign and independent, the best known being Sparta and Athens. Most Greek city-states were petty kingdoms ruled by tyrants of various sorts. It was not until the sixth century BC that citizen assemblies were introduced into government and a greater respect for the bearers of the armed forces was fostered. This gave rise over time to limited democracy for male Greek citizens in Athens, a political tradition which was rediscovered during the Renaissance period in Europe (Rhodes). At times the presence of an external threat constituted a reason for treaties between city-states that united them in order to ward off an enemy, yet frequently they engaged in wars against each other. It is important to note how weakened the individual city-states became when they fought lengthy wars with each other. The example of conflict between Sparta and Athens is notable here.

Greek philosophy remains the cornerstone of modern philosophical thought. The style of focused rational inquiry into the world shows clear lines running from Greece to Rome and up through the centuries into the contemporary secular sciences. One scholar has noted, "Western philosophy is just a series of footnotes in Plato" (Philosophy – "Series of Footnotes to Plato"). Martin West in *The Oxford History of Greece and the Hellenistic World* points to the intrinsic connection of the Greeks and philosophical reasoning when he says, "Philosophy as we understand it is a Greek creation" (140). Socrates believed that one's happiness was dependent on leading a moral life and reiterated that concepts of justice should predominate in government (Ancient Greece: Philosophy). Philosophers developed thought pertaining to ethics and how humans can lead good lives of virtue and excellence that are unobtrusive to others.

In literature the influence of Greek authors has also been inestimable. The Greek playwright Aeschylus changed the Western dramatic genre by the introduction into literary plays of dialogue and characters that interacted with each other (Gutzwiller). In fact, the artistic and intellectual influence of Greece on Rome was so large that the Roman poet Horace said, "Captive Greece took captive her fierce conqueror and instilled her arts in rustic Latium" (Horace).

### 2.3.2 Knowledge and Scientific Environment

The impact of Greek science on the civilized world cannot be underestimated. The history of science was born in the cradle of Greek philosophy's search for practical knowledge. Reason and empirical inquiry abounded alongside idealistic and speculative works. In these texts, the Greeks mused about divine power and the afterlife. Many inquiries were made into the creation and nature of the universe and how it worked. Thus natural philosophy was born. Before modern science was developed and widely used, natural philosophy was the prominent method for gaining knowledge. It served as a precursor of various natural sciences like physics. The modern understanding of "science" evolved only in the nineteenth century AD. The Greeks simply referred to knowledge and Greek natural philosophers provided stepping stones for the creation of modern science.

As with the Mesopotamians, the ancient Greeks played their part in the development of astronomy. Through natural observations they formed a workable and reliable calendar. Hesiod's *Works and Days* speaks of a calendar which enabled the farmer to regulate his activities according to the seasons using phases of the moon and the stars (Thurston 21). It is apparent that the Greeks were familiar with Mesopotamian astronomical theories and findings, which they studied and incorporated into their own schemes.

Along with the Egyptians, the Greeks made revolutionary discoveries in medicine. This is rather unsurprising for the Greeks, as it has already been established that their natural philosophy served as a basis for modern science. Interestingly, though, the medicine of the Greeks was not practised by a single profession, nor was there any licensing qualification. Rather, a wide spectrum of people performed the duties of physicians. These included herb collectors, midwives, drug sellers, gymnastic trainers, surgeons, and temple healers within the cult of Asclepius, all promoting themselves as qualified healers in their relevant area (Lloyd 38–39). While beneficial for raising standards of practise, this competition led to polemics. Physicians engaged in public verbal attacks against each other to encourage doubt among the populace towards a competitor. A prime example of this is the Hippocratic text about epilepsy, *On the Sacred Disease*, in which temple healers are criticized for their ignorance and greed. Hippocrates was well educated and knew that epilepsy was a natural illness, not caused through external influences or factors. Yet his ignorance about what the real cause was and what treatment was available showed him to be no more enlightened than his rivals (Lloyd 15–24). This points towards limitations and controversies within Greek medical practise.

The Greeks were prolific natural historians, who arguably were responsible for the advent of botany and zoology. Theophrastus wrote the first systematic books describing and classifying minerals, rocks, and plants, as well as the nature of animals. These ideas were later used by Pliny the Elder in the *Naturalis Historia* (77 AD), which has survived to this day and purports to cover the whole spectrum of ancient knowledge. What made Pliny's encyclopaedia important was its departure from mere notation. Pliny sought explanations, not just descriptions. Moreover, many of his assertions were correct. He stated that amber is fossilised resin from pine trees, a fact that was until then unknown and is now understood as true. There can be no doubt that modern science owes a great deal to the ancient Greeks. Without their investigations and discoveries in philosophy, primitive science, medicine, and other areas, contemporary knowledge would likely be less advanced.

### 2.3.3 General Management

The ancient Greeks were aware of and utilised some important management ideas and practises. For example, they knew that repetitious tasks could be made less onerous if they were accompanied by music, an ancient form of *job enrichment*. Flutes, drums, or song lyrics were used to help people keep time when working in unison. This stimulated them to work faster and longer, in addition to alleviating boredom (Glotz).

Power and leadership in ancient Greece belonged to the local rulers of the city-states and to the men who created empires. Historians consider Alexander the Great to be one of the greatest military leaders of all time. His armies conquered large parts of the world. Pericles was another military leader who advocated reform and social improvements for Greek citizens. In addition to political leaders, Greek philosophers had an impact on social ideas and forms of leadership. In *The Evolution of Management Thought* Daniel Wren points out that the Greeks were the first society to consistently allow leadership outside the military and politics. In other words, philosophers influenced society by contributing key ideas about management and the arrangement of social relations.

Around 400 BC, the philosopher Socrates analysed the relative similarities between public leadership (military and political) and private management. He viewed management as a distinct skill, different from knowledge and experience in any other technical arena. Socrates was also the first figure to document the importance of delegating authority and work. Under his lasting inspiration, Plato and Aristotle further developed his management theory to include specialisation of work and the division of labour (Wren 19).

Plato (428–348 BC) also considered specialization important and appreciated the distinctiveness of management. In *The Republic* he recommended that young men should be encouraged through training to develop a moral character and leadership skills (Pindur and Rogers). The Socratic method used in his dialogues was a major contribution to Western thinking. Plato applied this method to examining concepts in order to unmask a person's underlying beliefs and assumptions and show the extent of their knowledge or ignorance. This method decomposed a problem according to a sequence of questions. The responses to each question in the sequence worked to distil a solution. This approach to investigation and problem solving has strongly influenced the scientific method, which proposes an initial hypothesis and gradually eliminates alternatives. The Socratic Method eliminated hypotheses in a *negative* fashion. It discovered better hypotheses by identifying those that resulted in contradictions and eliminating them one by one. Through its design it forced participants to consider the feasibility of their views and thereby set knowledge on a more objective footing (Coppen).

During the Middle Ages Socrates' teachings were rediscovered, together with those of Plato and Aristotle, in both Medieval Europe and the Islamic Middle East. The Renaissance and the Enlightenment in Europe led to him achieving his full stature as a philosopher, when political theory and natural philosophy were rejuvenated under Locke, Bacon, and Newton.

The Greek historian Thucydides (460–395 BC) is often viewed as the first modern historian. His *History of the Peloponnesian War* serves as one of the first true treatises on leadership. His thesis that leadership was necessary for democracy but also dangerous to it sparked an intense debate that has survived well into the twentieth century (Warner 620).

The Greeks were the first Europeans to read and write with an alphabet. Thus their contributions to language and communication are easier for historians to measure. Their most important contributions to communication are in the realms of rhetoric, literature, and theatre, especially Greek tragedy and comedy. Historians believe that both were designed to spread Greek culture and values and promote a common identity among Greeks through diaspora. They functioned alongside the Greek art of military epics. Thus they have immense value as historical communication tools.

### 2.3.4 Construction Technology

We know most about Greek architecture of the late archaic period (550–500 BC), the Periclean age (450–430 BC), and the early to pure classical period (430–400 BC). What mostly survived from these times were temples rather than other buildings.

Greek examples will be compared to later Hellenistic and Roman examples (architecture in Rome drew heavily on the Greek model). In addition, there are important later sources such as the writings of Vitruvius (first century AD) that reflect an earlier period of architecture.

Greek architecture was more diverse than previous civilisations in that they utilised a more diverse array of materials. Supports and roof beams were made of wood; sinks and bathtubs were made of plaster. The walls of domestic dwellings consisted of unbaked brick. The columns and walls of larger public buildings were constructed of limestone and marble. Roofing was made out of thatch or "terracotta," which was also used ornamentally. In addition, metal, especially bronze, was used as decoration. There were five main types of building: religious, civic, domestic, funerary, and recreational.

The most widespread example of Greek public architecture is the temple. Greek altars were in the open air in what was called the *temenos* or sacred fane, which was frequently situated in front of the temple. Sacred objects associated with the god to whom the temple was dedicated were stored at the temple, and it was also where votive offerings were left by devotees of that particular cult, including weapons, helmets, and even statues. The interior of the temple, known as the *cella,* was often decorated with columns and most used for further storage and as a strong room. The orientation of some Greek temples was decided according to astronomical principles (Penrose 42–3).

## 1. Tiled Roof

There is evidence to support the theory that Greek monumental building methods enabled the development of the tiled roof. Earlier grand-scale buildings were constructed of mud-brick, with the exception of the Egyptian pyramids, whereas the Greeks used stone to build the walls of their monuments. The stone walls could support a weighty tiled roof, which mud-brick walls could not (Goldberg 305–10). The earliest documented evidence for roof tiling in archaic Greece, between 700 and 650 BC, comes from Corinth at the temples of Apollo and Poseidon, which were formerly roofed with thatch. This architectural advance spread rapidly. Within fifty years, roof tiles were being used at a significant range of sites in Greece, Italy, and western Asia Minor. These early roof tiles were S-shaped and were heavy, at around 30 kg. Since tiled roofs were more expensive to produce and more labour-intensive to build than those made of thatch, it is reasonable to assume that it was the desire for greater resistance to fire that ultimately led to their introduction (Wikander 285–90).

## 2. Columns

Another significant feature of ancient Greek building technology was the use of columns. There were three column types established in Greece (Benson 253–72). Doric columns were the most elementary. Their capital (the top or crown) was built of a circle mounted by a square. The shaft was plain and had twenty sides. The Doric order had no base. While plain, it was powerful-looking in its design and was popular in the construction of the long rectangular buildings of Greece. Above the column were items called friezes, metopes, and triglyphs. All architectural elements, these sections were often used to convey simple patterns interspersed with statues of gods or other favourite figures. The best-known example of the Doric style is the Parthenon in Athens. Modern-day construction projects draw inspiration from some elements of the Doric order (Thompson, Papadopoulou, and Vassiliou 531–43).

The Doric order is used in most of the ancient Greek buildings that remain to this day, such as the Parthenon and the Temple of Hephaestus in Athens. However, some are Ionic, such as the Erechtheum and the Temple of Athena on the Acropolis, and also the Library of Celsus in Turkey. The latter order achieved dominance in the Hellenistic period because its style was less restrained and more decorative.

## 3. Simple Machines

The ancient Greek philosopher Archimedes developed the idea of the "simple machine" through study of levers, pulleys, and screws. He learned that the lever offered a mechanical advantage (Ostdiek 123), although he did not comprehend more than the mere balancing of forces. Through the concept of mechanical advantage, the ratio of output to input force is proportionally increased, making a load easier to move (Anderson).

In the Hellenistic period Heron of Alexandria (ca. 10–75 AD), in his work *Mechanics,* lists five mechanisms that can be used to set a load in motion: winch, lever, pulley, wedge, and screw (Strizhsak 245). Heron was a mathematician, physicist, inventor, and engineer. His writings indicate that he taught at the Museum in Alexandria. Hydraulic, steam-, and air-operated machines are credited to Heron in addition to some sophisticated surveying tools. One surveying tool was the *dioptra,* which was used in civil engineering to determine the direction of roads, tunnels, or other structures (Lahanas). The Greeks were also familiar with other simple machines including the wheel and the inclined plane (Koloski 1025–30).

Simple machines transformed the enterprise of construction. They made work easier: things that would otherwise be difficult to move were made easier to manoeuvre through use of a simple machine (Singer, Holmyard, and Hall 320–34) that changed the direction or degree of force. The development of the winch and pulley, the watermill, the wheelbarrow, and the odometer all had enormous impacts on the progress of construction technology in ancient Greece.

## 4. Crane

The ancient Greeks invented the crane in the late sixth century BC to enable them to raise massive loads. Evidence for the crane comes from examination of peculiar holes in stone that indicate the use of a lifting mechanism. Archaeologists regard these holes as proof of the innovation of the crane. The cranes employed by the Greeks represented an earlier technology of crane evolution. These early cranes featured an elongated wooden beam, a "boom." The boom was attached to a rotating base and a rope was wound around a drum that was driven by a wheel or treadmill. The rope was attached with one end to the tip of the wooden beam. The other end of the rope had a hook which assisted in raising heavy loads, such as large stones, and even ships (Coulton 1–19).

Crane technology such as the winch and the pulley hoist replaced ramps as the main means of vertical lifting employed by the Mesopotamians and Egyptians. Heavy blocks used in stone buildings could be hoisted rather than pushed up a ramp into place. Stone size also decreased as construction technology advanced (Coulton 1–19). Like many innovations in technology, the winch and pulley system may have been a development out of military needs (Coulton 1-19). Indeed, the catapult and ballast in ancient Greek warfare were structured and operated on a winch and pulley system called the *gastraphete* (Marsden). The winch and pulley system was pivotal not only in building design, but also in the construction of civic works such as canals, government buildings, and temples.

#### 5. Watermill

The Greeks invented a device called the watermill. It was composed of a water wheel or turbine to power some mechanical process. Put more simply, it was the first harnessed use of hydropower in the Western world. Its technology is widely employed today (Wilson 1–32). Used from everything from processing food (grinding wheat) to powering a sawmill, it is likely that the supportive functions of the watermill were of enormous benefit in the development of ancient Greek construction technology.

In summary, Greek civilisation improved construction technologies and building practises immeasurably. It was the first to use simple machines like the pulley to lift and move stones, which decreased the amount of labour necessary. In addition, it added the crane and the watermill to the available tools. These inventions displaced the ramp, which fell into obsolescence as a construction method. New architectural structures evolved as well, including the tiled roof and the column made possible by stone construction.

### 2.3.5 Master Builder Tradition

While the Egyptians built the great pyramids using a large force of unskilled labour, the Greeks created a more organized, smaller force of skilled labour. In terms of organisation, the crane made possible a less extensive workforce. Small teams of skilled labour were preferred over large unskilled labour. Fewer people were required to shift and lift stones (Landels). Also because they used limestone and marble, the Greek master builders started to create groups of skilled stonemasons to use in projects. This eventually led to master craftsmen training others in a particular skill. These apprentices were then utilised as skilled artisans on other projects. Finer detail and design allowed selected skilled artisans to use their abilities in architecture. Construction history was never the same again (Jackson 5).

The Greek name for master builder was *architekton*, from which derives the Latin name *architectus*. Both words signify "master builder," which denotes the person in charge of the design and construction of a building and the management of the building environment. Today's English word "architect" is obviously the phonetic equivalent of these terms, although it has a different meaning. The old master builders are highly respected and venerated among contemporary architects (Ancient Master Builder).

Even 2,500 years ago sophisticated contracts were drawn up when a major building project was planned. For example, the master builder Kallicrates was given responsibility for the Long Walls in Athens, and he in turn assigned the work to ten different contractors. There were contracts specifying the work to be undertaken, guarantees to be given, and how the labour force were to be paid (Weaver 5). There were also specifications for completion time.

### 2.3.6 Building Projects

#### 1. Parthenon (490–432 BC)

The Parthenon sits elevated on the Acropolis. This naturally fortified site was the spiritual heart of classical Athens. It was the residence of early rulers and home to the chief Athenian gods (Pomeroy 169). Carpenter has convinced scholarship that the Parthenon was built by two architects. In its final form, it was an incorporation and enlargement of an earlier, partially completed temple that was supposed to be a monument to the Marathon victory. Pointing to embedded column drums and the foundation, Carpenter believes that the first temple was begun in or shortly after 490 BC, after the Athenian defeat of the Persians, only to be interrupted again when the Persians stormed it in 480 BC (Carpenter 28). Between 468 and 465 BC under Kimon, Kallikrates supervised the start of the old building. Internal political strife halted construction for about twenty years. When Pericles initiated the present Parthenon in 447 BC, he replaced Kallikrates with the architect Iktinos in 450 BC and the project grew more ambitious. The later version took only five years to build using the rubble and model of the earlier (Rhodes 41). It is, however, longer by a column and wider by two columns. This enlarged the *cella* and gave more focus to the temple's interior – needed, according to Rhodes, for the installation of the huge Pheidian statue of Athena (Rhodes 81–82). The Parthenon was structurally complete in 438 BC, with only the fine details of pediment sculptures to complete by 432 BC (Carpenter 67).

The blended Doric-Ionic temple was made of Pentelic marble quarried 16 km outside the city, and the marble roof tiles were supported by cypress timbers that spanned the *cella* and were placed in gable sockets (Belozerskaya and Lapatin 72). Its design, which did not involve an inventive departure from classical orders, was on a

9:4 geometrical ratio. There was no strict adherence to measurable ratios, but rather "the builders of the Parthenon worked empirically, trimming and fitting together the component marble blocks of the exterior and interior orders, of the tapering walls and coffered ceilings, quite as much by eye and by immediate need as by previous theoretical calculation" (Carpenter 13–4). Carpenter does not see the irregular spacing of the exterior columns or imprecision in the cornice block widths as evidence of careless workmanship, but rather as an intentional aesthetic deviation to bring life and elasticity to the building. Nuttgens adds, "The design of the Parthenon called for meticulous measurement; precision in calculation; mastery in masonry; and a unique fineness of perception and response" (97). The state treasury paid for its construction.

Plutarch's *Life of Pericles* lists the vast materials and human resources engaged in the project:

> *The materials to be employed were marble, bronze, ivory, gold, ebony, and cypress wood; while the craftsmen to work and utilise these were carpenters, moulders, bronze-casters, masons, dyers, goldsmiths and workers of ivory, painters, broiders, embossers, not to mention the furnishers and transporters of the materials, among which were dealers and sailors and steersmen by sea and wheelwrights and waggoners and breeders of yoke animals by land. Also there were rope-makers, weavers, leather-workers, road-builders, and miners. And since each craft and occupation had its own company of slave and free under its orders, one might say that every age and every capacity were marshaled into service (Plutarch).*

The extent of the workforce is evident, as are the types of skilled labourers employed.

The Parthenon's use of *entasis*, a swelling or convexity at the midpoints of the columns, is remarkable. The columns, thicker and closer together in the middle, tilt inwardly at the top and are tapered upwards harmonically. This curvature was a refinement of the temple platform, the stylobate, and the entablature (Rhodes 76). The meticulous carving and planning of stone gave an illusion of sagging horizontals or exaggerated perspective whose impracticality was not justified solely by drainage.

The pediments are what distinguished the Parthenon as unique and superior to other similar temples. These were designed by Pheidias, but carved by skilled workmen, including slaves (Belozerskaya and Lapatin 74). According to Palagia, marble was quarried from Mt. Pentelikon for the pediments. This involved "building roads and rolling the blocks down, then carting them to Athens and hoisting them up to sculpture workshops on the Acropolis" (7). She cites building accounts as evidence that "the sculptures were carved on the Acropolis, distributed among a number of workshops, and that quarrying and carving went on simultaneously" (7). The pediments were chiselled from single blocks or pieced together. Occasionally stonemasons trimmed the statues after they were hoisted. Individual carving methods can be discerned but mostly the work is uniform. There is little doubt that simple machines and cranes were used to carry out this impressive piece of architecture.

## 2.4 Roman Empire

### 2.4.1 Historical and Cultural Environment

#### 1. Background

Roman culture grew out of the agrarian-based Etruscan civilisation on and around the Italian peninsula and surrounded by the Mediterranean sea. The Romans were less important as innovators than as organizers and conquerors. Through military and political conquest they overran the Greek empire and moved west into the Iberian Peninsula and Britannia (England). By defeating Carthage in the Punic Wars, Rome became master of the Mediterranean. From the fifth century BC to the fifth century AD, Rome controlled the largest, most comprehensive empire in the ancient world. The territories under its control stretched north from Britain up to modern Germany, east almost to India, and south through northern Africa to the headwaters of the Nile (Scarre). However, due to political instability, lack of a solid military and political base, and attack by various rebellious tribes, the western part of the empire broke up into independent kingdoms and transferred whatever political hegemony was left to the Eastern Roman Empire of Byzantium (Elton).

#### 2. Relationship to Previous Period

Most of the culture of ancient Rome was inspired by and in many cases copied from Ancient Greece. The Greek culture was "modified" to fit Roman sentiments, politics, and culture. It is likely that the city of Rome was founded in the eighth century BC by Greek traders and artisans who settled and mingled with the native Etruscans. This blending eventually allowed Rome to subsume the Greek empire, although Greece continued to govern its own city-states locally while being a Roman province (Elton). Over the period of two centuries, from 509 BC to 281 BC, the Roman tribes subdued the Etruscans and then finally the Greek colonies in the southern part of the Italian Peninsula. This access to the sea allowed them to dominate the Phoenician colony of Carthage in the Three Punic Wars, and resulted in Rome's domination of the Mediterranean (Hooker).

#### 3. Contribution to Western Civilisation

Rome's imperial conquests ensured that its culture and civilisation would prosper. Because of its expansion and longevity, the Roman impact on modern Western civilisation was immense. The city of Rome rose to become the largest urban area in the Western world, with a population that exceeded one million people (an urban area not surpassed in the world until London in the nineteenth century). This mega-urban area required a hierarchical structure of organisation that could devote the time and effort necessary to govern provinces far away (Flower). This would not have been possible without a well-funded and trained military that could not only subdue and conquer, but establish and maintain order.

Military leadership and tactics evolved during the history of Rome. The Roman military was characterized by a leaner, more flexible operation utilising technology and organisation that had advanced beyond other civilisations (Goldsworthy). Many of the Greek and Egyptian technologies it adopted were lost in the Dark Age until they were revived in the Renaissance. In addition, Rome contributed much to politics, law, and civil society, not to mention the pervasive influence of the Latin language on history and modern European languages.

### 2.4.2 Knowledge and Scientific Environment

As with the Greeks, many Romans wanted to systemise scientific knowledge gained from the preceding Hellenistic period and to join it with knowledge from conquered areas. The *Naturalis Historia* of Pliny the Elder (23–79 AD) played a central role in gathering knowledge together. It organised knowledge like an encyclopaedia into distinct and sensible sections that included the organic world of plants and animals as well as the realm of inorganic matter. Pliny does not confine himself to scientific observations, but also includes comments on the inhumane treatment of animals. His work describes metals and minerals in extensive detail. All that was known of gold, silver, tin, iron, lead, and mercury is given, along with their alloys pewter and bronze. Pliny talks at length about the greed for gold, including the ridiculousness of using it for coins and its uniqueness in being far more malleable than any other known metal.

In discussing minerals, Pliny primarily expands on earlier authors such as Theophrastus. He adds a review of gemstones and man's obsession with luxurious items. This is not a superficial overview of these products, but a detailed analysis. Pliny talks about the properties of fluorspar, the shape and hardness of diamonds, and the use of diamonds by gem engravers to cut and polish other stones. Given such a detailed examination of mineralogy, metallurgy, zoology, and botany, it is easy to see why the Romans held his work in such high regard.

Claudius Ptolemaeus (Ptolemy) was another central figure. Ptolemy was an astrologer, astronomer, mathematician, and geographer who lived under Roman rule in Egypt. He influenced Roman science by systemising astronomy using knowledge discovered by those before him to create a firm empirical foundation for it as a science. He demonstrated a working relationship between astronomical observations and astronomical theory. Not only did his treatise, *Almagest,* define both the method and subject of future research into astronomy, his Ptolemaic system became the dominant model for understanding the movements of the heavens (Goldstein 1–12).

In anatomy and physiology, Galen systematized Hellenistic medical knowledge and generated new insights. He dissected various animals, from dogs to Barbary apes. He wrote detailed observations on the nervous system and organs, as well as on specific functions such as the role of arteries in carrying blood around the body.

His results became central in moving medical science forward. Much of the medical knowledge for a millennium after Galen was taken from his research.

Peculiarly though, despite the fact that the years of the Roman Empire saw science continue to expand in scope and direction, the Latin texts that were written were largely compilations of Greek works. This shows how deeply steeped in Greek science the Romans were. Greek was the language used for teaching and research, which hindered the spread of knowledge so much that after the fall of Roman Empire the majority of Greek texts did not become available in western Europe until the twelfth century. So there was a language barrier – they could only be translated by monastic scholars – but also, prior to that, Europe was in the Dark Ages.

### 2.4.3 General Management

The Roman Empire introduced the world to a new form of public leadership: the Senate. The Senate in Rome was designed to be a separate body of government from the emperor (Abbott 385). It is thought to be the world's first legislative body. Eventually, the ancient Romans established a republican form of government since they did not want one man to make all the laws. Their solution was to balance political power between three different branches: the executive, the legislative, and the judicial. The implications of this new form were immense.

Cato the Elder (234–149 BC) was an important Roman statesman, soldier, and historian. He was the first significant Latin prose writer, and the first to compile a Latin history of Italy. Only one of his works is extant in full, a manual on farm operations called *De Agri Cultura* (*On Farming*). This is a compilation of rules for husbandry and farm management, along with descriptions of rural life in the second century BC. Employed as a textbook during Roman agricultural expansion, the assumptions of the work include that slaves are used to run and staff the farm. This is important in signalling a change in farming practises towards increased business profitability. Cato advises large-scale farmers to hire gangs for the olive harvest. His book incorporates advice on slave management, such as how to keep slaves working continually, when to reduce rations given to slaves who are ill, and when to sell slaves who are old or incapacitated (Dalby). Cato's work was thus important for its discussion of management methods.

By all accounts, Julius Caesar (100–44 BC) was a master of political management. His own writings and other biographies tell us much about his management and leadership style. He was hailed as a master at political manoeuvring who built alliances that served him well and helped raise him to a leadership position within the Roman Empire. His reforms developed a system of public administration which is the basis for our modern-day, Western style of central government.

Diocletian (244–311 AD) was another crucial figure in the history of management, 400 years after Julius Caesar. Born of humble Illyrian status, Diocletian rose through the military ranks to become cavalry commander to the emperor Carus and eventually Roman emperor from AD 284 to 305. From the perspective of management,

Diocletian was an excellent delegator. He divided the scattered Roman Empire into 101 provinces, and then formed these into thirteen dioceses and four geographic divisions (History of Management). This tightened the ability to delegate authority and maintained the chain of command (Osigweh), enabling the managerial techniques practised in the city of Rome to extend throughout the empire.

Roman communication skills focused on education and literature. Greek was studied as well as Latin. Roman educators placed a high value on skills in oratory. Furthermore, Roman road building allowed for the expansion of Roman ideals and values by facilitating communication routes.

### 2.4.4 Construction Technology

Besides the tremendous system of highways the Romans built, many other types of structures show the genius of Roman construction technology. Roman aqueducts and public town baths used advanced concepts of hydrology and the recognition of gravitational force. The Romans made major advances in sanitation, which set the standard for urban planning in the Renaissance. Because of the crowded urban atmosphere, many Roman houses had indoor plumbing and flush toilets, while the towns often had a complex sewer system that predated sanitation technology by several hundred years (Bird). In other words, Roman building tackled pragmatic problems with vigour and invented important architectural features in response to these demands.

The building style of Rome was rooted in the Hellenistic tradition. The post and lintel system, previously the building form most often employed, was restricted in the load it could bear and the width of the span between the supports. What the Romans developed out of this Greek architectural style was the arch. The Roman arch was an architectural revolution, allowing for much greater load bearing than the previous system of columns.

#### 1. Arch

The strength of the arch enabled much larger structures to be erected. An arch was relatively easy to make using scaffolding and timber formwork. The support was held in place with a keystone. The arch form distributed weight more evenly down from the keystone toward the bottom stones, providing greater stability to the structure. The scaffolding and timberwork were easily reused to produce multiple arches of the same size (Onians 192–207).

The arch proved useful in the construction of many building types, including aqueducts. These carried water from the hills or reservoirs and mostly ran low to the ground or were underground; aqueduct bridges were built high over valleys or rivers. Typically these bridges were composed of staggered layers of arches. In fact, the arch became the dominant element of Roman architecture, inserted in most buildings as the primary supporting structure. This was true not only of exteriors but also of interiors, such as in Roman temples and basilicas, whose architecture is concentrated inside the building (Mark and Hutchinson 24–34). The Romans even constructed pure arches, such as the triumphal arch, where the arch was itself the whole structure (Alchermes 167–78). Thus, it was the development of the arch that made Roman architecture possible and gave it a unique and enduring quality in the history of building.

## 2. Concrete

During the Roman Empire, the most often used building material was concrete (*opus caementicium*), a mixture of quicklime, pozzolanic ash (pozzolana), and an aggregate of pumice. The widespread use of concrete freed Roman construction from the limitations of stone and brick, of which virtually all previous structures had been made. In addition, it permitted design innovations that were more elaborate and structurally complex (Lancaster). Laid into arches, vaults, and domes, concrete would harden into a rigid mass that was not susceptible to many of the internal forces and stress associated with material structures made of stone and brick (Robertson 233). As a result of the development of concrete, new opportunities up were opened for construction projects.

## 3. Concrete Dome

The development of the arch and concrete together made possible the concrete dome. This is a stepped dome with a drum base that tapers externally in stages to an oculus, a hole at its top where the concrete is thinner and lighter. Supported by thick walls on a circular foundation of concrete, the stepped dome does not in fact weigh as much as it may appear to, particularly since empty clay jugs and hidden smaller arches and niches were built into the upper sections to make it lighter and to enable the concrete to dry more quickly (MacDonald). The concrete dome demonstrates more than anything the spectacular advances made in Roman building using concrete and the arch. It is in the Pantheon where such a dome is most impressive.

## 4. *Vitruvius'* De Architectura

In addition to advanced architectural forms and materials, Roman civilisation contributed the single most important ancient text on architecture, Vitruvius' *De Architectura* (ca. 25 BC). Marcus Vitruvius Pollio (ca. 80–15 BC) was an engineer who wrote at length on the art and architecture of Rome. *De Architectura* is the only Roman text on classical architecture that remains intact. Divided into ten sections, it ranges over all aspects of Roman architecture, such as:

1. Town planning, architecture or civil engineering in general, and the qualifications required of an architect
2. Building materials
3. Temples and the orders of architecture
4. Continuation of book 3

5. Civil buildings
6. Domestic buildings
7. Pavements and decorative plasterwork
8. Water supplies and aqueducts
9. Sciences influencing architecture – geometry, mensuration, astronomy, sundial
10. Use and construction of machines – Roman siege engines, water mills, drainage machines, Roman technology, hoisting, pneumatics (Vitruvius)

Vitruvius mentions new uses for ropes, pulleys and winches, wheels, mills, and metal equipment. The text indicates much that was happening in Roman building and construction technology (Milani) and is a key source for contemporary knowledge of ancient Roman techniques.

The book was lost during the Medieval period and was rediscovered in 1414 by the Florentine humanist Poggio Bracciolini. Giovanni Sulpitius produced the first known Renaissance edition of Vitruvius in Rome in 1486. With its translation into other European languages soon thereafter, it was a significant source for Renaissance and Baroque architecture. *De Architectura* spurred Renaissance architects to formulate architecture as a scientific discipline. The work was also instrumental is emphasizing the skills of the artisan. Brunelleschi, for example, was prompted by this text and existing Roman monuments to invent a new device to enable him to hoist the large stones into place when building the dome of the cathedral in Florence. In terms of project management and scientific engineering, therefore, this Roman text had a significant impact on later generations.

## 5. Construction Machinery

The Greeks had used pulleys, cranes, and other machines. Roman builders adopted the same technologies. The pulley was used to direct force upwards or downwards, and horizontal or vertical winches also applied force. Such devices enabled the Romans to produce the various types of machinery necessary to meet their construction needs. One might expect metal to be used, but this was restricted to particular situations and projects (Heizer 821–30). Instead, many different styles of ropes were employed, some elastic on the model of the energy-conserving spring. For example, the catapult functioned on the tensile force created in the coils of ropes (Marsden). Some machinery could be massive in both size and strength. However, real machinery for moving and transportation operations was lacking. While no engines existed at the time, large stone sections would be carried great distances using teams of oxen, ramps, and manpower (Heizer 821–30).

In summary, the Romans made perhaps the greatest architectural advance of all time with their invention of concrete as a building material. In addition, they created the first structural arches, an engineering development that led further to the concrete dome. The arch contributed greatly to bridge and aqueduct construction over water. These forms were Roman additions to the Greek stone column. Machinery from earlier times was skilfully employed. Finally, in terms of theory, Vitruvius produced one of the most important texts on architectural theory and practise ever written, which gave insight into the building technology and construction management practises of the time.

### 2.4.5 Master Builder Tradition

The Roman Empire was a revolutionary period due to the dramatic changes that took place in engineering, architecture, and building science. Construction projects were ordered by the emperors, many of whom engaged in massive reconstruction and renovation projects in the cities. Not much changed in terms of labour, although its organisation based on Roman military practise would have been excellent. Often the skilled labour for projects came from the military, although no engineering corps as such existed. The new challenges of concrete building, such as arches and domes, stretched workers in new ways as they perfected such architectural forms through trial and error. At this time, the construction of aqueducts, bridges, and temples still required a large labour force, including slaves.

In terms of building tradition, master builders controlled large-scale projects, working with teams of surveyors and managers. The ancient master builders were skilled and ingenious in finding ways to address their needs (Merolla). In addition, the Romans used knowledgeable builders from the areas they conquered. The actual direction of the work, however, was done through a master builder who oversaw construction planning and progress, paying close attention to craftsmanship. The concept of the master builder took on greater significance because the master builder handled the design and supervision of the construction (Jackson 6). Furthermore, it is thought that guidebooks like *De Architectura* were drawn up based on thorough instructions from a master builder and then sent to a Roman outpost for a town to be built (Loulakis 46).

Marcus Vitruvius Pollio (born 80–70 BC, died after 15 BC) was one such master builder and his comments are instructive. He described the service of the *architectus* as consisting in craftsmanship and theory (*fabrica et ratiocinatione*) (Granger 7). Vitruvius wrote, “Craftsmanship is continued and familiar practise, which is carried out by the hands in such material as is necessary for the purpose of a design” (as quoted in Granger 7). Vitruvius goes on to warn that the master builder must beware of relying solely on theory while ignoring craftsmanship. In other words, the master builder must be trained in building with his own hands; that is, he must be trained in the tradition of artisanship and manual skill. Otherwise, Vitruvius says, he follows “a shadow and not reality” (as quoted in Granger 7). Vitruvius’ skill as an engineer and architect enabled him to develop designs, techniques, styles, and processes that served for centuries as the authority on building and design. While not scientific, his text created a model for architectural guidebooks.

### 2.4.6 Building Projects

#### 1. Caesar's Rhine Bridge (55 BC)

The Romans were not the first to build bridges. The earliest recorded major bridge was built by the King Nabopolassar of Chaldea over the river Euphrates at Babylon (O'Connor 139). However, the Romans produced the first true bridge engineers due to the high priority of such structures in the maintenance of the empire (in terms of efficiency, communications, and transport). Bennett says that Roman timber bridges were preserved by soaking wood in oil and resin as protection against dry rot, and coating them with alum for fireproofing (Bennett 14). In his view, the Romans knew that oak was the best for substructure work in the ground, alder was preferred for piles in water, and fir, cypress, and cedar were suitable for any superstructure. It is unlikely that these measures were taken in building Caesar's Rhine Bridge, which was meant only as a temporary structure.

Caesar himself describes the bridge construction (*Gallic War* 4.17). Its method involved pile driving thick timber piles, fastened two feet apart, obliquely (in the direction of the current) into the river at right angles to the bank. The same was done forty feet down river. These piles were joined by two-foot-wide beams fitted into the spaces between the two piles of the pair. A diagonal tie was arranged between pile pairs. The upper pair was kept at the right distance from the lower pair by iron braces. For protection against a floating attack, an additional pile was driven in front of each pair. Then planks were laid over the structure, allowing passage over the river. Supposing that the bridge was built at Coblenz, its length would have been at least 260 meters. Given the pier spacing, the work would have had to average three spans a day for it to be completed in the reported ten days. It is unclear what kind of equipment was used for lifting and pile driving.

Most remarkable was that the army could make six pile pairs a day and that the whole bridge was completed in ten days. Caesar's army crossed over the Rhine into "barbarian" territory (Gaul). Then they recrossed eighteen days later and destroyed the bridge. The purpose of the whole exercise seems to have been to demonstrate the speed of the Roman army, perhaps to awe the tribes, to show symbolically that Caesar was victorious over their river god, and to use this technical achievement for political means (to hurt the barbarians' morale). Caesar routinely built such bridges when going out with his army (e.g., later across the rivers Loire and Saone).

#### 2. Roman Colosseum (70–82 AD)

The Roman Colosseum is the amphitheatre situated on the site of the former lake of Nero's Golden Palace. It was commissioned by Vespasian in 75 AD, virtually completed by Titus in 81 AD, and a fourth story was added by Domitian in 82 AD. According to Bonde, Maines, and Richards, its foundation is a twelve-meter deep ring of concrete and stone blocks (Bonde, Maines, and Richards 29). It is 188 meters long by

156 meters wide. Around it are 80 arches with two annular corridors at ground level and three stories of stairs to various rings of seats. Encompassed within it are numerous subterranean chambers and passages. Most of the load-bearing structure consists of stone masonry (travertine and tufa), with concrete vaults and upper walls, and timber seating (Ward-Perkins 94). The joining surfaces of stone were cut and mortared. In lieu of mortar, iron cramps and dowels were used to fasten blocks together. The original structure was covered with a veneer of travertine, and its perimeter wall was made of marble ashlar with brick facings of pozzolan, concrete filled (Bond, Mark and Robison 82).

Taylor has done the most thorough study of the project's procedure. He presents a plausible explanation for a sequential process in building the Colosseum that entails slave forces for transporting materials and a highly skilled and specialized force of craftsmen working on the materials at the site (Taylor 137). He says that more than a dozen guilds of building specialists are consulted in the construction. His view is that the logistics were worked out beforehand, with efficient management of slaves and free workers, bricks already cured and fired, and quicklime slaked months in advance. He describes how during construction "legions of artisans were shaping the thousands of stones to be fitted" and how arches "would be laid out on templates, blocks carefully measured, sawed, and chiselled according to detailed specifications either of the architects or of a master stonemason working from plan and elevation diagrams" (Taylor 138). The final dressing of stones was done at the end. Taylor's study indicates a complex overlapping of tasks and stresses the material conditions that helped the flow of work through chambers and around material. He opts to see the crews working circumferentially, rather than vertically, which was more efficient in terms of the use of stone-hoisting cranes and ensured that work was being done on different parts simultaneously.

It is significant that the Romans employed cranes to lever stone blocks. Taylor's detailed book is crucial for understanding the Romans' use of shear or A-frame cranes to work in confined spaces around the building before they were situated on higher levels. Many cranes operated simultaneously and on multiple levels. He gives important details about the load capacity, the tilt, the reach, and the manoeuvrability of cranes during construction. Men and animals pulled the ropes. Scaffolding and formwork was only brought in for vaulting. He writes, "at this stage the cranes would be removed and timber formwork and scaffolding introduced" (Taylor 156). Because of the machines and labour power, the building was completed rapidly.

## 3. Pantheon (118–126 AD)

The Pantheon which means "all gods" in Greek was among the Emperor Hadrian's innumerable public buildings. Studies of its fabric and its brick stamps (most of which date to 120 AD) have shown conclusively that the building dates from Hadrian's reign (MacDonald 13). MacDonald's definitive study has outlined the building's history. He says, "it was begun sometime between July of 118 and the end of the following year and finished between 125 and 128" (96). After its dedication, it was used as an imperial audience hall and housed the Roman Senate, besides serving as a religious temple, which shows the multiple functionality of Roman buildings.

In terms of material and structure, most of the building is brick-faced concrete. Its foundation is a huge ring 4.5 meters deep of concrete and travertine fragments, with a further external circle. The porch façade is of gray Egyptian granite, the four inner columns of reddish Egyptian granite. All the original capitals and bases are of Pentelic marble. Marble and granite blocks are arranged in a design of circles and rectangles to form the porch pavement. The original roof was perhaps framed in timber. The rotunda's entranceway was barrel vaulted, elevated and surrounded by white marble pilasters. Its outer wall was probably covered in plaster. Under the dome, the colourful granite circles and squares of the convex ground (for drainage) form the "largest and best surviving example of an inlaid marble floor from ancient Rome" (Stamper 198). The Pantheon drew on predecessors such as the Temples of Jupiter Capitolinus and the Mars Ultor. However, as Stamper has remarked in his study of Roman temples, "it transcended these influences to a greater extent than we have previously seen, its architect achieving a new synthesis of innovation within the classical language and a redefinition of the temple as a building type" (Stamper 184).

What makes this building impressive is the method of constructing the dome. It was the largest vaulted concrete dome ever built, whose design and engineering problems far exceeded anything previously attempted. Its quick erection shows careful planning. It uses volcanic Pozzolana mortar throughout, which as Ward-Perkins says was a Roman finding that produced a lime mortar of unprecedented strength (100). MacDonald estimates that it was built "by pouring successive rings of concrete against a hemispherical dome of wood upon which the huge wooden forms for the coffers were first positioned. As the concrete was poured a grid of ribs was gradually built up between the coffer forms, strengthening the dome by virtue of their thickness" (110). To accomplish such a feat required massive timberwork twenty meters high. In addition, as Sear points out, material was carefully graded so that it lightened as the building moved upward. He says, "as the dome rises the fill becomes lighter until, near the oculus, it consists mainly of light volcanic pumice" (170). This was an innovative concept. Besides this selective grading of the cement, the whole succeeded on the strength of the mortar mix and foundations, and the numerous cavities placed within the drum body which facilitated drying and lightened the weight of the masonry (thus helping to relieve the arches). Each vault counteracted the lateral thrust of the adjacent vaults. Structurally, the dome had an obvious later influence on the Hagia Sophia, the Florence Baptistery, and St. Peter's Basilica.

Stamper has suggested various stages in the Pantheon's building (190–1). The awkward relationship of the *pronaos* and the intermediate block to the rotunda (unaligned cornices) indicates that the original design was for taller and wider columns. Because some of the Egyptian columns were lost at sea, Stamper sees a sign of a possible sudden change of plan during the construction due to a lack of the longer column shafts. He also sees a divergence from the *pycnostyle* and a problem with the pilaster-faced piers on the *pronaos* back wall, which are wider but with the same size capitals. His conclusion is that the design was changed during construction (Stamper 192). The discovery of full-size templates for the pediment and *pronaos* entablature in the pavement before the Augustus Mausoleum supports this conclusion and points to the fact that the marble used in its construction was unloaded at a port near to the Mausoleum, trimmed to the required size, and then transported to the site of the Pantheon.

According to MacDonald, "the combination of a domed cylinder lacking a peristyle with a monumental temple front" was a striking innovation (111). Its style was so innovative and successful – a portico with an unscreened rotunda – that it had an inestimable impact on later architecture. The Pantheon also experimented with dynamic optical corrections by slightly distorting the rosettes and slanting the front edge of the coffers outward inside the rotunda, corrections similar to those at the Parthenon. Much has been made as well of the symbolism of the eagle and oak laurel pediment (which links it to the imperial and family cult of Augustus) and the cosmic or geometrical symbolism of the dome. Sear gives an apt summary of the building's importance: "not only is it, by any reckoning, one of the great buildings of antiquity; not only does it mark the coming of age of the concrete-vaulted architecture which was Rome's unique contribution to the history of European architecture; but we can also see it very much as the Romans saw it in their own time" (Sear 98).

## 2.5 Byzantine Empire

### 2.5.1 Historical and Cultural Environment

#### 1. Background

The Byzantine Empire denotes the east of the Roman Empire after a political, cultural, and religious schism in the fourth century AD. Byzantium itself, located in a strategic area between the Adriatic and Black seas, was a major trading port founded by Greek traders. It was the strategic location of the city that allowed trade, commerce, and ultimately political hegemony to transfer power from West to East when it became apparent that Rome could no longer manage its political domain appropriately (Harris).

#### 2. Relationship to Previous Period

The separation of the Roman and Byzantine empires is really a current concept based on the idea that it was logical for Byzantium to take on the mantle of Rome when the culture of the Italian peninsula began to decay. In AD 324 the official capital of the Roman Empire was moved to Byzantium and renamed Constantinople (after Emperor Constantine) or "New Rome." Thus, Byzantium was a continuation of the Roman legacy, although with evolving technologies and, most importantly, the new officially sanctioned Christian religion (Adena).

The Byzantine Empire was a powerful 1,000-year empire whose influence in political, cultural, religious, economic, and military areas extended throughout the Mediterranean and Middle Eastern world. It provided a vehicle for the Greco-Roman cultural heritage to maintain power during a period in which much of western Europe was in turmoil. Many scholars believe that without the Byzantine Empire, many Western traditions may have been lost to the Islamic or Mongol empires. Yet as power in the West rose, Byzantium's power decreased, culminating in the Ottoman Turks' defeat of Constantinople in the fifteenth century (Halson).

### 3. Contribution to Western Civilisation

The Byzantine Empire was the only stable, long-term political and cultural system in Europe which both protected and isolated western Europe from the emerging Islamic empire. Its primary cultural importance lies in economics and religion. It had the most progressive economy in the area until the Renaissance. Its well-established trading network stretched across most of Eurasia and North Africa and incorporated the Silk Road. These economic trade routes were key to the dissemination of Western culture throughout the known world, as well as bringing into Byzantium Asian and Middle Eastern culture. It is likely that without the Byzantine trade routes and economy, there would not have been enough funding for the Crusades, which resulted in the redevelopment and revitalization of Europe (Laiou). The intricate network of interstate relations and treaties that formed the basis of Byzantine diplomacy allowed the rest of the world to assimilate its institutions, values, and attitudes (Neumann). The need for continual attacks on the Byzantine Empire gave rise to strong empires in the West, like Charlemagne's Holy Roman Empire. Out of Byzantine feudalism grew the incipient structures of economic capitalism.

Recent scholarship understands the Byzantine Empire as a complex blend of Rome and the East. This balanced historical approach seems to point to the fact that the various stages in medieval development would have been unlikely without the influence of Byzantium. Indeed, the Byzantine Empire is now viewed as equally dynamic and successful to Rome, with a far-reaching influence on the West (Angelov). By no means does it fit the description of a society of decadence and decay. In addition, it was an instrumental social force for the dissemination of Christianity. This had a radical impact on building in the West.

## 2.5.2 Knowledge and Scientific Environment

While the foundations of science were undoubtedly laid by ancient cultures, the Middle Ages proved to be a time where science moved out from under the wing of philosophy and became an independent discipline (Saliba 32). Byzantine knowledge and science preserved the writings of classical antiquity, particularly in philosophy and metaphysics (Anastos 410). The sophisticated Byzantine world preserved the previous Greco-Roman scientific discoveries and theories in medicine, mathematics, and science. The philosophical and scientific systems of Aristotle, Galen, and Ptolemy were spread around the empire to a new audience. Commentaries on their works proliferated and launched science through to the medieval period.

Nevertheless, after the sixth century AD and during the plague years and the Arab conquests, there were few novel contributions by Byzantine scholars (Cohen). Then, at the end of the first millennium, Byzantine scholars developed expertise in the astronomy, mathematics, and medicine of Persia and Arabia (Tatakes).

During the Byzantine Empire, religion proved unexpectedly to be no strong impediment to science and knowledge. Following the collapse of the Roman Empire, western Europe saw a huge loss of religious knowledge. In the East, however, the Christian church retained this knowledge. Scholars such as Aquinas and Buridan allowed the spirit of scientific inquiry to continue. Science was contained in their texts. Thanks to later translations of many of these medieval works in the Renaissance, Europe reclaimed this knowledge. The Scientific Revolution in Europe was based on it. The medieval period, in other words, allowed science to flourish because its philosophy focused on logic, encouraged empiricism, and viewed nature in terms of a set of existing natural laws that could be understood and explained through reason.

Despite the initial setback, the Byzantine Empire hosted some exciting scientific developments. For instance, Byzantine scientists actively put mathematics into practise, continuing the efforts of the ancient Greeks. In the field of architecture, early Byzantium watched Anthemius of Tralles and Isidore of Miletus construct the Hagia Sophia church using mathematical formulas. The significance of this building was enormous as it marked a technological breakthrough in its geometry, height, and design.

Perhaps the most important contribution the Byzantine Empire made to the progress of science was providing the medieval Islamic scholars with the ancient Greek works of mathematics and astronomy. These works were translated into Arabic, thus opening the Islamic world to a wealth of scientific information. This allowed Islamic countries not only to catch up scientifically, but to use the texts as a platform from which to devise their own theories and make fresh discoveries. As a result, the Islamic world became a scientific leader, extending knowledge in astronomy, mathematics, and other fields. The interchange of information between Byzantine Europe and the Arabic world fostered this trend. Byzantine scholars translated Arabic works into Byzantine Greek, thus continuing the exchange. The back-and-forth discovery and communication was beneficial for both and proved to be a sensational means of furthering human awareness and understanding of natural laws. Later, it was Byzantine grammarians who brought Ancient Greek grammar and literature to early Renaissance Italy.

One pertinent example of this process is the introduction into Europe of the Tusi-couple (named after Persian astronomer Nasr al-Din Tusi), an alternative to the equant put forth in Ptolemy's *Almagest*. It featured in the work of Nicolaus Copernicus, an astronomer who devised a working theory to demonstrate that the Earth is not the centre of the universe (Saliba 32). So important was Copernicus' theory that his *On the Revolutions of the Celestial Spheres* is not only considered the groundwork of modern astronomy, but the beginning of the Scientific Revolution itself.

In sum, the Byzantine Empire's influence on the progress of science was profound. It proved to be crucial to understanding natural laws and the universe. While Byzantine writers' contributions may not remain as well known as that of the Egyptians, we continue to use and employ their discoveries.

### 2.5.3 General Management

Despite the fact that monotheistic Christianity was the official religion of the Byzantine Empire, society did not progress forward in thinking with regard to government or management during this time (Cohen). Nonetheless, through writing and grammar the Byzantine Empire contributed significantly to the preservation and transmission of classical knowledge so that other societies could benefit from past systems (Anastos 410; Tatakes).

Communication in the Byzantine Empire was essentially religious in nature, and an austerely rigid religion at that. Art and literature took on the form of ecclesiastical and theological doctrine. Much of Byzantine art would serve as motivation for Renaissance artists. The Byzantine Empire instigated the Crusades, so effectively they laid the basis for most of the world's affairs for the next 800 years.

### 2.5.4 Construction Technology

The Byzantine Empire applied Roman technological advances in building its own grand projects. Yet there is also a detectable Eastern influence. Constantinople had a close relationship with the Greek East and Eastern culture made an important contribution to its architectural style, design, and construction elements (Van Milligan). The Byzantine builders adopted materials, tools, and machinery given to them from both West and East.

The key to changes in architecture during the Byzantine Empire was the development of a new type of church architecture, the most notable example of which was the Church of Holy Wisdom, or Hagia Sophia, in Constantinople, discussed at length below. Suffice it to note that its central plan with flanking domes was without antecedent, and that the necessary technology of ramps, levels, levers, pulleys, and winches, as well as the mathematics of angles and arches, were all utilised and expanded on during this great project (Ousterhout 165–76). Many of the important buildings of Constantinople were destroyed, though some examples exist throughout the provinces, mainly of religious architecture. However, the ruins of the fifth-century walls of the city itself do survive, consisting of outer and inner walls and ninety-six towers (VanMilligan).

## 1. Brick and Stone

The Eastern influence presents itself, for example, in twelfth-century churches' external brick walls. Brickwork was important in the Roman period and continued to be an important industry in the Byzantine Empire. Bricks were used for the facing of walls and piers, and in the exterior decoration of churches. They were sculpted and aligned so as to produce bands of ornamentation, a pattern likely borrowed from Persian influence. Brick was used also for vaulting in many buildings made otherwise of stone. The covering of exterior vaults and domes was of lead or tile, once again showing the evolutionary aspect of technological advancement and the utilisation of materials and methods from previous times (Hakim 4–25). Stone and brick were both used, alone and together. Iron clamps were used to tie stones supporting particularly heavy loads (Ousterhout 165–76).

## 2. Vault

There were some ingenious processes for building vaults, which were sometimes constructed of cut stone and sometimes of brick. There are some examples of vaults made by layering earthenware jars in a continuous spiral from the dome's foot to its top. Others were made without cent rings, likely a process learned from Assyria. Groined vaults "approximated the form of a dome by a longitudinal convexity upward in the intersecting vaults." The aisles of Hagia Sophia demonstrate different forms of vaulting technology (Osterhout 165–76).

## 3. Dome

The dome characterizes Byzantine architecture. An important technological advance was made in the discovery and use of pendentives to support the dome. According to Vanderpool, a pendentive can be conceived by thinking of "a hemisphere cut by five planes, four perpendicular to its base and bounding a square inscribed, while the fifth plane is parallel to the base and tangent to the semicircular intersections made by the first four" (552–69). In these conditions, only four triangular spaces remain of the original surface, and these are bounded by arcs or circles, which are the pendentives. Each masonry pendentive is convex and forms a type of arch. At the crown of the four arches, these pieces meet and form a circle. Vanderpool says that the pendentive is "perfectly stable and capable of sustaining any superstructure that does not by excessive weight disrupt the whole fabric by overthrowing the four arches which support it" (552–69). As a new technique for dome construction, this development was significant (Ballance 141–75). It meant several things. For one, it showed that domes could be built with any curvature. For another, it meant that a circular structure could be constructed on a square foundation and reach new heights.

### 4. Buttressing

The Byzantines understood the construction technology of buttressing. Their building designs incorporated internal abutments, which frequently carried on above the roofs of the side aisles to prop up the main vaults (Ballance 141–75). This followed the Roman employment of buttresses in saunas and temples, but it was used less often.

The impact of the Byzantine era on architecture was in some ways profound. The use of the buttress, the dome, and the vault reflected the earlier Roman period but passed that on through history by influencing early Islamic buildings. Islamic architecture utilised Byzantine architectural elements in building the Umayyad Great Mosque of Damascus and the Dome of the Rock in Jerusalem. Indeed, both structures borrowed Byzantine craftsmen and mosaicists to handle the decorative work. The West was impacted on a lesser scale, but Byzantine efforts paved the way for later Romanesque and Gothic architecture (Byzantine Legacy).

## 2.5.5 Master Builder Tradition

Until the sixth century the Byzantines used the term *mechanikos* to designate an architect and *mechanopois* to indicate an engineer. Builders during this period served patrons, who also took a hand in directing construction (Ousterhout 3–7). Nevertheless, the extent to which most patrons were involved is questionable. While they certainly provided funding, they probably had little control over actual construction. That was left to the master builder. Within the legal codes of the Middle Byzantine period, a manager acted as the conduit from the client to the workers. In a public works project, a government official who was not an architect was appointed to oversee the construction, with a master builder under his command (Ousterhout 43–8).

The Byzantine building team spanned several generations, with youths learning the trade as assistants, *mistbioi*, to the mature workers, *maistores*. The Byzantines used workshops as apprentice training schools for craftsmen. The skilled worker could work through the ranks from apprentice to journeyman. After some years it was possible to reach master mason level. The master mason would continue to improve and hone his technical and practical skills through building experience and study of existing structures. In his book *Master Builders of Byzantium*, Robert Ousterhout described the process:

> *Commonly, after a boy began an apprenticeship, he worked his way up through the various labours of construction. Often he started as a labourer in the quarry, cutting and removing stones. From there he could advance to become, successively, a layer of rough stone at the building site, a layer of finely carved stones, or perhaps a carver. If he had aptitude, he could become the apprentice to the master mason and learn design techniques. It was expected that a master mason would work his way step by step, through the workshop, to eventually possess considerable practical and technical knowledge of the*

*materials, as well as the skills necessary to work with them. His training was also supplemented by his personal experience and the study of monuments. (52)*

### 2.5.6 Building Projects

#### 1. Hagia Sophia (532–562 AD)

The Emperor Justinian commissioned Hagia Sophia in AD 532. The earliest church on the promontory had been the Constantinian church of Hagia Irene, or Holy Peace, which burnt down in AD 404. According to Mainstone, the foremost expert on Hagia Sophia, "no description of the form of the original church has survived apart from brief references to it as 'circus-like' or 'oblong'" (134). It was restored by Theodosius II in AD 415, but suffered its own fiery demise years later during the Nike riot of January 532 AD. This disaster gave Justinian the pretext for rebuilding a more magnificent church. The piers to carry the nave of the new structure were underway after only forty days of planning.

From Procopius we know that the architects of the project were two well-known Greek *mechanicoi*, Anthemius of Tralles (474 – 534 AD) and Isidore of Miletus. Both men had worked on key projects before and were "distinguished mathematical physicists" with extensive civil engineering experience (Freely and Cakmak 94). When Anthemius died in AD 534, Isidorus took over and completed the project in AD 537. Unfortunately, the church was built too rapidly, with the buttress foundations put down and built up to 42½ feet within a year and a half, and the upper parts of the buttresses, the arches, and the dome within three and a half years (Kähler 14). This speed affected the drying of the walls and the binding power of the mortar on the upper bricks. This structural weakness combined with an earthquake to collapse the dome partially in December 558 AD, along with part of the eastern semi-dome and the main eastern arch (Kato *et al.*).

Kähler believes that the flatness of the original dome created inordinate pressure and forced the walls of the pedestal outward, leading to collapse (32). This led to the first major reconstruction of the central dome from 558 to 562 AD, which added twenty feet to its height (Mainstone 126). Isidorus the Younger, Isidore's nephew, supervised this. He inserted a row of smaller arched windows around the dome. To prevent the same kind of meridional cracking as experienced by the Roman Pantheon, these window openings were an expedient for warding off cracking (Mark and Robison 151). The Hagia Sophia received its definitive form in AD 562 and was rededicated.

Scholars know very little about how workers were organized on this project, as almost nothing is said in the texts about builders' working methods (Ousterhout 39–57). Procopius does say that Justinian gathered artisans from all over the world without care for expense. He alludes to two teams of 5,000 workmen, each placed under 50 masters. They allegedly built the two sides in competition. The materials were interesting. According to Mainstone, mortar for the foundations was made "not with water, but with a broth of barley and the bark of elm" and special bricks for the arches and dome were manufactured on the island of Rhodes (85). Silentary's description shows that most of the columns were specially quarried and hewn in Thessaly (Freely and Cakmak 111–2). Procopius describes building the piers: "The courses of stone were laid down so as to form a four-cornered shape, the stones being rough by nature but worked smooth; and they were cut to the angles when they were destined to form the projecting corners of the sides of the pier, but when they chanced to be assigned to a position between the angles, they were cut in rectangles." He says they were not bound by lime or asphalt, but by lead poured into interstices and hardened in the joints. The ceiling was overlaid in gold – which is all we know about the mosaics from ancient sources (Kähler 47).

Where Hagia Sophia breaks new ground is in the way it uses pendentives. The transition from the square of the arches to the circular dome was made by these curving triangles, themselves buttressed by half-dome masonry. Nuttgens says, "Each beehive shape would start at the corner junction of two supporting arches, but stop when level with the top of the arches, forming curving triangles (the pendentives) that met in a ring poised on top of a canopy formed by the pillars and the arches" (143). The dome rested on this ring. Weight was thrust down onto the corner piers. This innovation, which its builders did not know would work, made the construction possible. In this revolutionary way, the congregational basilica was married to a vaulted double-shell dome in a spontaneous fusion of styles (Rodley 71).

## 2.6 Islamic Golden Age

### 2.6.1 Historical and Cultural Environment

#### 1. Background

The Islamic Golden Age is also known as the Caliphate of Islam or the Islamic Renaissance. The term refers to a system of political, cultural, and religious authority derived from the teachings of the Prophet Mohammed in the early sixth century AD. At its high point under the Abbassid Dynasty (eighth to thirteenth centuries AD), Islamic civilisation experienced a flourish of art and culture that blended Arab, Persian, Egyptian, and European elements (Kraemer). The result was an era of incredible intellectual and cultural advancements (Wiet). At the height of its power, the Caliphate controlled all of the present-day Middle East, all of northern Africa and into Spain, and as far east as the Indus Valley, making it among the largest empires of all time and one of the few states ever to extend direct rule over three continents (Kennedy).

#### 2. Relationship to Previous Period

Following the disintegration of the great Middle Eastern empires (Babylonian, Assyrian, Egyptian), the Arab world was not unified and remained a series of nomadic tribes under the nominal control of various warlords. Mohammed and his followers understood that real incentives were needed to increase agricultural production (Chaudry). As a result, Islam became a force for social transformation that made economic stability a reality. This allowed various tribes to coalesce into a community, or *umma*, united under religious teaching. After unifying, the leaders began a sweeping conquest of all surrounding lands. During the Islamic Golden Age, the Roman Empire transferred most of its political power to Constantinople. The population of Europe was loosely organized under feudalism.

### 3. Contribution to Western Civilisation

The Islamic Golden Age extended its rule to Spain and Sicily around AD 700, moving as far north as southern France by AD 730. Through this channel, Islamic arts and sciences entered European consciousness. Al-Hakam II, a ruler of Muslim Spain, gathered as many books as possible from Arab countries and put them in a library. This library became a translation centre for the texts to be rewritten in Latin (Lindberg 57–8). In this way, older knowledge was reintroduced into Europe. Influence was also exerted by the relocation of Arab scholars to Europe. Many had studied Greek texts in their home countries, so they brought those ideas with them (Laughlin 120). In other words, Islamic civilisation contributed to Western civilisation by preserving its own intellectual heritage and reintroducing it at a later date.

Furthermore, the European invasions of the Middle East during the Crusades created instability in the Islamic Empire beginning in the eleventh century, but also allowed a sharing of culture. The crusaders often returned with culture and technology brought from Islamic civilisation. In addition, the Islamic Golden Age kept alive the advances and texts of ancient Greece and Rome. What is most clear is that Islamic civilisation was rife with artists, scholars, philosophers, poets, physicians, and engineers who made significant contributions to the arts and sciences. So valued was the idea of learning during this period that Turner wrote, "Muslim artists and scientists, princes and labourers together made a unique culture that has directly and indirectly influenced societies on every continent" (as quoted in Saliba 270).

### 2.6.2 Knowledge and Scientific Environment

The Islamic world played a robust role in preserving and developing science during its Golden Age. Its discoveries and theories were passed back to medieval and Byzantine Europe through translations. This included the retranslation of many Western texts previously lost to Europe back into Latin or Greek from the Arabic (Lebedel 109). In this fruitful exchange, Islamic scholars reawakened the ancient Greek philosophical texts, especially Aristotle. Islamic mathematicians developed algebra and algorithms. They added trigonometry to Euclidian geometry. The decimal point was instituted and led to a redevelopment of the Arabic numeric system. In medicine Islamic physicians evolved the germ theory and made pharmacological advances (O'Leary).

Muslim scientists developed quantitative, empirical, and experimental approaches to scientific inquiry. A number of scholars believe that they provided the platform for modern science (Durant 162–86). For example, Al-Haytham (965–1039 AD) introduced and vigorously pursued the scientific method (Steffens). He was considered one of the great pioneers of experimental physics (Gorini, Durant 53–5). He authored the *Book of Optics,* which proved, using empirical evidence, that light rays entering the eye are responsible for sight. He demonstrated this using an invention known as the *camera obscura,* which showed the physical nature of light rays (Lindberg 154–76). He also conducted groundbreaking psychological work in visual perception that is regarded as the basis for psychophysics (Khaleefa).

From the Islamic world came a number of new technologies that were later adopted in Europe. Some of these inventions were astronomical instruments, including the quadrant, sextant, and observation tube. The latter was influential in creating the telescope (Morelon 9–10). Aside from astronomical technologies, the Islamic world created street lamps, waste disposal facilities (Artz 148–50), ethanol (Hassan), and more than 200 surgical instruments.

Another contribution from the Islamic world was its modifications to libraries. The libraries in Muslim countries had collections of ancient manuscripts that made the scientific discoveries of ancient cultures accessible. In addition, they introduced the public library and the ability to borrow books on loan, thus giving some the opportunity to increase their knowledge. Libraries also served as places to discuss scientific theories and discoveries, rendering science more understandable to the public. Finally, the organisation of books into categories and genres in a catalogue was first introduced in medieval Islamic libraries (Françoise 988–91).

The Islamic Golden Age nourished public education by creating the university. The world's oldest university to grant diplomas is at Al-Karaouine in Morocco. No doubt different than European universities, the early Islamic institutions were a major influence on their later European counterparts (Makdisi 175–82). The doctorate degree was conceived in the medieval Islamic system of legal education. Makdisi mentions other Muslim influences on the university. He says that "the fact that we still talk of professors holding the 'Chair' of their subject" comes from the "traditional Islamic pattern of teaching where the professor sits on a chair and the students sit around him." He explains that "practices such as delivering inaugural lectures, wearing academic robes, obtaining doctorates by defending a thesis, and even the idea of academic freedom are also modelled on Islamic custom." Thus, the Islamic Golden Age not only furthered the scientific method, but also enhanced public learning through pedagogical methods that are still intact today.

Transmission of Greek Philosophy is another important Islamic contribution. The collapse of the Roman Empire had a knock-on effect whereby many texts of classical antiquity came into the possession of the Europeans. As explained in the section exploring the Byzantine Empire, many of these texts had previously been provided to the Islamic countries. This goodwill gesture led to an unpredictable turn of fate, as during the Middle Ages many of these texts were translated from Arabic back into European languages. Thus, while the original copies in Europe were lost, the passing of the texts to the Middle East led to retranslated texts, which allowed the works of philosophers such as Aristotle to be known once again to the Europeans (Lebedel 109).

Another way in which Greek ideas were reintroduced to Europe was through the expansion of Islam from the Middle East to Europe. Sicily and Spain were conquered in approximately AD 700, with southern France becoming populated by Muslims by AD 730. Al-Hakam II gathered as many books as possible from Arab countries and placed them in a library, which later became a translation centre for the texts to be rewritten in Latin (Lindberg 57–8). Their reintroduction was also furthered by the relocation of Arab scholars who, having studied the Greek texts in their home countries, moved to Europe and brought Greek ideas with them (Laughlin 120).

### 2.6.3 General Management

Islamic scholars sought out scientific, rational, and humanistic writings in their quest for information. Many of these men were open to humanistic notions like individualism, liberalism, religious freedom, and cross-cultural exchange (Hassan). Among them, Al-Ghazali (1058–1111) had a significant influence on leadership and management. In his important book *Nasihat*, or *Advice to Kings*, he dealt with subjects such as the qualities required in kings, and the character of ministers and deputies. The *Nasihat* ("Advice") was part of a genre of writings about political authority and leadership. One of Al-Ghazali's arguments is that communication with the leadership needs to be maintained so that the leadership remains involved in the organisation as a whole. Good leadership was a sacred duty, which led to God's pleasure when it was undertaken well. The following three paragraphs summarize the contents of Al-Ghazali's *Advice to Kings*:

1. On good conduct
   The burden of establishing the right model of behaviour is placed on the shoulders of the king.
2. On accessibility
   Leaders who are not accessible to their people restrict open communication throughout an organisation. Information is significant for the leader to comprehend the organisation's strengths and weaknesses, but also to be in possession of all information that influences the management of the enterprise.
3. On trustworthiness and self-denial
   Giving an example from the life of the Caliph Umar bin Abdul Aziz, Al-Ghazali relates that the Caliph was awake one evening studying the government's daily report by the light of a lamp. One of his servants came in to discuss some household problems. Aziz ordered that he extinguish the light, because the oil was paid for by the public and the people's property should only be used for public business.
4. On appointing deputies

Al-Ghazali wrote about deputies in the context of ministerial posts at the Sultan's court. He compared a minister to one of the companions of the Prophet. Good ministers were important for a ruler in the same way that even the Prophet had to consult the learned and wise among his companions. (Chowdhry)

### 2.6.4 Construction Technology

Islamic architects borrowed heavily from the Byzantine Empire's practise of building domes and arches. They used surveying tools such as plumb bobs and levels. Cranes, ramps, levers, and wheels were in use in the construction machinery of the Islamic Golden Age, as available and necessary techniques to build large and heavy structures. An example is the Dome of the Rock in Jerusalem. The structure is octagonal. It is made up of a dome of wood with a diameter of approximately sixty feet, set on a raised drum, which in turn comprises a circle of sixteen piers and columns, with a surrounding octagonal arcade of further piers and columns. Without question, therefore, the structure of the Dome of the Rock shows the progressively expanding knowledge base of the methods used to construct domes and arches (Kostof).

In general, mosques consisted of covered walkways, columns, and arches, a small niche or *mihrab*, and a fountain placed in an open courtyard used for purification. Islamic architecture pioneered the minaret built beside the main structure. The minaret was a large tower typically used by muezzins for the call to prayer, which sometimes doubled as a watchtower. The building materials of the Islamic Golden Age were taken from previous periods and from the environment. Mostly they built using marble, stone, and brick, combined with other mortar composites, tar, and metals for various project applications. Islamic builders utilised building examples from the Byzantines and the Romans (Banister 571). Advancements in glass made glass windows possible. Other significant contributions to construction technology must be noted in the area of skilled tradesmen and craftsmen, in using decorative techniques in sculpting, in metallurgy, and in other forms of material artwork (Ousterhout 165–76).

The Mosque of the Prophet, *Al-Masjid al-Nabawi* (622–781 AD), was situated on the site of Mohammed's house in Medina. For that reason, it has been called an "accidental prototype for the mosque" since the mosque grew out of his house (Ettinghausen, Graber and Jenkins-Medina 7). Mohammed himself is said to have shared in the construction work, carrying clay. This sanctuary generated almost all subsequent Islamic mosque architecture and construction technique. From it evolved the Islamic congregational mosque. Its basic plan was replicated in virtually all other significant mosques throughout the world and became the nuclear edifice of Islamic cities from which all other streets and structures radiated.

The original structure was simple. According to Hoag, these mosques were "essentially rectilinear forum-like enclosures oriented in the direction of Mecca, with a roofed columnar hall like a Greek stoa or better yet an Achaemenid *apadana*" (10). It was built of unfired mud brick (*libn*) with palm columns supporting the palm frond roof (King 82). There was a walled courtyard and an unpaved floor. The structure was expanded in AD 628, which "doubled the floorspace of the Mosque" and added an "Honorable Room" in which Mohammed's tomb was later placed (Ismā'īl 38).

The Medina mosque was rebuilt in stone in AD 649–50 by Caliph Uthmān bin Affan, replete with a new roof made of imported teak and doors of local *ar'ar* (King 82). The new structure used chiselled stone with lime mortar rather than sun-dried mud-bricks and palm columns. Arches were constructed from the east to the west side over the new columns. The building was rebuilt again in AD 706 using eighty Coptic and Syrian artisans. All the columns were covered with plaster, rubbed, and polished so as to look like white marble (Creswell 43). Their capitals were carved and gilded. A lead-covered roof was put over the gilded teak ceiling panels. There were marble window grilles and a cornice with floral decorations. The "Honorable Room" was rebuilt in carved basalt.

Several important changes occurred in the new mosque that would have consequences for future mosques. The mosque was adorned with mosaic stones. The pulpit or throne-chair gained prominence by being heightened with nine steps. The mosque introduced the minaret and the *mihrab* (Ettinghausen, Graybar and Jenkins-Medina 21; Hoag 11). A dome was placed in front of it, which makes it the earliest reference we have to a dome in front of a *mihrab*. In summary, the axial nave, the concave *mihrab*, the *minbar*, and the dome in front of the *mihrab* were destined to play an important port in the history of Islamic architecture (Ettinghausen, Graybar and Jenkins-Medina 25).

What is important about the construction history of the Medina Mosque is how it became the architectural model for subsequent mosques. Religion shaped to a great degree the techniques used in architecture and building in the Islamic Golden Age. The unique development of the minaret, the domed *mihrab*, often with elaborate mosaic tiles decorating the domed area, the *minbar*, and the arcaded courtyard were key contributions of early Islamic architecture. Later the Muslims pioneered the revolutionary pointed arch that would play such a large role in Gothic architecture. In general, from the Mosque of Damascus (706–715 AD) and the Mosque at Qairouan (820–836 AD) to the much later mosques like the Taj Mahal, the impact of Islamic religious architecture shines through the centuries.

### 2.6.5 Master Builder Tradition

Religious and social needs impelled Islamic architects to develop their own creative stylistic features (Architecture). The Islamic style that can be found in Spain, North Africa, and the Middle East eventually influenced the Classical and medieval periods in Europe (Architecture).

In the Islamic Golden Age, the existence of several different styles, materials, and techniques enabled the builders to be creative and selective. Most of the masonry structures were in arched, vaulted, or domed form, continuing Roman and Byzantine building traditions (Banister 571).

The Byzantine model for domes assisted Islamic builders with roof construction and timber engineering. Unbaked bricks along with lime and gypsum for stabilization were significant, since most buildings were achieved by earth walling. The character of Islamic buildings must include the techniques used by masons for climate control in the hot and dry Middle East. They were basic techniques for the most part, such as small window openings in thick walls. But the development of window scoops was sophisticated, resulting in a mastery of technique by Islamic builders. They also crafted buildings that were less susceptible to earthquakes. The Islamic pointed arch and the horseshoe arch were central features of Islamic structures and would later be used in Gothic architecture (Banister 571).

### 2.6.6 Building Project

#### 1. Grand Mosque of Damascus (706–715 AD)

A mosque was built for Damascus by Umayyad Caliph Al-Walid in AD 706. This became the Great Mosque of Damascus with its transept, dome, four *maharib*, double-tiered arcades around the courtyard, marble window grilles of geometric shapes, gilt column capitals, white and colour-veined marble pavement and wall panelling, and mosaics. It is the oldest congregational mosque in the Muslim world and was constructed on an old Roman sacred platform, which survives in the large masonry blocks and pilasters (Hoag 22). The old site had four large towers at its corners and arcades around the edge that opened onto a rectangular courtyard. Under Theodosius (379–95 AD), Christianity apparently took over this precinct as a Byzantine church that lasted until the Islamic conquest.

In AD 706, the church was demolished and the mosque built along the southern wall. Its layout consisted of three aisles and a *qibla* wall with a raised transept. On the south façade was the *mihrab*. There was a two-story arcade along the courtyard's east, north, and west sides, with tiled roofs over wooden beams. The arcades display different arch forms (pointed, horseshoe, round, semi-circular), while the glass mosaics decorating the walls resemble those of the Dome of the Rock. In the transept centre was a wooden dome. The treasury was an octagonal chamber on eight columns, over a pool. According to Ibn Shakir, this incredible structure was finished in 714–715 AD (Creswell 46).

Petersen attributes the mosque's form to earlier architectural styles. He writes, "the form of the mosque, particularly the sanctuary façade, was probably derived from Byzantine palatial architecture, possibly the Chalci palace in Constantinople" (61–2). Hoag highlights the use of a similar style of mosaics between Theodoric's Ravenna palace and the mosque's prayer hall façade (25). He concludes, "sometimes, as in the Great Mosque at Damascus, secular Byzantine forms were used in an Islamic religious context – probably because that building was so intimately related to the Caliph himself, but also perhaps because the institution of the Friday mosque still had the political connotations of a forum as well as a place of prayer" (32).

What makes these comparisons more plausible is that the craftwork done in building the mosque came from Byzantium. Yeomans says, "The historian al-Tabari

(839–923 AD) said that al-Walid sought help from the Byzantine emperor for his building projects: the emperor sent one hundred workmen and forty loads of mosaic *tesserai,* so despite periodic Arab attacks on Constantinople good diplomatic and cultural contact was maintained" (34).

There is little doubt that the Damascus Mosque was influential in later Islamic architecture, perhaps to an unparalleled extent. For one thing, the four towers of the precinct served as minarets for the first time in Islam. Other architectural features with lasting influence were its three axial entrances, its transept, its alternation of piers and columns, its three-deep sanctuary aisles, and its two-tiered arcades (Creswell 72). The same style was repeated to various degrees in the mosques of Cordoba, Aleppo, Harran, and Hamma. Damascus was quite simply the model for all later congregational mosques, more influential than the Dome of the Rock because of its representation of a covered prayer hall adjacent to a large courtyard surrounded on three sides by cloistered arcades (based itself on the Medina model but on a much grander scale). Yeomans gives an important perspective on the spatial equilibrium of this mosque and how it is an improvement over Christian basilicas: "The impact of an uncluttered, continuous floor plane, enlivened by densely patterned carpets, is one of the most distinctive and striking features of the interior spatial organization of this and any other mosque – it is one of the keynotes of Islamic architecture" (35).

## 2.7 Crusades

### 2.7.1 Historical and Cultural Environment

#### 1. Background

In 1095 Pope Urban II announced the First Crusade. The actual reasons for the Crusades – the series of religiously sanctioned military campaigns waged from 1095 to 1291 AD in the Middle East – remain controversial. The 200-year war was reputedly fought to restore Christian control over the Holy Land. However, modern scholarship has uncovered numerous other motives: feudalism was morphing into capitalism, which meant that new markets and exploited lands were required; the populations in Europe needed a cause in order to allow control to continue by royalty and the Catholic Church; and the Papacy needed a way to establish control over the kings of Europe and have a private army to dispense with its enemies (Riley-Smith). Perhaps all of these reasons combined initiated the Crusades.

The routes taken by the Crusading armies, whether by land through Greece, Constantinople, and into the Middle East, or by sea through Alexandria or Tyre, contributed to the expansion of European influence. Furthermore, armies required regular provisions, and with the movement of so many troops and supplies it was necessary to improve shipbuilding, food technology, military arms, navigation, and geography (Asbridge).

## 2. Relationship to Previous Period

The so-called fall of the Western Roman Empire in the AD 400s and the transfer of complete power to Constantinople eventually resulted in a power vacuum in Western Europe. This vacuum was filled by a series of rulers who vied with the Papacy for control. The Crusades united Europe under one idea and increased adherence to the doctrine of Christianity. However, because there were so many different agendas, many of the Crusade armies were deflected from their original purpose. For instance, Constantinople was sacked following the Fourth Crusade, and the Sixth Crusade left Europe without the blessing of the Papacy. Islamic forces triumphed in the Seventh through Ninth Crusades. The last, in 1271–2, resulted in the collapse of the remaining Crusader strongholds along the Mediterranean coast. With the technological revival in Europe, however, Europeans were now more interested in trading eastward and re-establishing their own hegemony (Madden).

## 3. Contribution to Western Civilisation

The Crusades were by and large a dismal failure for the European monarchs and the Papacy. However, there were some benefits. Political improvements in Europe after the Crusades led to a consolidation of power in the major European capitals and a general unification under the Papacy that may not otherwise have happened. The Crusades also brought knowledge of the East back into Europe and re-established traffic between East and West (*New Catholic Encyclopedia* 508).

The political and cultural strife engendered by the Crusades is still apparent in global foreign policy surrounding Israel. Even in the twenty-first century, many Arabs view the Crusades as savage invasions by Christian fundamentalists, and the modern Arab independence movement and Pan-Islamic organisations trace their beginnings to the desire to rid their culture of European influences (The Crusades – Crusade Legacy). The Crusades established the foundations of the modern nation-state. They also exposed Europe to Islamic culture, technology, and science. Most of all, they opened up the idea of trade and exploration into Asia, Africa, and the New World, eventually resulting in the discovery and European exploitation of these continents (Stark).

## 2.7.2 Knowledge and Scientific Environment

The Crusades themselves did little to advance science and knowledge outside of military warfare. However, as noted, they did bring the European West into intimate contact with the Islamic Middle and Near East. Although Europe had been exposed to Islamic culture for centuries through contacts in the Iberian Peninsula and Sicily, much knowledge in areas such as science, medicine, and architecture was transferred from the Islamic to the Western world during the Crusade era. In addition, the Crusades are seen as having opened up European culture to the world:

> *The Crusades brought about results of which the popes had never dreamed, and which were perhaps the most, important of all. They re-established traffic between the East and West, which, after having been suspended for several centuries, was then resumed with even greater energy; they were the means of bringing from the depths of their respective provinces and introducing into the most civilized Asiatic countries Western knights, to whom a new world was thus revealed, and who returned to their native land filled with novel ideas.... If, indeed, the Christian civilization of Europe has become universal culture, in the highest sense, the glory redounds, in no small measure, to the Crusades. ( Crusades.-The New Catholic Encyclopedia 508)*

The need to raise, transport and supply large armies led to a flourishing of trade throughout Europe. Roads largely unused since Roman times saw significant increases in traffic as local merchants began to expand their horizons. Along with trade, new scientific discoveries and inventions made their way east or west. The result of this conjunction was significant for Western knowledge, since it partially enabled Europeans to reconnect with Islamic science, which at the time was flourishing. Many of the Islamic advances previously discussed, such as algebra, optics, and the university system, entered the Western world when the Crusaders returned. These contributed greatly to the subsequent European Renaissance.

### 2.7.3 General Management

Chivalry was the most important guiding model for behaviour during the Crusades. As will be explained, the concepts underlying chivalry link directly to management. Medieval knights followed a code that had roots in earlier centuries but flourished during the Crusades. Later it dwindled except among the nobility during the Renaissance (The Chivalry Code), when wealthy merchants sent their sons for training to aristocratic courts and read guides to gentlemen's manners (Sweeny). During the Crusades, the Catholic Church's tolerance of war as a means of defending the faith was forced to increase. The Theory of Just War experienced a revival. Religious rituals developed around blessing a knight's sword, along with purifying baths (Sweeny). The notion of being a "knight of Christ" (*miles Christi*) vitalized the European imagination in the eleventh century, making the era of the Crusades one of specifically religious chivalry.

In his book *States of Political Discourse*, Constantinou sees chivalry as a symbol for authority in management. It derived from ideas about horsemanship, including the handling and training of horses (169). In other words, chivalry had to do with managing and controlling something else with a certain system and spirit. Referring to the exemplary image of King Arthur's roundtable, Manch and Henning write, "the table's round shape did not allow for hierarchy or a singular leader" (41). All were equal partners in defending the Christian faith, fighting injustice, and relieving oppression. This model of leadership is based on a distribution of authority. It functions more closely to the idea of partnership. While associated with feudalism and a class structure, chivalry was not hereditary, as was feudalism.

Chivalry was a clearly understood although unwritten code of conduct. In retrospect, Léon Gautier (1832–1897) has formulated its principles:

1. Thou shalt believe all the Church teaches and shalt obey her commandments.
2. Thou shalt defend the Church.
3. Thou shalt respect all weaknesses and shalt constitute thyself the defender of them.
4. Thou shalt not recoil before thine enemy.
5. Thou shalt make war against the infidel without cessation and without mercy.
6. Thou shalt perform scrupulously thy feudal duties, if they be not contrary to the laws of God.
7. Thou shalt never lie, and shalt remain faithful to thy pledged word.
8. Thou shalt be generous, and give largesse to everyone.
9. Thou shalt be everywhere and always the champion of the Right and the Good against Injustice and Evil. (as quoted in "The Code of Chivalry")

This code clearly emphasises the importance of honour, courage, spoken integrity, and concern for the less fortunate. The moral attitude it endorses has a lot to do with ideas of leadership. It also shows the controlling and managerial force of religious ideas.

### 2.7.4 Construction Technology

The period of the Crusades was characterized by religious warfare. This twin influence of religion and military concerns influenced to a great degree the progress of construction technology. Much was decided by strategic considerations. Military fortifications advanced to a new level given the importance of castles for military strategy and success. Castles in Europe at the time were rather rudimentary. The First Crusade created such a problem that builders began changing castle building from wood and earth to stone. This was in response to the lack of and inadequacy of timber, which meant a need to build shorter towers that were insufficient for defence. Stone became the primary material for building, which enabled higher and stronger walls and towers. In addition, the Norman keep was essentially designed for passive defence that required only sufficient food and cleanliness to allow those within to survive attack until relief forces arrived.

When the Crusaders reached Constantinople, they were faced with Byzantine fortifications that included double-banked ditches, towers, and more enormous walls than they had ever seen. Many Crusaders returned home, taking with them their knowledge of Byzantine defensive structures. Of major importance, for example, was the idea of using round towers instead of square towers, and a concentric design. This allowed the Crusaders to employ multiple defences and opened the door to architects for further exploration in design (Crusader History 3).

Because the Christian Europeans had limited manpower in foreign lands, they were unable to maintain garrisons (Smail 133–49). Their military fortifications had to be sturdy enough, with thick, tall walls to withstand larger attacking forces. Stone was used and sites were selected to maximize military advantage and natural protection. Often construction was done on hills, not merely for protection but to ensure that signalling was possible from the walls and raised areas. Inside the fortress, provisions had to be made to endure a siege. There needed to be food storage rooms and access to water. Many castles were built over wells dug into stone (Ellenblum).

War machines employed existing technology, with ropes, tension, torques, and force to maximise destruction. Tools were made to suit the application at hand, whether it was for building or weaponry (Erlich 85–93). As such, the necessary machinery evolved, notably the crane, ramps, pulleys, and winches. Craft stone masonry was employed, with its associated tools often made to meet the immediate need.

The Crusaders were sometimes accompanied by their wives and even children, so castles functioned as homes as well as centres of government and military strongholds. The Crusaders developed the style of castles from the normal Western solid square keeps to round towers, which better withstood attack and gave them a more effective firing range. They also incorporated other features such as offices, the portcullis, and interior chapels (Williams). A crucial contribution to military architecture was the box machicolation, evident first in the Krak de Chevaliers, which pierced holes in the wall to allow missiles to be thrown with a protective covering. In sum, while the design of Crusader castles was primarily for military purposes, there were additional elements that took shape on the basis of family living, religious practise, and government administration.

### 2.7.5 Master Builder Tradition

The Crusader master builders were skilled in the construction of impressive castles and towers geared towards protection and withstanding assault. They came from Europe, where feudalism and Roman influence had already led to numerous Norman-style keeps and castles. The barons ruled their lands and domains from these fortified structures. The master builders designed them with enough complexity to be used for defence, administration, and personal home comforts. When they oversaw the Crusaders' castles, the conditions were a little different and the aims were to maximize fortification against the Islamic threat. The builders often took over previous castles and added various structural improvements for warfare. They did not neglect spiritual and aesthetic concerns, however, and the interior rooms of halls, chapels, and living quarters were designed with beauty and character. Thus they learned to combine various styles to meet different needs.

Design and construction of the Crusaders' castles was often done by the knights themselves. This is evident in the Krak de Chevaliers, which was built by the Knights Hospitaller. The Knights of Malta formed another important group of warriors and master builders. These brotherhoods provided the skilled design and master craftsmen for building the innovative Crusader castles.

Little survives of architectural theory from the time of the Crusades. Much of the writing was theological, and any comments on architecture are notes on structures in the biblical text. Abbot Suger's *Liber de rebus in administratione sua gestis* (*The book on what was done under his administration*) comments on and emerged with Gothic architecture (Crusader History 1). While it is assumed that architectural knowledge was transmitted both verbally and in writing, the most important way in which the master building tradition was handed down occurred technically, in master builders' lodges.

There is no evidence that imported labour was involved in building during the Crusades, and many of the castles are in isolated and difficult places, away from towns. The skill required to build these structures would have been tremendous given the challenging lay of the land, often sloping on elevated hills, and considerations of military strategy that included defence against attack and siege. The builders learned quickly to change from wood and earth building to stone. They adapted innovations from the Byzantine Empire. Thus, the master builders are seen as engaged in a dynamic dialogue with their own contemporary architecture and the military needs for which they were constructing.

### 2.7.6 Building Project

#### 1. Krak de Chevaliers, Syria (ca. 1144–1250 AD)

Located on the site of a former Kurdish or Arab fortress, Krak de Chevaliers was built on an elevation 700 meters above the countryside to control access to the Orontes valley. Stierlin describes its origins: "during the Crusades, in 1142, Raymond II, Count of Tripoli, donated this site, which controlled access to the plain of Bekaa, to the Knights Hospitaller" (Stierlin 6). The small fortress was in an important location and seemed to the builders and warriors to be in a good defensive position overseeing the plain (Tyerman 198). The Knights Hospitaller immediately set about doubling the thickness of the limestone walls (to eighty feet) and installing defensive machicolations to repel Muslim invaders. Who, other than the knights themselves, contributed to its building is unclear, however. Lawrence hypothesizes several building stages: "in the inner ward the wall from the tower of entry L to the tower with buttress-machicoulis P, including the chapel M, appears earlier than the rest of the inner ward. Of the outer ward the whole south front is Arab, and the western side so far as tower D" (94).

This great stronghold was undoubtedly a military advancement. Claster speaks of impregnable walls, interior accommodations for 2,000 knights, and a well-supplied source of water and a cavernous undercroft for storage of a five-year supply of food (263). Its strategically designed position atop steep-sided slopes was enhanced with surrounding double walls, a moat with a drawbridge, and semi-circular towers. The towers were connected by a long vaulted passage "that enabled mounted knights to ride straight up into the impregnable heart of the fortress" (Billings 83). All of this is expected from what historians know of the requirements of Crusader castle architecture. Stylistically it is a Gothic fortress. Yet it is important for another advance: the covered box machicolation. The master builder chose for the first time to employ this architectural feature. From these covered overhanging floor slots, missiles (stones) could be fired downward against scaling attempts. This is important, as Lawrence says, for "assailants could never get underneath the fire of the defenders on the fighting platform" (97). The machicolation was an innovative advance in military building and design. Combined with the other typical and accentuated features of the massive stone fortress, its architecture perfectly exemplifies the castle-constructing mastery of the Crusader builders.

In addition to the imposing exterior there was a pleasant interior. Harrison speaks of a fusion of religious and military architecture, by which he means fortifications guided by religious design, construction, and function (4). He says, "what is not usually appreciated is that the inner enceinte contains a monastic core of knights' hall, dormitory, cloister and chapel; here the warrior monk was totally isolated from the outside world and lived a life that could be separated from lay servants and mercenary soldiers" (Harrison 5). The great hall and cloister had ribbed architecture, while friezes, bosses, and capitals softened the façade of the central courtyard (Harrison 42). According to Billings, "the Castellan of the Order had his splendid gothic chamber, delicately carved and decorated, in the south-west tower; and in the courtyard below, you can still enter the Romanesque chapel and the refectory where crowned heads of Europe on crusade would have been entertained" (83). In other words, Krak de Chevaliers had stylish charm and Gothic spirit as well as structural strength.

## 2.8 Romanesque

### 2.8.1 Historical and Cultural Environment

#### 1. Background

The term *Romanesque* is an architectural category that refers to the art and architecture of the Mid–Late Medieval Period in Europe (1000 to 1240 AD). It was coined in the nineteenth century to delineate features of the post-Roman Empire style. The Romanesque period saw the decline and downfall of the Roman Empire, a vacuum that was filled by the Roman Catholic Church. During this time, cathedrals and castles connected with the church and the Crusades sprang up in stone. Their Romanesque elements comprise round-headed arches, barrel vaults, apses, and decorations, and in southern Europe are often blended with Byzantine elements (Atrisgerinko). Additionally, the Romanesque style developed to reflect a rebirth of art, science, and culture in the High Middle Ages. This European intellectual revival came with a great deal of social, political, and economic transformation (Benson). There was also a renewal in scholasticism that coincided with the Romanesque architecture and its new technologies.

## 2. Relationship to Previous Period

The Romanesque period is considered a furthering of the traditions of the Roman and Byzantine empires. Through feudalism, Europe became more prosperous and experienced urbanisation. This placed more emphasis on urban art and architecture related to the church, which was the cultural centre of every European town. The church continued as the vehicle for spiritual art and building, but gave artists new opportunities to experiment with past trends and designs.

Politically, Europe was divided and not as robust or unified a civilisation as that of the Islamic World. However, by the twelfth century the Hanseatic League had been founded, and the Holy Roman Empire had taken on the overall political administration of the old Carolingian (from Charlemagne) structure (Grant). Added to this were the Eastern artistic, cultural, and scientific influences brought back to Europe by the Crusaders. One scholar has written:

> *The twelfth century in Europe was in many respects an age of fresh and vigorous life. The epoch of the Crusades, of the rise of towns, and of the earliest bureaucratic states of the West, it saw the culmination of Romanesque art and the beginnings of Gothic; the emergence of the vernacular literatures; the revival of the Latin classics and of Latin poetry and Roman law; the recovery of Greek science, with its Arabic additions, and of much of Greek philosophy; and the origin of the first European universities. The twelfth century left its signature on higher education, on the scholastic philosophy, on European systems of law, on architecture and sculpture, on the liturgical drama, on Latin and vernacular poetry. (Haskin viii)*

This important summary of the period by historian Charles H. Haskins describes the major features of the High Middle Age renaissance at the end of the eleventh century and its important connections with other periods and movements.

Essentially, the Carolingian renaissance was historically grounded in previous periods, especially the Islamic Golden Age and the Byzantine Empire with their contributions to the rediscovery of Greek science. It heralded later literary, artistic, and scientific achievements in the fifteenth-century Italian Renaissance and the seventeenth-century Scientific Revolution.

## 3. Contribution to Western Civilisation

The twefth-century renaissance that accompanied the development of the Romanesque style was international in scope. For example, wandering scholars travelled from country to country developing their own genre of poetry (Sommerville). There were social, political, and economic transformations too. For example, the new institution of the university altered higher education, providing innovative techniques of thought and speech. Scholars working within the universities and monasteries created fresh approaches to ancient intellectual problems (Middle Ages).

### 2.8.2 Knowledge and Scientific Environment

The twelfth-century renaissance also entailed a revitalization of intellectualism in Western Europe. This revival was influenced by the recovery of Ancient Greek philosophical and scientific texts. The centres of this intellectual movement were the monasteries and the new European universities. By the outset of the thirteenth century, these centres had produced accurate Latin translations of these texts, which allowed the transfer of scientific ideas. Ancient ideas on the natural sciences began to spread. Scholastics like Robert Grosseteste, Albertus Magnus, and Roger Bacon commented and expanded on the Greek works, creating a new context for the elaboration of science. Numerous commentaries on Aristotle's writings framed these intellectual debates (Grant 127–31). In addition, other texts were sought out for translation. The Greek Church Fathers became popular writers and a broad interest in the Qur'an and Islamic scientific texts (d'Alverny 429–30) and literary texts (Irwin 93) enflamed the quest for knowledge. This interest in Islamic thought was illustrated by Gerard of Cremona's journey to Toledo, where he found in the library numerous Arabic books on every subject matter and set about learning Arabic to translate them (Burnett 255). Science and knowledge exploded as a result of such efforts to make texts accessible.

Thus, the renaissance of the twelfth century played an integral part in fostering scientific methodology as it forced a renewed interest in Arabic texts, which themselves had been transferred from Europe prior to the demise of the Roman Empire. The Arabic translations once again allowed the works of antiquity to be rediscovered by the Europeans.

### 2.8.3 General Management

The institution of the university reorganized higher education in the intellectual world. Nevertheless, this was perhaps not as important for construction management as for other social conditions. For most of the medieval period, travel was arduous and extremely rare. Transportation systems were unreliable, expensive, or dangerous. People generally stayed in their towns and worked in their homes or on farms. Most of those who were not involved in agriculture did not commute to work. This is important because of the rise of cottage industries.

Trade guilds were formed by skilled tradesmen, including leather goods makers, furniture makers, and blacksmiths. The precursor to labour unions, these guilds organized the specialized labour necessary for society to stay in operation. Typically the craftsmen worked out of their shops, which were located in or next to their homes (History of Organization of Work). Cottage industry, for example that involved in the manufacture of textiles, was organised among families, whose homes were often located in a semi-circle, allowing each family to complete a particular stage in production and then to pass it to the next until production was complete. There would be a division of labour for each activity, such as shearing the sheep, cleaning the wool, combing, bleaching, and dying it, spinning the yarn, and weaving the yarn into cloth.

The whole organisation of activity occurred without commuting, bosses, regulation, common buildings, and other modern forms of work structure. Such groups of workers were inextensive and self-organising, thus there was little need for management (History of Organization of Work).

### 2.8.4 Construction Technology

Romanesque architecture draws on the design features of the Roman Empire period, including the following characteristics:

- harmonious proportions
- stone barrel vault or groin vault
- thick and heavy walls
- thick and heavy pillars
- small windows
- round arches supporting the roof
- round "blind arches" used extensively for decoration inside and out
- nave with side aisles
- galleries above the side aisles, separated from the nave by a triforium
- a transept (section crossing the nave at a right angle, giving the church a cross shape)
- an apse (semicircular niche, usually in the east end)
- an ambulatory (often with radiating chapels) around the apse
- multiple towers, usually at the west end and over the transept crossing
- sculptured decoration on portals, capitals and other surfaces
- painted decoration throughout the interior (Sacred Destinations).

Romanesque work typically included rounded arch windows, arched doors, and arched entrances. The important rose and wheel styles of window are Romanesque (Browne 13–20).

Most of the Romanesque masterpieces are cathedrals, since the Roman Catholic Church was the principal force behind construction projects in Europe. These cathedrals were built on the military model prevalent at a time during which warfare was perpetual and castles were the other major type of monumental building. Like the Crusader castles, the Romanesque cathedrals were built to be heavy and strong, as though fortified for the same strategic defensive purposes. Their thick, weight-bearing walls created a dark and gloomy atmosphere. It was this type of austere ambience that medieval builders thought was conducive to the experience of God's presence. Beauty was not the most important criterion for building. The cathedrals normally had triple arches that symbolized the Trinity (Edson 173–88).

The Romanesque builders incorporated structural advances in technology into their architecture to enable larger and taller buildings with new features and decorative styling. For instance, the arch was used in a new form. The semi-circular arch, which evolved into the Gothic style, was the first major improvement in building techniques since the Roman Empire. This form of arch increased building strength and load-bearing capability. The stone vault ceiling and buttress were also employed on a wider scale (Castles Architecture). Similarly, the use of symmetrical planning and ratio in design demonstrated a keen application of mathematical knowledge to building technology (Banister).

Design took into account interior factors as well. Concepts of the use of space were changed (Carlsson 91–114). Interior planning utilised mathematics, knowledge of materials, and specialized tools to create personal living spaces inside fortified buildings. According to Williams, this "heralded a new idea in the design of 'comfort'" that forced designers to think out technical issues of indoor plumbing, water, and insulation from heat and cold. Objects and architectural features often had both functional and aesthetic value. During the Crusades, the use of Middle Eastern rugs became fashionable. At first they were employed for decorative purposes rather than to cover floors. The stone walls began to be plastered to insulate them against both heat and cold, which in turn made possible the painting of frescoes for decoration (Erlich 85–93). Aesthetically, enamel and ivory work, as well as detailed bronze and gold sculptures, were utilised as stylish adornments. Stained glass and embroidery were extensive and detailed (Toman). The Normans also hung their walls with tapestries. These utilities mitigated to some extent the often harsh, dark, and heavy stone appearance of the Romanesque castles and cathedrals.

The length of time required to complete the grand Romanesque cathedrals gives some indication of how massive these projects were. Often they took generations to build, exceeding by many years the time it took to complete the Roman projects. The techniques were massive as well, surpassing those used in several hundred prior years. Large-scale machinery was used alongside human capital and material resources (Sacred Destinations). Due to the longevity of the construction process and advances in architectural techniques, there were frequent additions to the original plans. These design changes resulted in a mixed look within the structure (Conant). In general, the Romanesque period was important in introducing a heavy and bulky style of building into Western architecture that included the semi-circular arch while retaining ties with the past.

### 2.8.5 Master Builder Tradition

The Romanesque period includes the rise of the guilds throughout Europe, from approximately 1100 to 1426 AD. During that time craftsmen formed guilds as a means of organisation and there are some extant written contracts, particularly those relating to church structures. Architects were normally described as master masons, or *Magister lathomorum* (The Medieval Builder).

Some cities did not use guilds and were deemed "free." The pooling of labour in the trades made the guilds a powerful force. Part of the idea was job security, so that out of the guilds developed the idea of lifetime progression (a career) within a particular trade or craft. The progression was from apprentice through journeyman to master craftsman, just as it is today. The problem with a guild was that non-members were shut out of the trade. There were historical cases of struggle between greater guilds and the lesser artisan guilds. What is significant is that where the guilds functioned they held a monopoly on trade in that particular craft (Guild). In addition, master builders would often apprentice their sons and grandsons to their projects, allowing for continuity and a sort of family craft to persist.

## 2.8.6 Building Projects

### 1. Pisa Cathedral (1063–1118 AD)

Begun in AD 1063, Pisa Cathedral was dedicated by Pope Gelasius II in AD 1118 long before it was finished in AD 1350. Nothing is known of the original architect or builder, although it was generally believed to be Buscheto. What is clear is that the building took centuries to complete and involved numerous master builders along the way to bring the project to completion. The length of time indicates the slow working methods required for such a large project, although certainly the technology used in terms of lifting mechanisms, tools, and skilled masonry and marble work were adequate to the times.

The structure consists of the cathedral itself and two buildings that were not absorbed into the church, a baptistery and a campanile (or tower). Kostof says that the building "typifies the highest accomplishment of Italy in the Romanesque period" (314). The exterior is beautiful Tuscan marble. It is distinguished from the Gothic style by having no façade and no apocalyptic scenes over the portals or on its capitals. It falls into its own unique Pisan Romanesque style that combines the influences of Islamic pointed arches and Byzantine mosaics. The cathedral has arcaded galleries, round-headed arches, a coffered ceiling over the nave, reused classical columns of granite or marble, and an ellipsoidal dome at the crossing. Around 1180, a bronze door with biblical scenes designed by Bonnano Pisano was installed. On the interior, the decagonal white marble pulpit carved from 1302 to 1311 AD by Giovanni Pisano is one of the most impressive features. The granite, Corinthian-style columns that separate the nave and the aisles were pulled from the Palermo mosque once the Pisans had taken it in AD 1063. Obviously the cathedral was a combination of working labour and highly skilled artisanship.

The baptistery building was started in 1152 or 1153 but was not completed until the fourteenth century. The involvement of master builder Diotisalvi is known only from his name on an interior pillar. The pulpit is hexagonal and was completed in AD 1260 by Nicola Pisano. A central fountain was designed in AD 1246 by Guido Bigarelli da Como. The entire structure, inside and out, is a precursor of the Renaissance.

The famous campanile is a warning tower. It was probably the work of Diotisalvi, who laid its foundations in AD 1173. Others took it to seven stories – the eighth story, with its bell, was added in the mid-fourteenth century by Tommaso di Andrea Pisano

(Altet 178). Several men have been proposed as the main early architects, including Gerardo di Gerardo, Guglielmo, Bonanno, and Diotisalvi. Scholarship leans in the direction of Diotisalvi, given similarities of style with his other works and temporal proximity (Pierroti).

Bonde, Maines, and Richards explain the lean of the campanile (a failure of footing) by reference to its exceeding the bearing capacity of the underlying soil: "the so-called Leaning Tower adjoining the cathedral at Pisa, built between 1174 and 1370, is the best-known medieval example of this type of catastrophic failure" (24). In other words, soil has crept below the shallow foundations, causing excessive settlement and rotation due to the low shear strength of the soil. Apparently Bonanno was not unaware of this possibility. After AD 1178 the building began to sink and construction operations were halted, not least due to political strife and ongoing military engagements with other Italian city-states. Construction began again from 1272 to 1284 under the supervision of Giovanni di Simone. Again, progress was halted owing to war and defeat by the Genoans. The final tower was finished late in the fourteenth century.

## 2.9 Gothic

### 2.9.1 Historical and Cultural Environment

#### 1. Background

Gothic art and architecture evolved out of the Romanesque style in the early thirteenth century. The development began in France and spread throughout Europe, but centred in Northern and Western Europe. Many European cathedrals and abbeys are Gothic, but this architectural approach is also evident in universities, castles, guild halls, town halls, and palaces. The Gothic provided a natural stylistic transition from the Romanesque to the Renaissance. Its popularity lasted into the fifteenth century (Charles).

#### 2. Relationship to Previous Period

The transition from Romanesque to Gothic is not marked by an unambiguous event or change; rather, it was a gradual progression. Gothic figures slowly became more animated and precise in relation to backgrounds or scenery. As with the Romanesque, the Gothic kept the predominance of religious subject matter in its sculptural, painted, and glass expressions. In architecture, the Gothic style continued the Romanesque challenge of building larger cathedrals (Gothic Art). However, its emphasis was different. The Gothic Period was typified by "vast space and lots of light to create an impression of reverence" (Branner 327–33). This contrasted with the dark, bulky, and gloomy Romanesque churches.

The Gothic style correlated with social and cultural changes throughout Europe. Its foundations lay in Christianity, of course, and monumental Gothic art and sculpture was used educationally to tell biblical stories. Yet it arose, as did the Romanesque, in a European environment of increased urbanisation, proliferation of the university system, and facilitation of trade within Europe and externally. Europe was moving toward a capital-based economy. Increased literacy and the establishment of a middle class that could afford to patronize art propelled Gothic into the mainstream (Cahill). Craftsmen artists experienced a new level of exposure.

## 3. Contribution to Western Civilisation

The Gothic style, which is still in evidence today, shaped human perceptions. The Gothic became a different way of viewing the human condition. Punter describes this difference skilfully:

> *In painting and sculpture, just as in literature and poetry, figures become more animated and lifelike, more realistically aligned to the background, and without the exaggeration of previous ages. The use of light and shadow to define the subject in art, the use of subtleness of character in literature all gave the Gothic artist a more humanistic palate from which to draw – certainly a legacy that helped transition from the overt focus on religiosity to a more secular approach to human culture. (Punter)*

Beyond this, the idea that the average household could utilise art such as woodcuts to decorate their homes was an important movement away from feudal drudgery toward a more humanistic appreciation of life (Lilley).

## 2.9.2 Knowledge and Scientific Environment

Christian natural philosophers at the end of the Middle Ages were involved in a search for the natural causes of events, rather than being content to rely on explanations of forces and processes that referenced supernatural intervention. For example, the fourteenth-century Catholic natural philosopher Nicole Oresme discussed natural wonders, saying, “there is no reason to take recourse to the heavens, the last refuge of the weak, or demons, or to our glorious God as if He would produce these effects directly, more so than those effects whose causes we believe are well known to us” (as quoted in Numbers 267).

The various waves of plague that swept through Europe affected the progress of knowledge. A third of Europe’s population was wiped out in AD 1348, including many towns that were the repositories of scientific information and innovation. Coupled with the plague were destructive famines and numerous violent peasant uprisings, especially in Germany, that significantly distressed European society (Blickle). Given this sequence of events, it is little wonder that scientific development ground temporarily to a halt, not to be revived until the fifteenth-century, a period known as the Renaissance.

### 2.9.3 General Management

In the late twelfth century, wealth and prosperity drove economic progress. New commercial centres sprang up. The period was dominated in Western and Northern Europe by ecclesiastical construction projects in towns. Over several hundred years, cities in Western Europe strove to outdo each other in creating the most splendid Gothic cathedral. There was a mercantile component to this competition. Building a grand cathedral was one way to attract pilgrims, and thus prosperity and importance to a city. Therefore, the merchants added their resources to those of the Catholic Church (Lesson-from-History). In other words, cathedral construction was influenced by economic motives. At the same time, because of the time invested in building Gothic cathedrals, massive funding was required along with supervision through a project governance structure. By today's estimates the Chartres Cathedral project cost around $1 billion, and the project was subject to a constant cycle of stops and starts as funding ran out (Lesson-from-History).

Time was another important management consideration. Gothic cathedral projects took generations to complete. Often work continued for over 100 years. Therefore, from a management perspective, these projects required long-range planning. The output had to be built with painstaking precision and detailed complexity to minimize project risk, increase safety, and prevent collapsed or failed structures that would require more time to rebuild. An administrative structure was paramount to keep the project going over such a long time. There was an expectation that no single master builder could finish a project. Chartres Cathedral, for example, involved nine master builders. With each transition to a new master builder, different standards of measurement were used. Therefore, the project had continually to adjust its calculations based on previous project work (Lesson-from-History).

### 2.9.4 Construction Technology

Gothic building participated in the evolution of the design process. As with the medieval Romanesque, accumulated knowledge was handed down through the apprenticeship system. Over time, authentic "gothic"-style designs were clearly discernible based on this accumulated experiential knowledge. Small-scale modelling began to be utilised in analogy to full-scale building. These models permitted the builders to test the stability of a plan or structure on a small scale prior to attempting it in reality. Branner writes, "close examination was produced 'on the job', by constructing the cathedral one bay at a time, while applying tested elements from past plans" (Branner 327–33). This sort of testing using mock-ups was important in determining the stability required for the innovative and complex Gothic arches. All the elements of Gothic architecture were worked out progressively as the builders noticed problems and modified their structures when necessary.

Among the structurally definitive elements of Gothic architecture are flying buttresses, rib vaults, and pointed arches. All of these were employed as solutions to the requirement to build high structures while retaining sufficient light in the interior (Wilson 1–32).

## 1. Pointed Arch

The pointed arch evolved in Gothic cathedrals to replace the rounded Roman arch. The rounded arch was good for spherical domes, but not more complicated roofs. Through the pointed arch, earlier adopted from Islamic architecture but now given more prominence, more complex shapes for steeper and taller buildings could be constructed (Vanderpool 552–69).. According to one theory, the introduction of the pointed arch in Europe which roughly coincided with the Norman conquest of Islamic Sicily in AD 1090, the Crusades which began in 1096, and the Islamic presence in Spain, brought about a knowledge of this significant structural device. (Warren 59–65) In terms of the evolution of technology, this change in European architecture came about in response to the demands of architectural monuments. Demand pushed technology, even while technology made possible new construction methods. The relationship is dialectical.

## 2. Ribbed vault

During the twelfth century, ribbed vault technology evolved that removed the requirement for walls to carry loads. The skeleton of the Gothic church was constructed using ribbed vaults that bore all the weight. Extra walls between the ribbed vaults were unnecessary. This innovation permitted builders to use more audacious designs, such as putting glass in the spaces between pillars and ribs (Arch 8–18) or the sexpartite design used to distribute the load through the vaults, as at Bourges Cathedral (Erdogmas, Boothby and Smith 9–17). Additionally, curves filled the gaps between the arches. Beyond this, rubble fill was needed to stabilize the vaults and increase pressure (Branner 327–33).

## 3. Flying Buttress

The flying buttress evolved through trial and error as builders experimented with different designs to counteract outward pressure. The first use of the flying buttress appears to be at Notre Dame de Paris around AD 1180. This architectural innovation distributed weight diagonally rather than vertically by using half-arches to support the outside walls. Forces ran sideways to counteract the proclivity of the nave vaulting and walls to swell from lateral pressure. Only when it reached the pier buttress, which braced the flying buttresses, did the force travel downwards (Erdogmas, Boothby and Smith 9–17). In addition, the buttresses were attached to the exterior of the building, which was a stylistic transformation. As with the other Gothic elements, the flying buttress promoted taller and more complicated building designs that enabled less density and more open spaces (Turnbull 315–40).

The evolution of the flying buttress also made possible a new architectural grandeur. The height reached by Gothic cathedrals and spires was a more graceful form of religious architecture than the Romanesque. The tall arches were formed in a beautifully balanced scheme (Macaulay). Their magnificence was enhanced by the light they permitted to enter the church by contrast with their dark predecessors. Along with the other technical arrangements such as the ribbed vault and pointed arch, Gothic architects challenged conventions and pushed the limits of construction toward positive growth.

### 4. Treadwheel

During the Roman Empire the treadwheel (*magna rota*) crane had ceased to be used, but it was brought back in the High Middle Ages for major building projects. It consisted of a wheel made out of wood that was large enough for two people to walk beside the shaft. Matthies gives a more nuanced description:

> *While the earlier 'compass-arm' wheel had spokes directly driven into the central shaft, the more advanced 'clasp-arm' type featured arms arranged as chords to the wheel rim, giving the possibility of using a thinner shaft and providing thus a greater mechanical advantage(510–47).*

References to treadwheel and to harbour and mine cranes start to appear in literature beginning around AD 1225. These cranes were crucial for the vertical transport of material. They played a pivotal role in Gothic construction, without fully displacing labour-intensive methods. New machinery and older manual methods of work (climbing ladders, using hand barrows) seem to have coexisted on medieval construction sites (Matthies 510–47).

In summary, the Gothic tradition was important for introducing and combining the new technology of ribbed vaults and flying buttresses. In addition, it imported the pointed arch to Europe from Islamic architecture. All of these structural elements made possible higher and better-lit buildings, and contributed to a recognizable style that included the rose window and twin towers. None of this would have been possible, however, without the crucial reintroduction into building of treadwheel crane technology.

### 2.9.5 Master Builder Tradition

The goal of the Gothic cathedral was to allow more light to enter the interior. This necessitated new types of vaults, arches, and buttresses. Equally important were the skilled managers and workers who knew how to construct such objects. During the Gothic Period, trade guilds flourished. These guilds sent men to work on construction projects. Already with better literacy, more accurate record keeping, and a system of patronage, the reputation of some artists was increasing (Cahill).

To give some indication of the challenge for master builders, it is helpful to examine the working site. Macaulay has described a possible scenario at the construction site for a Gothic cathedral. After excavation with shovels, carts, hoists, and sledge hammers, the master mason would use his level and plumb line to ensure that the foundation was level. Once it had dried, the walls would begin to rise. An army of masons and labourers would be present, mixing mortar and laying stones. Machines would be ranged over the site. Cranes, winches and pulleys, ramps, levers, and wheel-driven machinery were employed. As the cranes moved stones, skilled workers who stood on scaffolding with tools would use hoists to pull materials up to the walls. The vaults and arches would materialise over the course of the years. Macaulay says, "all in all, the construction of the Gothic Cathedral was a massive building effort, involving scores of labourers, skilled craftsmen, cutting-edge machinery, specialized tools, and incredible engineering design" (Macaulay). Supervising the whole feat were the master builders.

The Dominican doctor and churchman Albertus Magnus (1193–1280) had an impact on Gothic building. He was also known as Albert the Great, teacher of master builders and the medieval stonemason's lodge documents the idea of the "Albertian Manner" or "Albertus System." He drew up the original plans for Amiens Cathedral in Cologne and his name is mentioned as the first clerk of the works in Cologne and in the Chronicles of Cologne and the book *Life of Albert the Great* (The Masonic Trowel). These texts all refer to a master architect, designer, and planner of great skill who may have influenced Gothic construction.

### 2.9.6 Building Projects

#### 1. Notre Dame de Paris (1163–1260 AD)

Using large personal and Catholic coffers, the Bishop of Paris, Maurice de Sully, decided to rebuild the old cathedral on the Ile-de-France (Temko 97). The foundation stone of the new edifice was laid in AD 1163 and Notre Dame de Paris was begun. Construction was long and took place in several stages. By most estimates, at least five master builders contributed to the finished product over the decades.

The building's construction history is complicated (Jantzen). The choir and apse were built first from 1163 to 1182, taking about twenty years. The nave occupied another two decades from 1182 to 1200. The west façade was nearing completion by AD 1204, and the portals were being worked on by AD 1208. The rose window and flanking bays took from about 1220 to 1225. Work on the towers, which remained without spires, lasted until about AD 1245, with the southern tower finished ca. AD 1240 and the northern later, in AD 1245. According to Cheam, there were no original plans for attached chapels, so "when these were added in the 13th century, they were accommodated, unobtrusively, between the buttresses" (39). Erlande-Brandenburg says that after AD 1250 there was a decision to install a façade with a portal and rose window (217). In about AD 1260 the transept fronts were rebuilt and lengthened by Jean de

Chelles. The project perhaps encompassed as many as four or five anonymous master builders who directed the actual construction on behalf of the church and the state.

As has been discussed, cranes, winches and pulleys, ramps, levers, and wheel-driven machinery were all employed as the 'work horses' of the industry. "Although the master builders operated in a preindustrial age they had a variety of technical equipment at their disposal: the winch and the windlass, the inclined plane, the lever and the jack" (Temko 140). Some of the hoisting gear for heaving and positioning the vault stones sat on the roof. Fitchen has shown how scaffolding, shoring, and centring were used by Gothic builders, whether in conjunction with existing masonry or independent of it (17–8). His book is doubtless the classic reference on Gothic construction methods regarding formwork and vault construction.

First the site had to be excavated, which required labourers with shovels, carts, hoists for large loads of sediment, and sledge hammers to break rock. Masons were at hand with the mortar-mixer labourers, and while the masons worked the stones to be laid, the mortar men mixed the lime and sand. The master mason used his level and plumb line constantly to ensure that the foundation was level and the walls were true vertical. The construction of the walls commenced once the foundation had been laid and the foundation mortar had dried. Walls were typically six to eight feet thick, crowned by arches and domes, with flying buttresses to support the walls bowed outward by the weight of the domes (Arch 8–18). Cranes were a common feature on the worksite, moving stones of massive size. Scaffolds were built as the walls were constructed, strong enough to hold a team of men and their tools. They were hung from the walls as the walls progressed, since wood was a precious commodity and not available for building large scaffolds. Hoists were used to move material up and down the scaffolds. Cement was mixed on site and lifted up to fill the spaces between the wall stones. Ladders were not typically used, as spiral staircases were built into the walls as they were constructed. Pointed vaults and arches crowned the walls, and decorative gargoyles were placed on the buttresses. All in all, the construction of a Gothic cathedral was a massive building effort, involving scores of labourers, skilled craftsmen, cutting-edge machinery, specialized tools, and incredible engineering design (Macaulay).

Bruzelius gives the most cogent revision of the previous building sequence based on her remeasuring of the masonry and moulding. Her main revision is that the choir elevation was changed during building as a refinement by a second master builder and included the addition of flying buttresses (540–69). The nave was started around AD 1170 as the choir was in progress, and was designed from the beginning under the premise of buttresses. This shifts the dates forward significantly and emphasizes the simultaneous construction of various parts of the building. Bruzelius points to subtle structural, technical, and aesthetic modifications, not overall stylistic changes. She asserts that there were five master masons between AD 1160 and 1245. The first planned and set out the lower choir story; the second completed the choir, started the nave and initiated work on the north side of the west façade; the third thickened the west side (1190–1220); the fourth was inconsequential; and the fifth remodelled the flyers and clerestory, and inserted the chapels.

In terms of workforce, there must have been a veritable army of craftsmen. Conservative estimates state 5,000 workers and several hundred craft masters. Temko writes, "A safe guess is that the majority of the men who built the Cathedral had been trained in the guilds of Paris" (106). Stone was quarried outside of Paris, "dressed on the spot, hoisted out of the pit by winches and levers, and loaded on long, two wheeled oxcarts" (Temko 107). In addition to an onsite planning office, the whole site was a bustling workshop of smiths hammering clamps and hinges, a foundry in which bells were cast, kilns smoking lime, and glassmen laying out patterns on chalk tables.

Notre Dame de Paris demonstrates the movement toward Gothic architecture, emphasising luminosity and weightlessness over heavier, darker Romanesque churches. The flying buttress was the Gothic solution for thrust and compression of high walls. The cathedral's use of thin-wall construction made flying buttresses necessary to prevent collapse of the high nave vaults by supporting the wall on the outside (Jantzen 90). Weight was distributed transversely and diagonally like umbrella spokes rather than straight down, which meant that greater height could be achieved. The pointed arch was employed expertly. In addition, the cross-ribbed vault was utilised. Jantzen describes its impact: "its superiority and originality in comparison with other forms, like the barrel, ribbed and domical vaults, which were also employed in Western sacred architecture, lie in the effects of thrust and compression being absorbed in the wall structure" (29). Finally, Notre Dame displays the commonplace Gothic twin towers on its façade.

## 2.10 Renaissance

### 2.10.1 Historical and Cultural Environment

#### 1. Background

The European Renaissance between the fifteenth and seventeeth centuries began in Florence. It was not a sudden rebirth from the Dark Ages, but approximates more a refocusing outward politically and intellectually. Europe had become more than a series of small principalities vying for hegemony. There were larger cities, a more educated population, and a growing technology that allowed states to concentrate on growth and improvement. Italian cities were freed from feudalism, and were more mercantile and less hinged around a monarch (Skinner 69). On a cultural level, the Renaissance signalled a rebirth of learning and educational reform. People returned to classical works and revised their position on Christianity. There was a rise in realism among artists, who used light and perspective in a more natural way. Philosophers such as Machiavelli portrayed political life realistically rather than idealistically. The change in mindset affected the political structure and management of the European people. It was a three-centuries-long cultural, social, and political movement and a revolutionary period for art, architecture, and literature (Leonard da Vinci – Renaissance Man).

## 2. Relationship to Previous Period

The Renaissance continued the medieval rediscovery of the Roman and Greek traditions. It advanced technologies that changed the way populations congregated so that the urbanizing trend continued and increased. In art, realism prospered. The move toward capitalism and away from feudalism made further progress. Europe expanded through colonisation and trade. The Italian city-states thrived. In all these qualities the Renaissance gradually evolved from and moved along the same trajectory as the earlier medieval period (Starn 122–4).

## 3. Contribution to Western Civilisation

Much of the debate regarding the Renaissance swirls around whether it was an improvement over Medieval European culture. The cultural legacy of the Renaissance was to expand the European worldview. The world became a large, complex, and discoverable place. Exploration became a leading idea. On the other hand, there was warfare, political persecution, and disease. Still, most of the artists and writers within the culture fully believed their era was completely new and different than anything that had gone before (Looking at the Renaissance). The gradual re-examination of the Roman and Greek heritage led directly to the modern age, and thus represented a significant Renaissance legacy in contemporary culture and thought. Figures such as Leonardo da Vinci paved the way for modernity (Osborne).

## 2.10.2 Knowledge and Scientific Environment

The single greatest achievement of the Renaissance period could be said to be not a discovery or a theory, but the *scientific method* (Brotton). This emphasized observable empirical evidence as the way towards discovering and understanding natural laws and true causes. Use of the scientific method advanced biology, astronomy, and physics during the Renaissance. For example, dissection and a mechanistic view of anatomy gained popularity with Vesalius' *De humani corporis fabrica.* Many of the Renaissance discoveries remain basic to today's knowledge.

Although a religious perspective still held sway during the Renaissance, as seen in its artwork, many Renaissance theologians were influenced by the rising tide of humanism. Humanists expanded the study of texts to incorporate Greek, reading them in the original languages. This led to a more precise understanding of Greek philosophy. Significantly, Renaissance humanism shaped the intellectual landscape through the humanities, such disciplines as moral philosophy, history, and rhetoric. Humanism and Christianity merged in a fruitful and harmonious union. Pope Pius II was an example of this unity in which the teaching of humanism and Christianity were reconciled (Löffler 538–42). Translations of the Bible were improved and less Catholic orthodoxy was used to interpret the texts. This laid the foundation for the rise of vernacular translations and the Protestant Reformation, which turned toward individualism.

Galileo Galilei (1564–1642) was an influential mathematical scientist. In his book, *II Saggiatore*, he validates experimental empiricism. He writes,

> *"philosophy [i.e., physics] is written in this grand book – I mean the universe – which stands continually open to our gaze, but it cannot be understood unless one first learns to comprehend the language and interpret the characters in which it is written. It is written in the language of mathematics, and its characters are triangles, circles, and other geometrical figures, without which it is humanly impossible to understand a single word of it; without these, one is wandering around in a dark labyrinth" (237–8).*

Galileo promoted knowledge for knowledge's sake and discovered, contrary to Catholic teaching, that the Earth was not the centre of the universe. This finding revolutionized astronomy, although he was persecuted for it (Singer 217).

Galileo used experiments as a research tool to verify truths rather than following the Aristotelian practise of demonstrating science from first principles. He gave mathematical demonstrations of his arguments. As mathematics did not readily lead to the discovery of causes, Aristotelian science's main concern, its usefulness was not immediately obvious (Feldhay 80–133). He shied away from presenting his experimental results, but gave them in supplementary Italian dialogues on the theory of motion. Charles Van Doren has concluded that the Copernican Revolution is actually the Galilean Revolution because of the scale of change introduced by Galileo's work.

The Renaissance revitalized science, religion, and art. Many of the theories and discoveries of the time had an enormous impact; they have endured to the present day.

### 2.10.3 General Management

The invention of modern printing by Johannes Gutenberg (ca. 1398–1468) was an inestimable moment for the Renaissance and all subsequent human history. His mechanized process of movable type allowed books to be mass produced. This invention laid the foundation for a modern knowledge-based economy (Eisenstein). It accelerated the accessibility of learning within society and had an immediate impact on education, communication, and the organisation of information. Thus it was crucial for general management.

In political theory, Niccolò Machiavelli (1469–1527) simultaneously revived the idea of a republican government and proposed a new way of viewing political leadership. His concept of virtue in *The Prince* (1513) reversed traditional moral values by placing self-interest and political power at its core. His realistic theory urged rulers to act without a moral view if that would lead to the downfall of the state. Rather they should use arms, deceit, or any other expedient means to acquire and maintain their authority, but without neglecting to present an image of traditional virtue. This did not entail the mistreatment of constituents, for the prince must above all avoid being hated by the populace. Equally, Machiavelli believed that being feared was politically safer than being loved. For instance, having a reputation for cruelty was not bad if it kept the troops and people in a cohesive and powerful unity. He justified rule by force rather than by law, or at least thought that law was worthless without backing by force (Anglo). He asserted, in addition, that the prince must dedicate himself wholly to the discipline of war. From the management perspective, *The Prince* was a book about social cohesiveness, power, and leadership in organisations (George). It has been an influential theory of management style and effectiveness since its publication.

The Protestant Reformation, which followed closely on the Renaissance, was also important for management ideas. In his book, *The History of Management Thought*, Daniel Wren points out that the Protestant work ethic, a sociological concept developed by Max Weber, had a significant influence on the historical development of modern management (25–8). This refers to the Calvinist stress on hard work as a route to salvation. Work was an individual and social duty, just as worldly success was the outward sign of personal salvation. The Protestant reformers in this way effectively transferred the notion of good works into the obligation of hard work to prove that a person had received divine grace (Weber 9–12). In economic terms this meant that work was not evil when done in the service of God. Nor was there a division between secular and sacred work. Anything a person did was both secular and sacred. It was accompanied by earthly benefits and it glorified God when the attitude toward work was joyful. This moral style gave work an intrinsic and positive value, inverting the notion of work as a necessary evil. It led directly, according to Weber, into capitalism, since it allowed people to endorse the idea that hard work paid dividends in wealth without contradicting spirituality.

Besides the Protestant work ethic, reductionism and individualism took hold during this time. These were the precursors of modern management. Reductionism entails, first, removing unnecessary elements of a process and, second, reducing it to its smallest tasks in order to grasp how the process works. Individualism assumes that humans are independent agents with the ability to manage risks and come up with ideas. Social actions turn such ideas into reality as long as there is an available descriptive language. According to Patrick Weaver, these three major ideas – reductionism, individualism, and the Protestant work ethic – were incorporated into seventeenth-century scientific Newtonianism and eighteenth-century liberalism and capitalism (Weaver 2). Thus they had an impact on both the Scientific Revolution and the Industrial Revolution. In addition, he argues in his important research paper, "The Origins of Modern Project Management," that Frederick Taylor's classic school of Scientific Management is rooted in this same philosophical tradition.

### 2.10.4 Construction Technology

In the Renaissance, the ideas of regularity, symmetry, and harmony were reintroduced as classical ideals. Milo argues that the Renaissance builders believed these principles could be actualised and "seamlessly applied to architecture" by a scientific mastery of geometry (Milo). This shows how much construction was inspired by classicism and mathematics.

As in other eras of Western architecture, the most notable structures of the Renaissance were cathedrals, churches, and chapels. Their architects were extravagant, but they did not depart from their classical roots. Renaissance construction projects imitate Greco-Roman building (Betts 5–25), as demonstrated by their incorporation of columns, domes, and arches. The builders sought to apply classical principles of design and proportion in numerous Christian structures (Ackerman 3–11). Greco-Roman forms were employed in Renaissance palaces as well, especially in Florence and Rome, and in the beautiful street façades of many cities (Partridge). It is perhaps this extensive borrowing from the Greek and Roman styles that most marks out the Renaissance. Its guiding aesthetic principle was based in the classical world (Walker).

Finally, an impressive range of machinery was employed in Renaissance construction technology. The Institute and Museum of the History of Science gives a good catalogue of such machines. Large construction machinery included the reversible hoist, a mobile crane on rollers with a hoist, a lifting device with pincers, a bell-lifting device with a counterweight, screw-operated lifting devices, and pile drivers (The Sienese Engineers). To power such devices, human and animal labour was used, sometimes in conjunction with plows, hoes, and steam power. The Renaissance builders understood how to employ hydraulic power. They experimented with wind power as well, but it is unclear if any wind power instruments were important for construction technology.

### 2.10.5 Master Builder Tradition

Perhaps the most prominent example of a Renaissance master builder was the Florentine architect Filippo Brunelleschi (1337–1446). Before he created the Renaissance architectural style, this man steeped himself in the structural system of classical architecture, trying to figure out how to transfer its principles into his own age. He was first a clock maker and sculptor. Out of the blue he won a competition to build the dome of Florence Cathedral. As a good Renaissance man, his design was based on Roman structural solutions (Walker). The solution he devised was ingenious and ranks as the greatest structural achievement of the fifteenth century (Loulakis 46). He also invented numerous mechanical devices that transformed the way building was conducted. Leonardo da Vinci, among others, was fascinated by his new design and built an ox hoist that sped up the building process tremendously. Brunelleschi's first truly Renaissance work was the Foundling Hospital built between 1419 and 1424 (Wittkower 257–291).

Brunelleschi's rival was Leon Battista Alberti (1404–1472), another good example of a Renaissance master builder who made operational changes in the field of procedure. He was the first true predecessor of today's architects. Alberti claimed that he could direct master craftsmen without being directly involved in construction, just by providing highly specified creative designs and models. He gave the plans of his buildings but frequently did not become involved in the actual construction project. In other words, he remained a designer who drew up plans, but was not engaged in work production or direct supervision of the building. He simply handed his sketches and models over to the *compomastro*, who transferred them to the worksite where another master builder would implement them. According to Jackson, "his new philosophy was the first that would result in the separation of design and construction as completely different concepts" (Jackson 7). This new technique was exemplified in Alberti's façade for Florence's Santa Maria Novella. It was the first known project for which the designer was not the builder.

During the Renaissance, therefore, there were competing notions of what constituted a master builder. Alberti represented the separatist view. He desired a complete separation between design and building. In fact, he wrote a book, *De Re Aedificatoria* (On Edifices), in which he describes his own design process and distinguished it from the builder's role (Loulakis 47). Thus, Alberti was the founder of a line of architects who sought to make architectural design distinct from engineering as a science and building as a craft. Brunelleschi, by contrast, was an integrationist. He believed that the structural designer should also be the manager of construction. This view is closer to the traditional role of the master builder who was involved in the management of trade contractors and was not merely the draughtsman intellect behind the building design. Brunelleschi got his hands dirty, while Alberti stayed aloof. Those who followed Brunelleschi's model were viewed as part of the master builder camp (Loulakis 47). They viewed buildings as working machines, whereas the separationists treated buildings more like static objects, since they divorced design from the operational procedure of construction. Alberti's model stayed in the minority until the Industrial Revolution, when the balance shifted decisively towards independent architectural design separated from the implementation of the designer's vision.

### 2.10.6 Building Projects

## 1. Dome of Florence Cathedral (1420–1436 AD)

The pre-history of Brunelleschi's greatest work is well known. Arnolfi di Cambio was the original designer of the new church, although there is no evidence for his design. The foundation stone was laid in AD 1296 on the site of the Basilica of Santa Reparata. After di Cambio's death in AD 1302, building work stopped for fifty years. Under Talenti it resumed and the original design of the choir end was augmented. In AD 1347 a Genoese fleet returned carrying the plague, which decimated Florence. In AD 1355 only the façade and the nave walls were built. Building resumed in AD 1366 after the city recovered and the nave was vaulted and the east end planned. There was a competition at this time between Giovanni di Lapo Ghini and Neri di Fioravanti for the dome design, presided over by the consuls of the wool guild who controlled the building. Ghini won and out of this, in AD 1367, a thirty-foot stone model was built by a commission of master builders. This was to be the basic plan. In AD 1415 Giovanni d'Ambrogio built the massive drum. Still no one knew how to execute the high and wide dome that was planned.

Brunelleschi entered the picture first with the famous competition to design the door of the baptistery of San Giovanni in AD 1401. Another bout of plague had ended. In celebration, some renovations were planned for the cathedral, including a new design for the door. The contest required a bronze illustration of the sacrifice of Isaac in the framed shape of a Gothic quatrefoil (four stylized leaves). Some take this contest to symbolize an entrance to the Renaissance. Gärtner writes, "the very fact that a competition was announced represents a change in the way that art was perceived and also a change in attitude toward artists" (14). Brunelleschi's design was more dynamic than Ghiberti's, but he lost out.

Brunelleschi won the next competition, announced in AD 1418 by the cathedral stonemason's lodge, which decided who would build the dome. This time Brunelleschi's model beat out Ghiberti's. What was notable was that Brunelleschi was neither a mason nor a carpenter, but a goldsmith and clock maker. Even more amazing, says Gärtner, was how he proposed to build the dome: "the incredible feature of his proposed solution was that he intended to build the dome *senza armadura*, without scaffolding" (86). The technique for doing this was almost inconceivable at the time. Others had proposed wooden scaffolding or stone towers to support the work. Nor could Brunelleschi prove by pointing to previous experience that he could accomplish this feat. As a safety net, Ghiberti was appointed co-architect along with Brunelleschi, but out of rivalry it is almost certain that Ghiberti did very little. Construction began on Brunelleschi's dome on 7 August 1420. It was consecrated on 30 August 1436.

Its form is the novel Tuscan double-skinned dome. The exterior and interior of the domes are separate entities, leading to dominating grandeur outside but good proportions inside. According to Gärtner, there was no precedent for this type of structure (88). What makes it important, furthermore, is its octagonal vault form that stands without buttresses and transverse chains. It is a combination of Gothic and Renaissance styles, combining innovation and tradition. By contrast with earlier domes, Walker says, "the heavy Roman cupolas, set into massive masonry supports, have nothing in common with the lofty, gently curving dome in Florence" (78). What Brunelleschi did was to free the cupola supports from the wall structure and make them into a separate framework, which prepared the way for the twenty-four-ribbed structure of the cathedral dome. Thus, the system of struts supporting the cupola is transformed into a self-supporting skeleton of ribs. This style of dome definitively ended the medieval period of architecture. Walker notes, "with it the 'monumental' form of modern architecture was born. . . . Thus Brunelleschi's edifice has to be seen as *the* 'modern' building which marked the end of the medieval period" (77). It influenced architecture inestimably, and was taken up at St. Peter's and in many American capitol buildings.

The methods used to erect the dome were revolutionary. Saalman has given the definitive description of the process and instruments used. It was the first dome undertaken without the use of centring. This was so amazing that Alberti thought that "hanging centering" may have been used, although there is no evidence of this (Saalman 161). For one thing, he used herringbone masonry by which stones were laid sloping inwards, not horizontally. For another, the building procedure went in rings. A new ring was started only once the last ring had been completed. Without scaffolding, there were eight teams of masons. King says that "the masons simply moved around the perimeter of the cupola on *ponti* (narrow platforms made from willow withes and supported on wooden rods inserted into the masonry) while below them yawned the chasm" (96). For safety and to prevent the masons from looking down nervously, Brunelleschi built a balcony inside the vault. Workers wore leather safety harnesses and were not allowed to swing in or to carry tools up in hoisting tubs. The result was an incredible safety record, with only three recorded deaths during the project.

More significant, perhaps, were the devices Brunelleschi invented for the transportation upwards and laterally of the sandstone beams and marble slabs. He took sixty-seven days to build a new kind of ox-driven hoist with a reversible gear that could raise heavy loads using less power and greater speed than ever previously. King says, "in this task it probably excelled any hoist ever constructed, for one or two oxen were able to raise loads that before had taken as many as six pairs" (67). Apparently, the specialist knowledge to build such a machine had not previously been available. Brunelleschi's mechanical and engineering techniques exceeded those available in the Middle Ages. Saalman and King have described the ox-hoist in detail. King writes, "the hoist that he created was to become one of the most celebrated machines of the Renaissance, a device that would be studied and sketched by numerous other architects and engineers, including Leonardo da Vinci" (59). In addition, for lateral positioning of material Brunelleschi built a new kind of crane that operated once the stone reached the upper working level. All of these were radical innovations that contributed to the future of engineering.

In summary, Brunelleschi's construction of the Dome of Florence Cathedral began Renaissance architecture, both in terms of its design of structures and its execution using new technologies. Gärtner says, "There can be no doubt that the early Renaissance begins with his buildings" (11). It is safe to say that there is a consensus on this point.

## 2. Façade of Santa Maria Novella (1456–1470 AD)

Orlandi gives the following sequence of events (Orlandi 6–7). The original church on the site dated from the ninth century AD. It was enlarged in AD 1094 by the patronage of the church canons. In November 1221 it was ceded to Giovanni of Salerno, who wanted to build a new church. The inauguration stone for the new church was laid on 18 October 1279, by Cardinal Fra Latina Malabrance, who was in Florence to make peace between the rival families of Guelph and Ghibelline. Inspired by a Cistercian Gothic style, the church was designed by two lay brothers, Sisto Florentine and Ristoro da Campi, but built by a series of other builders. Da Campi, in around AD 1330, constructed the campanile. Talenti completed the church under the direction of Jacopo Passavanti. Orlandi says, "S. Maria Novella was the first large gothic church in

Florence, since the first stone of S. Croce was laid in 1294, and that of the Duomo in 1298" (7). Pope Martin V consecrated the church in 1420.

The architect Alberti created the façade, although he did not design the actual building. The original façade was begun near the beginning of the fourteenth century and left incomplete around AD 1350. It comprised six arch tombs (*avelli*) and three Gothic portals, as well as the marble squares and arches up to the level of the frieze. The Papal court resided in the cloisters of Santa Maria Novella between AD 1434 and 1443, just before Giovanni Rucellai commissioned Alberti's new façade design. It was paid for using money from an estate sale whose stipulation was that it be spent on patronizing ecclesiastical building. That is when Alberti took over, although the chronology is uncertain. The upper frieze gives Rucellai's name and a date of 1470. According to Tavernor, this "does not denote the start of construction, which was 1458, when Giovanni was also purchasing the house next to his palazzo" (99). In AD 1478 the entry portal and right-hand scroll still needed work. Orlandi writes, "Between 1458 and 1470, Leon Battista Alberti, commissioned by Giovanni di Paolo Rucellai (whose name can be seen in large letters below the tympanum), designed the magnificent central portal (executed by Giovanni di Bertino) and the upper part of the façade, admirably harmonizing the pre-existent Gothic elements with the new Renaissance style" (4). One thing Alberti did was to hide the sloping roofs of the aisles with two upturned volutes, the first examples of this architectural motif. The whole façade merges the lower Gothic elements with the upper Renaissance elements.

In terms of architectural style, the façade is based on the triumphal arch, thus showing a Greco-Roman influence. Its architectural elements comprise a temple-like pedimented upper story with triangular panels and scrolls on a broad base. Disciplined classical shapes with Florentine ornamentation are fitted into a medieval structure. There are possible influences of the Florentine Baptistery of San Giovanni and di Cambio's original design for Florence Cathedral (Grafton 103). The proportions of the façade were widened with thick end pillars of banded white and green marble, paired with Corinthian columns matching the portal frame. The portal was remodelled to make it reminiscent of the Pantheon with its fluted pilaster door frame and coffered entrance vault with rosettes. The pre-existing rose window had to be incorporated, but it is too low to function as an "eye." Grafton summarizes Alberti's work this way: "in practise, however, Alberti was above all an artist of facades – a creator of exteriors that radically altered the appearance of a building but did not directly express its internal organisation as an organic, living system" (325).

Tavernor explains how the building was built without supervision from Alberti. He writes, "according to a dedication written by Fra Giovanni di Carlo, a friar at the church, to Cristoforo Landino, Alberti designed the marble inlay on the façade, and this was executed by Giovanni di Bertino, a mason skilled in this art" (99). He goes on to say: "Presumably a wooden model was build of the façade. Indeed, it is possible that models were made of all the buildings Giovanni planned to build in Florence, and that they were designed by Alberti as an ensemble, at the same time. The models would have provided the masons on site with details of Alberti's designs well into the future, and would have allowed Giovanni to employ different masons for each project, when he was ready to build. This may be a factor that has contributed to the uncertainty surrounding Alberti's role in Giovanni's projects" (99). Apparently, then, Alberti was able to provide design models to the work site, but was not present for the actual building of the façade. This represented a change in building methods.

## 3. St. Peter's Basilica (1506–1626 AD)

Bonde, Mark, and Robison write, "The first proposal to replace the old basilica came in the 1450s during the pontificate of Nicholas V" (Bonde, Mark and Robison 129). The cornerstone for the new domed basilica was laid in 1506. It incorporated the tomb where St. Peter's body was believed to be laid. Taking almost the entire sixteenth century and into the seventeenth century to complete, St. Peter's Basilica is the end product of the labours of many architects and builders rather than the unique expression of one.

Pope Sixtus V decided that he wanted a new symbol to magnetize the Catholic world. Under this impetus, he masterminded the energy for the new basilica while consulting with the first main architect Domenico Fontana (1543–1607). Little fruit came out of this partnership in terms of building, but the idea remained. It was up to Pope Julius and the second architect Donato Bramante (1444–1514) to go full throttle on the building. Bramante's plan for the structure was a Greek cross superimposed on a square with a central hemispherical dome supported on four massive piers. He experimented with Roman concrete for the piers and arches (Nuttgens 184). The first problem he encountered was an inability to move St. Peter's tomb. As a result, Bramante's church had to be grafted onto the earlier Constantinian basilica "by sacrificing one of the apsed arms of the cross, that to the east" (Kostof 503).

Bramante's original scheme was altered due to the succession of architects after him who directed construction (Bond, Mark and Robison 173). It was apparent after Bramante's death that the centralized choir could never be wedded to the Constantinian nave. The new architect Sangallo was left with two options: revive the original cross plan or design a new nave in harmony with the spatial grandeur of Bramante's choir. According to Kostof, "the second solution, more traditional liturgically, became the clear favourite in the recessive, authoritarian decades of the Counter-Reformation" (504). Sangallo strengthened the pillars, and built the nave vault and pendentives to support the proposed dome. Bramante had been accused of using inferior materials for the piers of the dome support in order to progress more quickly. Bonde, Mark, and Robison believe that this was merely because he had not previously worked on a project of this scale. As a result, they say, Antonio da Sangallo (ca. 1483–1546) "would spend much time and effort increasing the size of the piers" (Bonde, Mark and Robison 131). There were structural changes in the piers and a general simplification of Bramante's plan shifted the church toward sturdiness and compactness.

Then Michelangelo Buonarroti (1475–1564) was designated as architect in 1546 and he applied himself to recognizing Bramante's centralized design once more.

Buonarroti worked on St. Peter's for nearly the last twenty years of his life (1546–64). He created a bold, simple volume for the church that was to be covered by a hemispherical dome with prominently projected ribs. Kostof says that Buonarroti took the messy system, unified by only the concept of a piered dome and a trilobe system of apses, and did three things: abandoned lesser cruciform units but retained domed cores and a square ambulatory between the bay and the apses; eliminated corner towers (reducing the total area); and wrapped a moulded wall around the structure (Kostof 504). He built a spiral staircase in the thick wall that was used by small draft animals to aid in carrying building materials for the dome up to the roof (Bonde, Mark and Robison 131).

Buonarroti designed the dome, but left it and the east end unresolved at his death. After him, "the change of popes brought about a suspension of work for the twenty-four-year period after his death, and when work on the basilica was resumed by Giacomo della Porta (1533–1602), the dome was given a more pointed profile, mainly to increase its visibility from the piazza in front" (Bonde, Mark and Robison 174). Della Porta was concerned about the stability of the main piers and foundations as a result of cracks noticed in the dome. He used iron chains to compensate for this problem, but his solution was inadequate and more correction was needed later. He accomplished the circular dome, which was made in two shells, internally brick shaped out of orange-peel segments tied by ribs held with three iron chains (Nuttgens 185).

A decision was made in AD 1612 to add towers to the basilica façade. Flanking bays were built, but they were unable to bear the load so the towers were scrapped. The final architect of St. Peter's was Bernini, who took the structure to completion in AD 1626 and turned to the square.

## 2.11 Baroque

### 2.11.1 Historical and Cultural Environment

#### 1. Background

The term "Baroque" refers to an artistic and architectural style that arose in the late seventeenth century and lasted until the early eighteenth century. It is usually described in terms of its florid, dynamic movement, its overt emotion, and its secularism. However, the success of Baroque art resulted from its ties to Catholicism and its architectural use in churches. The Baroque was the Catholic response to Protestant simplicity (Culture in the Baroque Era). It produced architecture that was emotionally accessible and was a demonstration of church's power and wealth. It also assumed a secular expression in grand palaces such as Mansart's Château de Maisons (1642) near Paris (Baroque Architecture).

The Baroque period coincided with the Scientific Revolution, a time at which new forms of logical reasoning flourished. Like the Romanesque and Gothic before it, the Baroque style entailed a mindset. It was not just a less religious view of society and the human condition. Its worldview allowed for far more risks in utilising the past to propel building forward toward the future (Friedell).

## 2. Relationship to Previous Period

It is relatively easy to view a gradual evolution of art, music, and architecture from the Romanesque to the Gothic to the Baroque. In retrospect, they can be seen as three different mature styles. Of course, the basic principles of Baroque were firmly established in previous eras and its expression was really an experimental advance that stretched the bounds of knowledge.

Many define this period as the beginning of the Age of Humanism as a way of learning. For example, in the Middle Ages and early Renaissance, learning focused on resolving rational contradictions between ideas and authors through debate. The Baroque period used a more logical, empiricist approach. Burckhardt described this as taking the known curriculum, applying the principles set forth in a book or treatise, defining what is observable, repeatable, and logical, and then coming up with the truth. In doing so, the interpretation was thought to provide more reliability and accuracy, merging textual interpretation with observation (Burckhardt).

## 3. Contribution to Western Civilisation

The Baroque style is still occasionally seen in architecture from the previous century. In the arts, it established a basis for the modern era as a transition away from Medieval and Renaissance traditions (Buci-Glucksmann). Modern conceptions of the individual's relationship to and responsibility for the state are products of this age. Dante's *Inferno* was a clear example of Baroque thinking. In it, religious thoughts were important but not primary, and human nature is juxtaposed with a new definition of society (Rolbiecki).

## 2.11.2 Knowledge and Scientific Environment

The Scientific Revolution was built on the foundation of all previous learning. It drew from the ancient Greeks, Romans, Byzantines, Medieval European and Islamic schools, and the Renaissance (Grant 29–30). It was based predominantly in the Aristotelian tradition, which provided the intellectual framework of the seventeenth century (Grant 42–7).

What was crucial was that attitudes changed regarding science and technology. Scholars became more willing to question previously held truths. They rejected the prevailing scientific doctrines that had been transmitted from previous ages (Butterfield viii). Out of this attitude of questioning, new questions and answers to scientific problems could arise. Unprecedented advances in knowledge were made. Science was placed on a new footing.

A number of revolutionary ideas gained currency in the Scientific Revolution. One such idea was the heliocentric view of astronomy. The realization that the Sun, not the Earth, was the centre of the solar system had detrimental effects on religion. It highlighted the fact that humans are not the centre of everything and challenged their priority in the universe. Another advance came when Antonie van Leeuwenhoek viewed bacteria under a microscope. This instrumental technology greatly furthered knowledge of germs, bacteria, and life itself, altering the field of biology. The list of scientific and technological breakthroughs during this time is almost endless. Wilhelm Schickard created one of the first calculating machines in 1623. The barometer was invented around the same time by Evangelista Torricelli. Franciscus Vieta gave the world modern algebra, while John Napier created logarithms. Edmund Gunter invented logarithmic scales, which were later used by William Oughtred in 1622 to invent the slide rule. Blaise Pascal constructed mechanical calculators and clarified the concepts of pressure and vacuum by studying fluids. The mathematician John Hadley built a Gregorian telescope with correctly shaped mirrors and the first parabolic Newtonian telescope (King 77).

Another major figure in the Scientific Revolution was Sir Francis Bacon (1561–1626). He introduced inductive reasoning in his *Novum Organum* (1620). This thinking method involved gathering all available evidence and reaching conclusions using facts alone. Data must be collected using measurable and observable evidence. Bacon believed in rigorously testing hypotheses. It was his inductive reasoning that became known as the scientific method and permitted the rapid acceleration of development in the Scientific Revolution.

The philosopher Rene Descartes (1596–1650) developed the notion of deductive reasoning, in which a premise is proposed and evidence for or against it is rationally sifted, leaving the researcher only with supporting evidence. Like Bacon, his desire was to put scientific thinking on a footing that was not deceived by the mind or the senses. Bacon's view of knowledge was empirical, Descartes' metaphysical.

Perhaps of supreme importance was the work of Sir Isaac Newton (1642–1727). His *Philosophiæ Naturalis Principia Mathematica* (1687) laid the groundwork for most of classical mechanics, including universal gravitation and the three natural laws of motion. He demonstrated the similarity between his theory of gravitation and Kepler's rules of the motion of the planets to prove that objects on Earth and celestial bodies are subject to the same natural laws. This eliminated any doubt as to heliocentrism. Newton favoured Bacon's empirical method over Descartes' rationalism and threw his weight in the former's direction in the *Principia* with the four "rules of reasoning" (Newton 974). However, he did not go so far as to believe that any person or age could explain all of nature (Westfall 643).

Newton's work became a model for other sciences and his inductive approach formed the basis for much of natural philosophy afterwards. The Scientific Revolution was an explosive time for scientific advancement. Its achievements shaped human knowledge and technology decisively.

### 2.11.3 General Management

During the Baroque period that coincided with the Scientific Revolution of the seventeenth century, two fundamental ideas influenced how individuals viewed the world. First was the notion that the universe and everything within it functions according to the laws of nature, which are set by a divine being. Nothing is random. All things work in an orderly and regular fashion. Second, reason became the strongest tool in the search for truth. It was believed that reason could discover the laws of nature. Humans could use reason to reach an understanding of the workings of the world. The management theory that derived from this worldview emphasized the ability to make choices, obedience to known laws, questioning the unknown, and adherence to moral standards.

### 2.11.4 Construction Technology

The Baroque design style was permeated with the representation of power and influence (Hersey). It aspired to show the might and superiority of the Catholic Church. In doing so, its structures appeared more fluid, using moving elements such as curvature in construction. Spiral-shaped columns deviated from Renaissance ideals. Curves replaced the Renaissance idea of straight lines in a deliberate design move meant to imply fashion and energy (Partridge). Building features were given more convexity and concavity. Architects decorated colonnades to create an impression of spaciousness. This meant new opportunities for architectural form to shape the feeling of a building, to make it bigger and richer. The use of risalits in façades was an innovation which required a change in planning the supports, strength of materials, and use of other general design elements (Cohen).

As a result of these shifts, different techniques of craftsmanship were required. Marconi writes, "the most popular techniques of the Roman Baroque building practises are the methods used to increase the masonry mortar setting time; the employment of unique mechanical devices; the innovative techniques in brick manufacture and laying; and the practises used in the supply and the working of lime, plaster and freestone" (10). Hence the field of construction technology responded to another evolution in mastery over materials and the development of tools (Hersey).

Baroque innovations in construction technology had little to do with revolutionizing the machinery involved in construction. Ropes, pulleys, winches, levers, ramps, and other devices for construction technology did not change. Rather, developments had to do with the idea of displaying power through building projects combined with Renaissance structural features such as buttresses, arches, and supports. Yet the Baroque was different than its predecessor. The use of risalits exemplifies this desire to convey strength for strength's sake. Cohen writes, "it is at this point, with the 'idea' of power and strength as seen as more than just utilitarian notions to convey to the masses, that architecture and building technology become truly separate concepts with more esoteric meaning, with physical realities of technology belonging to the engineers" (Cohen). In other words, the gap widened between the architect and the builder-engineers in the Baroque period. It moved slightly in the direction of Alberti's Renaissance idea. Overall, the Baroque signalled a paradigm shift in how metaphysical ideas were presented and interpreted in the physical world of materials and machines.

### 2.11.5 Master Builder Tradition

Up to the eighteenth century, architect and master builder are regarded as the same profession. Howard Davis, professor of architecture at the University of Oregon, explained in his book *The Culture of Building*:

> *In traditional society, the builder combined the functions of design and construction that are now assumed by separate professionals, and the system of apprenticeship taught people to take these functions on in a way that combined thinking and doing. The word architect, when it was used up to the eighteenth century, usually referred not to an architect in the present-day sense of the word but to someone who assumed overall responsibility for design and construction. Almost invariably, these master builders came out of the building trades, and their responsibility lay not only in the production of drawings but also in work on the building site – work that included the organization of trades and the supervision of workers. Their work was in fact an extension of the role of the craftsman. (108)*

He goes on to list the responsibilities that were contained in the one person, the master builder:

1. Responsibility for design – encompassing deep artistic abilities; drawing skills; profound understanding about how people live and dwell; art/design knowledge for actual shaping, constructing all elements of the built environment (including buildings – parts of buildings, interiors, exterior landscapes, urban environments).
2. Responsibility for construction – encompassing expert craftsmanship in the building arts; knowledge about how a beautiful building (or other environment) is built, as gained from actual construction experience; on-site project management (involving leadership, organizing-supervising workers, financial oversight, artistic discernment).
3. Complete and total authority on the building site – authority over on-site design-construction decisions; authority over all workers; unquestioned authority over the entire construction phase from start to finish. (108)

In Baroque architecture, Sir Christopher Wren (1632–1723) in London completely embodied this master builder tradition. He was given precisely these forms of responsibility and authority when he was commissioned to rebuild St. Paul's Cathedral. Wren both designed the new cathedral and worked with a team to manage the actual on-site construction. He was given the freedom to make design alterations throughout the process. He proposed several models along the way, which were subject to approval by city and church authorities, but it was clear that the authority rested in him to participate fully in hands-on aspects of engineering and building of the project. The following section elaborates on his role and interactions with those involved in the building process.

### 2.11.6 Building Projects

#### 1. St. Paul's Cathedral (1667–1711 AD)

The old St. Paul's church fell within the part of London that was severely damaged by fire in AD 1666. Three years earlier in AD 1663, Christopher Wren had been asked to give his assessment of its condition, as were other prominent masons, joiners, and architects. In AD 1667, Wren was put in charge of rebuilding the cathedral along with many of London's other buildings. He was primarily the designer, working with a large staff employed in an office. Little of Wren's correspondence and drawings related to this project has survived. What is known is that an initial repair authorized by the cathedral authorities partially collapsed in AD 1668, which allowed Wren to push for a completely new construction (Sutcliffe 34). The building was partially paid for through taxies levied on coal imports (Beard 25).

There is nothing simple about the timeline and construction history of this building. It is perhaps most interesting in terms of the history of design models rather than building techniques. Sutcliffe writes, "there was no English design context for the new cathedral, owing to the lack of church building since Henry VIII's break with Rome in the 1530s and this gave considerable freedom to Wren" (34). All parties agreed on a classical model, which was presented in AD 1670 (the First Model). This model was altered over time, contemplating a domed church on a traditional plan (the Great Model) versus a domed cross design with a large central space (the Greek Cross Model). The latter design was favoured and presented in a model in AD 1673. It was quite obviously aligned with St. Peter's in the Vatican. However, it was rejected as being overly dark and non-processional, as well as too Catholic. Demolition work was already under way by this time (Beard 25), thus a final design was needed quickly. In AD 1675 a combination of the warrant and great model designs was approved amid much political wrangling, rivalry, and discussion of expense (Sutcliffe 36). The significance of this whole design controversy is summarized by Soo: "the sequence of schemes for St. Paul's demonstrates Wren's empirical, almost arbitrary approach to design" (462). During construction, the design was continually altered, noticeably affecting the unity of the building (interior–exterior and visual–actual structure).

The foundation stone was laid in AD 1675 and contracts signed for sand and lime supplies and masonry. Beard writes, "in all, across the years of building, 1675–1709, 41 contracts were entered into for mason's work, supplies of stone, bricks and bricklayers, carpenters, plumbers, smiths, sand, lime, carving, paving, gilding, and the Great

Organ" (28). All were entered into a contracts book and signed by the com As a brief summary, Beard believes that by AD 1678 the choir was eigh and preparations were being made for dome support; by the 1690s, me and woodcarving for the interiors were on-going and the organ had been ordered; the final solution for the dome came in 1704; and the upper stories of the cathedral with its balustrade were completed in 1718. The painting of the dome, chosen through competition, was not begun until June 1715. While there were many who worked on the building, Downes is able to write: "probably no English cathedral previously had been designed entirely by one man; certainly none had been completed to one man's design and in his life-time" (15). He notes that construction was constantly changing, but simultaneously limiting the design possibilities as the building went up. He adds, "the dome and towers in particular represent, in their final form designed about 1704, the line of contact between on the one hand an imagination without limits and, on the other, a range of statical options that was constantly narrowed by the progress of construction" (23).

St. Paul's Cathedral was completed in AD 1711. What was most impressive in terms of engineering was the dome. "The dome, with its timber structure, false interior, and cone carrying the heavy stone pinnacle, was as much a triumph of engineering as a work of art" (Sutcliffe 36). It was a three-shell structure of brick cone hidden within an inner masonry shell and outer timber shell, hemispherical, and with their own decorative scheme. It did not exceed St. Peter's dome in height. Wren was disappointed with the length of the balustrades, which were added by a new surveyor, although he liked the tower additions. Soo gives a good summary: "as the result of a compromise between native medieval tradition and continental classicism, reconciled by creating a disunity between appearances and reality, the final design of St. Paul's is a clear reflection of social values and scientific philosophy in late-17th-century England" (462).

## 2.12 Industrial Revolution

### 2.12.1 Historical and Cultural Environment

#### 1. Background

During the Industrial Revolution machines changed the way people lived and their ways of manufacturing. The advent of steam power and its associated machinery in the eighteenth and nineteenth centuries spurred significant changes in farming, manufacturing, mining, and transport. Beginning in England, these developments started a process of using vast natural resources to power economic change, for example in such areas as the manufacture of cloth and in the use of locomotive engines in transportation (Schivelbusch). Europe's socioeconomic and cultural conditions were transformed (More). Technology introduced mechanised production systems that replaced manual labour. The use of steam and water power created the train and the steamship, which revolutionised the market and the transportation of goods

(Lorenzen). Factories altered the landscape. The military industrial machine also developed new technologies for war.

## 2. Relationship to Previous Period

Once machinery had been introduced, tradition production systems vanished. Larger middle and artisan classes meant political and sociological changes. The move from human- and animal-based technology to the use of machines required a number of scientific advances. More control than previously was asserted on national boundaries. Childhood mortality decreased, creating a larger workforce. Health and hygiene improved. Food production became more efficient, eliminating waste and the threat of famine. A switch from rural to urban suggested new needs. The refinement of the steam engine made transportation and travel easier, quicker, and accessible to more people. This change from the previous period allowed for a continuous cycle of improvement and a rise in the general standard of living for most Europeans (Mumford).

## 3. Contribution to Western Civilisation

The modern world was born with the Industrial Revolution. It created the conditions and technologies for global expansion, exploration, colonisation, capitalism, and European economic hegemony. Social movements such as Marxism were created in response to capitalism. Unique artistic trends were also produced. The modern conception of the individual and of human rights developed out of the Industrial Revolution. The contributions of this era have been so enormous that contemporary life, with all its technologies, comforts, stresses, political debates, and tragedies, would be inconceivable without it.

## 2.12.2 Knowledge and Scientific Environment

The Industrial Revolution progressed naturally out of the Scientific Revolution. Science provided the tools and technological developments that allowed for certain tasks to be conducted on a larger scale, such as agriculture. The Industrial Revolution was based on applied scientific achievements, and its social implications were also vast. For example, industries such as textiles, milling, and mining were mechanized using applied knowledge of machinery.

One of the more recognizable names from the Industrial Revolution is Hans Christian Ørsted (1777–1851). In his *Philosophisk Repertorium* he stated, "in order to achieve completeness in our knowledge of nature, we must start from two extremes, from experience and from the intellect itself. . . . When the empiricist in his regression towards general laws of nature meets the metaphysician in his progression, science will reach its perfection." Ørsted's view represents a fusion of scientific rationalism and empiricism, a scientist's dream. His research on electromagnetism led him to the realization that electricity is propagated by fluctuation. His discovery linking electricity and magnetism sent shockwaves through the physics community, leading to a large upsurge of research into electrodynamics.

Others made significant contributions at this time. William Whewell (1794–1866) was a disciple of Bacon. He developed the hypothetico-deductive method of scientific logic, which attempted to unite ideas with facts. He also coined the term "scientist" (William Whewell -Encyclopedia Britannica). Another empirical philosopher, John Stuart Mill (1806–1873), developed utilitarianism into a moral doctrine. Charles Sanders Peirce (1839–1941) helped to found pragmatism and statistics. He also invented the concepts of blind and controlled randomized experiments, now a staple of epidemiology (Management). In "How to Make Our Ideas Clear" (1878), Peirce outlined a method to test the truth of knowledge through logical pragmatism, which fuses induction and deduction rather than using them in competition. Secondly, Peirce proposes a scheme for testing hypotheses that still holds sway, and the abductive, deductive, and inductive inference modes of reasoning (286–302).

### 2.12.3 General Management

In analysing why the Industrial Revolution occurred, some commentators think that the British made advancements because its entrepreneurs held to a belief in the work ethic, the use of technology, and the importance of progress. Information could also be exchanged rapidly in England due to its network of informal philosophical societies. Furthermore, magazines and periodicals describing technology began in the early 1800s. Additionally, the middle class of industrialists and businessmen were beginning to have more power than the land-owning nobles (Hudson 138–44).

One of the central figures in management during the Industrial Revolution was Adam Smith (1723–1790), an economist who penned *The Wealth of Nations*. His economic ideas were the foundation for the laissez-faire management doctrine. He asserted the presence of an "invisible hand" that worked over the market, naturally controlling prices and competition. His thoughts on the division of labour were fundamental to the principles of the efficient organisation of work, including notions of increased specialisation, work simplification, and time studies. For example, Smith described process changes to improve productivity in pin manufacturing. Seeing that an individual could make 200 pins a day, through an analysis of the stages of manufacturing Smith was able to propose a process of specialisation in which ten people could produce 48,000 pins per day (Mejia 20).

Other economists and manufacturers contributed to the theory of management. Mill justified theoretically the notions of resource allocation, production, and pricing. Innovators like Eli Whitney (1765–1825), James Watt (1736–1819), and Matthew Boulton (1728–1809) were responsible for standardization of production, acknowledgment of the importance of quality control, the development of cost accounting, planning of work, and the notion of interchangeable components. Charles Babbage (1792–1871) was a pioneer in manufacturing technology. In 1822 he created a mechanical calculator which was the world's first computer. Babbage supervised how his invention was used and was interested in the labour division in manufacturing. He also invented equipment to monitor workers' output, which was then used to generate a profit-sharing system involving workers being paid a bonus from company profits (Management: Historical Perspectives).

Robert Owen (1771–1858) was a trendsetter in management practises. He viewed the progression of the Industrial Revolution as chaotic and sought to bring increased order to the system. His management philosophy was based on the idea that better observation could maintain order in a factory. He rejected corporal punishment or threats of redundancy as disciplinary procedures and chose rather to appeal to an individual worker's morality. This system elevated rewards over punishments as a motivation for productive employment. Owen gave his superintendents coloured markers to place at the workstations of good workers. At the end of each day, the workers would stand by their units so any person passing by could note the performance of each employee. This was designed to encourage those not exerting their full effort, while attempting to maintain sustained effort from the higher achievers.

By the late nineteenth century, economists such as Alfred Marshall (1842–1924) and Léon Walras (1834–1910) were developing theories of management style. Joseph Wharton presented the first management training seminar in 1881. This evolution of management theory led, by the 1900s, to managers attempting to place management on a scientific basis, for example founded on Henry R. Towne's *Science of Management*. The culmination of these efforts during the Industrial Revolution was Frederick Winslow Taylor's *The Principles of Scientific Management* (1911), which was a summary of a management theory he had proposed earlier.

In 1899 Taylor wanted to increase the productivity of labourers offloading steel into gondolas at the Bethlehem (PA) Steel Plant (Stewart). His experiment was to offer the incentive of higher wages to workers who achieved their quotas. Productivity increased, but total company savings were minimal compared to the non-incentive methods of worker motivation (Wrege and Hodgetts 1283–1291). Nonetheless, his principles were noticed.

Taylor's *The Principles of Scientific Management*, was a pivotal monograph that became the starting point for the study of modern organisation. Its principles of managerial motivation are quite simple:

1. Decompose work into tasks, or "elements" and develop "a science" for each one;
2. Select and train workers according to a scientific approach;
3. Create cooperation between workers and managers to ensure the work is being done according to the developed science; and
4. Divide the work between managers and workers, so that each performs the tasks to which they are respectively suited. (Taylor)

Taylor's work was significant because it marked historically the felt social need created by the Industrial Revolution for a class of professional managers (Warner and Witzel 263–76). It responded to the circumstance that ownership and management were separate.

### 2.12.4 Construction Technology

Technological development in the Industrial Revolution radicalized construction. This age saw the development of new machines, materials, and work processes. As described above, the new machines harnessed and used natural energy such as coal and steam to power engines (Houston and Snell 473–92). Such engine power produced far-ranging effects.

For one thing, it combined with the new management techniques to alter the way materials were manufactured. Machines facilitated better methods for building tools, manipulating materials, and building parts for larger construction machinery (Greenburg 693–714). The mechanization of industries meant that materials could be produced more quickly with less manpower. Innovations in organisational procedures meant streamlining and increased worker productivity in manufacturing facilities related to the construction industry. Specialisation became a key component as scientific knowledge was systematically applied to the manufacturing process for all kinds of goods. Material resources could also be acquired more easily as a result; thus, they were available in quantities previously unknown, reducing their cost. Merchants of construction materials could supply sufficient goods to their expanding markets. Furthermore, the process of prefabricating parts for machines and buildings was developed, leading to the possibility of interchangeable parts and the development of machine tools (Carlsson 91–114). Steam power in factories was eventually replaced by electric power, which allowed further progress in the efficient production of machined tools (Asif 1388–413). Factories situated near natural resources were built all over the countryside and in the cities. This meant an important change in the relationship between factories, transportation, and the management of a construction site that received the materials.

Another impact of this revolution was in transportation. The construction of canals and railroads progressed because of the smelting of iron. They made it easier to transport coal (via canal barges) and to extend the railroad system widely across the land. Steam-powered locomotives on railways could transport heavy materials quickly and cost-effectively, such as lumber, iron, steel, and other necessary construction items (Evans 1–34). This ability to transfer raw materials to the construction site quickly and through mechanisation rather than human labour had an enormous impact on the building projects of the time, including bridge construction, roads, railways, and barges (Schivelbusch).

Materials themselves changed. Stone, wood, brick, and concrete were still widely used, but iron and plate glass became viable options that challenged the viability of these other materials. Iron had the advantage of strength and lightness, whereas advances in plate glass technology and manufacturing strengthened its ability to be used in large-scale construction projects. Reinforced concrete improved that material. When lumber was used, it could be milled more efficiently by machine than by hand and easily transported by barge, railway, or ship. Industrial paints were mass-produced. Generally, steel, iron, and brass were available in large quantities for city construction. The Industrial Revolution made such materials available and accessible, thus rendering possible this period's notable structures.

The types of buildings also changed. Increased urbanisation during the Industrial Revolution created great demand for city construction. New problems in designing and creating buildings that housed many people made different engineering modalities necessary (Houston and Snell 473–792). High-rise commercial and residential buildings were facilitated. Urban industrial centres rose up using the machine-driven impulse. The tunnel shield for subaqueous tunnelling came into use (Landow). Iron suspension bridges and other types of large exhibition halls and towers were conceived based on the new technology, materials, and engineering advances. A good example of the use of innovative materials and building techniques to create new buildings was the celebrated Crystal Palace, erected in London in 1851 out of iron and prefabricated glass.

Finally, at worksites organisation had to be efficient and machines did most of the physical work, replacing the dominance of hand tools and human muscle. The steam engine supplied the power where previously human and animal brawn had done the work. For example, steam-powered cranes hoisted and handled materials with ease. Steam shovels were used extensively for the excavation of building sites, eliminating the need for large teams of labourers for digging. They also facilitated the construction of roads for transportation (Asif 1388–413). These changes meant less manpower and more energy output.

On the whole, building during the Industrial Revolution was driven by new energies and new forms of commerce (Landow). The church or religion was not a factor; rather, machine-driven ideals and automation inspired this period of radical advancement in building: the confluence of steam-powered engines to do the work; the creation of the factory system with its distribution networks to the building site; the improvement in metal and tool production processes; the advent of new materials for building such as iron and plate glass; and the complete overhaul and acceleration of transportation made possible by canals and railroads. All contributed to this powerful instantiation of construction technology.

### 2.12.5 Master Builder Tradition

The Industrial Revolution had clear effects on both architecture and construction management. The separation of construction and design was an on-going dynamic within building, where designers and builders functioned more independently from one another. The use of modern physics, mathematics, thermodynamics, and chemistry caused the emergence of building science as a discipline (engineering). This contrasted with architecture and the actual craft of doing the building work. In other words, the building professions remained complex but became even more specialised and defined into set roles. This was a general trend rising from the particular social changes in the industrial environment, just as specialisation was happening in the factories.

There were changes in the way the work and worksites were managed. The Industrial Revolution meant the rise of large contractors and the decline of small craft organisations for big building projects. These large contractors assembled and managed projects as a whole, from the labour and equipment to the materials and implementation of the design. In other words, each smaller subcontractor was overseen by and responsible to the general contractor, exactly as it is today. This did not, however, mean the end of master builders. Nonetheless, there was a progressive decline of such master builders and an elevation of the design aspect. People came to identify buildings with the architectural designer rather than the actual building contractors.

Thomas Telford (1757–1834) was a Scottish civil engineer, architect, and stonemason. He was well known for his bridge and canal construction projects as the surveyor of public works in Shropshire (Bellis). Telford managed the design and construction of the Ellesmere and the Shrewsbury canals. His work was important in extending new design techniques, based on knowledge of materials, into the area of iron building.

A similar type of industrial innovator in the field of building was the English engineer Isambard Kingdom Brunel (1806–1859). He was the mastermind behind the Great Western Railway, but also designed and built famous steamships, including the first propeller-driven iron transatlantic steamship in 1843 (the SS *Great Britain*). His ships were instrumental in laying the transatlantic telegraph cable. He also constructed many important bridges and tunnels, including the first subaqueous tunnel under a large river (Wilson 202–3). His designs revolutionised public transportation in particular, and by extension, all of engineering. Brunel's projects often contained innovative solutions to long-standing engineering problems (Wilson 202–03).

One French architect who influenced the architectural design process of the Industrial Revolution was Jean-Nicolau-Louis Durand. An instructor at the Ecole Polytechnique in Paris from 1794 to 1833, Durand actually discussed the design process itself in architecture. In other words, his designs did not merely present the finished building, but led through the construction process. The modern-day design process was addressed in 1873 by another Frenchman, Eugene Emmanuel Viollet-le-Duc. He developed simple but important guidelines for a good design process, stated as follows:

1. Identify the need;
2. Develop a detailed program statement for the project;
3. Explore alternatives that satisfy the program statement;
4. Execute the project based on the selected alternative that satisfies the program statement;
5. Learn from the completed project: What went right and what went wrong? (Ramroth 8–12)

This was an example of how master builders may have conceived of themselves and their role.

The master builder, now conceived of as general contract manager, was often in charge of delegating tasks according to the specialisation needs of jobsite functions.

The jobsite itself would house management offices from which the builder would work. The move towards work specialisation was compatible with the concept of separating design from construction. The clarity of this separation between design and construction professionals – between architect and builder-engineer – became evident in the mid-nineteenth century. The Royal Institute of British Architects was founded in 1835 in London, followed by the American Institute of Architects in 1857. The movement of professional architecture away from direct participation in construction was mirrored by the organisation of construction contractors. For example, in 1887 an organisation called the Associated General Contractors of America was formed. (Loulakis 48).

This clear division between responsibility for design and responsibility for building was the fruit of the new industrial demands. Yet it was the heir of the Renaissance debate between Alberti and Brunelleschi. Alberti's separatist movement had argued against Brunelleschi's integrationist view, clamouring for a distinction between architectural design art and engineering science or building technology. In the Industrial Revolution, the conceptualisation and practise of professional construction management swung Alberti's way. The implications of this were huge. Essentially the Industrial Revolution, by adopting this specialist attitude, led to the disappearance of the traditional master builder in the twentieth century.

The emergence in nineteenth-century England of the general contractor, who was a new kind of businessman, aided in the disappearance of the master builder. Another influence was professional architect Sir John Soane. He declaimed that the architect ought to be completely separate from construction, saying, "with what propriety can his situation and that of the builder, or the contractor be united?" (Kostof 194). In the place of the master builder role were the architect proper and the general contractor. The architect became responsible for design *only*. The problem with this system was that the architect might not really know much about construction. The general contractor became responsible for construction *only*. An analogous problem was created, since the contractor might have no genuine knowledge of design.

In summary, the functions were separated and no longer united in one figure. The architect–contractor system of division created problems, however (Cuff 33). Only the general contractor, not the architect, has authority on the jobsite. Previously in the master builder tradition, the master builder had retained power to change and to implement designs at the jobsite. In the modern industrial age, however, this was no longer true. While obligated to comply with owners' requests, the contractor was no longer legally obligated during construction to comply with what the architect decided regarding the design of the building (Cuff 33).

### 2.12.6 Building Projects

### 1. Menai Suspension Bridge (1819–1825)

The Menai Straits Suspension Bridge was built from 1819 to 1825 by Thomas Telford, who was the Surveyor of Bridges to the County of Shropshire prior to working on the

Ellesmere Canal. Colvin describes his career as an architect: "as a bridge-builder he was not slow to realize the possibilities of iron, already demonstrated by T. F. Pritchard at Coalbrookdale, and his iron bridge at Buildwas was one of the pioneer structures of its kind" (970). His later bridges, the Menai and Conway suspension bridges in Wales and the Craigellachie Bridge over the Spey River in Scotland, are among the best-known iron bridges.

Telford dominated British bridge building during this period. For the Menai Straits Bridge, he followed the pattern of Derby and Pritchard's bridge, which was the first of its kind (in 1779) to use a single semicircular arch composed of five cast-iron ribs. The parts were assembled on this bridge not using bolts but through interlocking joints and wedges. In the Menai Straits Bridge, Telford applied the principle of suspension to the huge span of 177 meters. It was a roadbed hung from wrought-iron chains that are slung over towers and buried in rock at both ends. For rust proofing, all the links were pre-treated in hot linseed oil before being dried in a stove. What anchored the roadbed were the massive masonry arches below. None of this was brand new; the techniques were already known. What was significant was his application of the new principle of suspension to iron bridge building on a larger scale.

Aesthetically, Telford was important also. According to Kostof, "Telford's distinction was to endow metal bridges with architectural grace" (599). On his bridges, the metal was elaborated with decorative designs and the masonry abutments were picturesque. Kostof evaluates the Menai construction thus: "Telford's contribution, again, was to approach this as an architectural problem, making it feasible on a large scale" (599). Soon the chains would be supplanted by wire ropes or cables. Telford's bridge was a step in this direction.

## 2. Crystal Palace (1850–1851)

The Crystal Palace was constructed at a time after the Gothic revival in an age "when mass production was beginning to alter the age-old habits of the building industry" (Kostof 594) This was the new mechanical age of iron, the age of world exhibitions for which it was originally built. The Victorian age was on the way out. Middleton and Watkin write, "iron and glass were not generally applicable to Victorian architectural needs" (359). The building signalled social change. Highways and railways were constructed into the countryside, beside slag heaps from which mines were accumulating. The increasing use of iron and glass was in some eyes the most radical advance in building material technology since the Roman invention and use of concrete (Kostof 595). Iron was cheaper, more resilient, and less bulky than stone masonry. It was used to strengthen walls, floors, and domes. Plate glass developments in the 1840s made possible the complete glazing of a building. The floor of the Crystal Palace was clay tiled and the roof glazed, but masonry had disappeared. There remained only iron latticework supporting wood-framed sheets of glass.

Several things are significant for the Crystal Palace in its representation of building in the Industrial Revolution. One, Joseph Paxton designed it on the model of the greenhouses he remembered as a gardener. Two, it was designed with an internal skeleton of cast- and wrought-iron stanchions and beams. Iron structures created columns and framework for the five-aisled building. This type of framework was innovative and became typical afterwards. Three, it was prefabricated, thus pointing to the new industrial arrangement and organisation of construction. This meant that it could be disassembled and transported. Kostof writes, "the casting process was geared to prefabrication in bulk, so that members could be shipped to the site ready-made and assembled with ease" (594). Apparently it was assembled in six months from thousands of prefabricated parts. Because its parts were light, transparent, and pre-made, Nuttgens believes that its form was indeterminate, unconventional, and revolutionary: "there was no reason why it should not be made bigger or smaller, longer or wider" (246). Four, its erection depended on the availability of railway transport and a sophisticated site organisation. As a result, the premanufacturing and mechanisation of the worksite at the Crystal Palace project changed building practises. They led to the replacement of craft guilds by large contractors. Finally, new internal systems were implemented. Nuttgens states, "the needs of industry led to the development of new technical services in heating, ventilation and sanitation, which began to be applied to domestic architecture as well" (245).

## 3. Eiffel Tower (1887–1889)

Intended as the gateway to the 1889 World Exhibition in Paris, the Eiffel Tower was the world's tallest structure at that time (over 300 meters). Its designer was Gustave Eiffel, who had extensive experience building arched wrought-iron bridges for railways and viaducts in France. His firm's design was chosen as the winner from over 100 contestants in 1886. Echols writes, "under the architectural preparation of Maurice Koechlin and the guidance of structural calculations by Emile Nougier, workers began construction on the Eiffel Tower on 26 January 1887" (229). It took about two years to complete. It was made out of 12,000 pieces of prefabricated wrought-iron parts (on the model of the Crystal Palace) that were connected with 2.5 million bolts and rivets to form a framework.

The earliest idea for such a tall tower was apparently that of Richard Trevithick in 1832 (Steiner 117). His design, which was never carried out, included a central elevator. However, his proposed cast-iron panels would have been too heavy to succeed, even with a hole in them to reduce weight. This was nonetheless the initial inspiration for French notions of a tall tower.

What is impressive about the Eiffel Tower is the relationship between strength and lightness. Echols states, "the tower was designed so that the structure applied a foundation load no greater than that of a person sitting in a chair per square unit of measure" (229). It applied a principle similar to the rigid frame truss designed by Henri de Dion to cover the Galerie des Machines, "in which there is complete union of 'stanchion' and 'beam'" (Steiner 95). Weight on the foundations was "less than that of a stone wall nine meters high" (Steiner 119). It was carefully planned with consideration for the soil. Eiffel composed a stratum of plastic clay sixteen meters deep and covered it over with gravel and sand. As to the frame, there were four piers and sixteen iron ribs, each of which rested on its own stone and concrete foundation. Steiner writes, "in order to ensure against unequal settling, a hydraulic press of 800 tons was built into the cast-iron shoe of each of the ribs" (119).

Given its height, wind was a major concern for the tower's structural integrity and stability. Echols states, "Eiffel resolved this potential problem by providing diagonal framing within the structure, and by incorporating a system of windbreaks" (229). As is obvious by looking at it, the tower is full of space in a sort of open construction that allows wind to pass through it, thus minimizing wind resistance. Echols comments, "the mathematical precision of the tower's components and the lightness of its lacy design made the tower a sophisticated product much ahead of its time" (229).

Steiner has outlined some of the important points about the Eiffel Tower's erection (Steiner 119–20). The first 25 meters were built in cantilever, using derricks and windlasses. Above this, timber scaffolding was used to the first level. Beyond this first-level platform (which ties the piers together structurally), the scaffolding continued to be used as materials were raised by the piered elevators. Since its completion, there have been repairs that have increased the tower's weight, but in the late twentieth century its load was lightened with the substitution of steel alloy for some of the iron.

## 2.13 Summary

The literature review is now complete. It constitutes the raw material from which the remaining analysis will be done. Twelve periods of architecture have been covered from a historical perspective. General background information has been culled from literary sources on the cultural, social, and scientific aspects of each period. A more detailed and precise collection of historical research was conducted into the management theories and construction technologies for all twelve eras. In addition, pivotal examples of twenty particular buildings have been discussed historically as exemplary of their respective architectural periods. It remains now to present, analyse, and interpret this data so that significant results, findings, conclusions, and recommendations can be drawn together with respect to the history of project management and the contemporary understanding of project management as a discipline.

# Chapter 3

# History of the Areas of Expertise and their Application to Project Activities

## 3.0 Introduction

The literature review conducted in chapter 2 can now be presented and analysed. This chapter will consider and summarize the data given there. The data will be investigated with a view to obtaining significant results concerning development within the various historical periods. The same guiding categories will be utilised to arrange the analysis, namely:

1. Historical and cultural environment
2. Knowledge and scientific environment
3. General management
4. Construction technology
5. Master builder tradition
6. Analysis of building projects

In practise, these items are closely interrelated and interact to form project management as a whole; they are separated here and throughout chapter 3 only for ease of presentation. The analytical presentation provided in this chapter will be used to develop the interpretive synthesis of the history of project management in the next chapter. Through a careful study of events and practises related to these research categories, the research will trace circumstances at different historical periods that affected the development of the areas of expertise and their application to project activities. As a continuation of the previous chapters, the goals are to recapitulate the historical data and extend its clarity and significance. By understanding the historical development of the areas of expertise and their application to project activities in this way, the history of project management will be detailed and unfolded.

Science and technology have advanced over the centuries, so as the cultural environment and management skill. It is these types of changes that ultimately this research attempts to analyse and synthesise using historical examples of buildings to examine how historical circumstances have influenced construction and professional tradition down through the various ages. This chapter will end with the analytical summary of the contribution of these buildings and look forward to the next chapter's synthetic perspective.

## 3.1 The Historical and Cultural Environment

### 3.1.0 Introduction

Project activities are performed within a particular historical and cultural, social and economic environment. When we study history, we tend to look at each different society as if it were essentially autonomous: there were the Egyptians, and the Greeks, and then the Romans, and so forth. But while, of course, there are core practises, habits, and beliefs – and historical moments – that distinguish these and other societies from each other, there are many key connections as well. Societies borrow from each other all the time; indeed, one might argue that the level of "borrowing" from one culture to the next is at the level of grand larceny.

When one thinks about it, though, there is every reason for societies to borrow from each other in the same way that one generation learns from its predecessor, and passes on what it has learned. Some of what different societies passed along to each other took the form of technological advancements, so that European builders took the technology of Romanesque building and developed it into the Gothic style, enabling taller, more delicate structures. Europeans who travelled East during the Crusades came into contact with the Arab sophistication and developments in math and science, bringing them back to Europe, where this knowledge helped to spark the Renaissance.

These cultural advancements would in turn lead to the Industrial Revolution of the nineteenth century, which would fundamentally change the entire world, shifting us not only from the labour of humans to that of machines and loosening the grip of tradition across all cultures, but also allowing for further changes in politics, art, and the very concept of the human condition. In the cities that were themselves in part a result of the Industrial Revolution, people would begin to live longer and experience a wider horizon than those in any previous society would have had the possibility even to imagine. This section examines cultural development from ancient societies to the Industrial Revolution.

### 3.1.1 Historical and Cultural Environment from the Earliest Times to the Classical Antiquity

Mesopotamia was the birthplace of civilisation. It was in all likelihood home to the first settled agrarian-based society, the first domestication of plants and animals, and the first city (Dlott). Human society prior to this time exists only in the shade, since there is no substantial documentation of previous civilizations. It is assumed as certain by scholars that the progenitors of Mesopotamian civilization were hunter-gatherers (Dalling). This transition from a nomadic mountain- and forest-based hunter-gatherer existence to stable plains-based and urban arrangements with surrounding farms was of inestimable importance for the development and viability of new kinds of culture, social techniques, technologies, and the need for permanent structures. In turn, this stability must have encouraged changes in thinking and innovation. Many of the other important aspects of modern civilisation had their origins during the Sumerian period in the Middle East. These included mathematics, writing systems, legal systems, and medicine (Pollock). They likely grew out of the practises of priests connected with royalty. During this period, of course, there were a number of peaks and valleys in the degree of civilisation, so one must be careful about drawing a line of sheer progress and enlightenment. Nevertheless, without question many of the basic qualities of modern culture were established within that time period.

The Egyptians were dependent on the river Nile. In particular, they needed to be able to predict its rise and fall. Because of this attention to flooding and subsidence, they developed sophisticated mathematics, recorded their observations in writing systems, and created a well-established division of labour. This paralleled developments among the Mesopotamians. The Egyptians surpassed the Mesopotamians, however, by creating a more sophisticated social and legal system than Sumer and a far more complex calendar system (James). Both ancient Mesopotamia and ancient Egypt contributed to the civilisations that followed. Connected through the Mediterranean Sea, the Greeks took up the learning, artistry, and culture of what came before them, and through this process of historical transmission and influence, knowledge and culture of the ancient world passed to Rome (Siliotto).

The ancient Greeks were a seafaring people who incorporated much of the knowledge and technology of older cultures, especially that of Egypt, but also of Phoenicia and Babylon (Freeman). Greek society spread farther through trade routes that the Romans would later take over (Hansen). The complex relationship among the different subcultures gave rise to the political organisation of democracy, which was one of the Greeks' enduring legacies to human society (Rhodes). Equally, the huge size of the empire made it subject to political upheaval and the Hellenistic Greeks could not retain their power (Elton).The entire edifice of Western philosophy rests on the foundation of Greek thought. Therein almost every philosophical subject matter was defined, from natural philosophy to epistemology and ethics. In addition, Greek literature and art were formative for later European conceptions of art. Greek drama still influences contemporary theatre (Gutzwiller). Greece synthesised all of the most sophisticated aspects of Eastern and Near Eastern civilisations and in turn passed these on to later societies. The Roman poet and orator Horace described the influence of Greece on philosophy, architecture, medicine, politics, literature, and education, and Roman civilisation and culture are inconceivable without Greek influences.

The Romans borrowed heavily from all past cultures and used this knowledge and know-how to build a geographically expansive empire through well-honed organisational skills. They replaced the Greeks as lords of the Mediterranean. The size of the Roman Empire required a well-disciplined army that not only conquered people across Europe but then established and maintained Roman law and culture in each new colony (Goldsworthy).

Rome took Greek and Egyptian technologies to new levels. For example, Roman houses had indoor plumbing, including flush toilets, and a sophisticated system of aqueducts that brought water to the cities for baths and to irrigate crops. Roman cities were clean and well organised (Bird). However, much of Roman learning and technology was lost after the fall of the empire and not recovered until the Renaissance. Nevertheless, even in the Dark Ages there were glimmers of Roman cultural achievement. For example, their language, Latin, forms the basis of many modern European languages (Thinkquest.org).

### 3.1.2 Historical and Cultural Environment of the Medieval Period

The Byzantine Empire lasted for a millennium and its influence allowed for the continuation of Greco-Roman cultural heritage and learning. These traditions were kept alive as most of Europe fell into the Dark Ages. Until its defeat by the Ottoman Turks in the fifteenth century (Halson), the Byzantine Empire provided a sanctuary for Western learning and culture. If it had not been strong, Byzantium would have been unable to withstand the emerging power of the Islamic empire. Primarily because it was such an important trading locus, the economy of the empire blossomed. Its trade routes (like the Silk Road) also spread the culture, art, and learning of Constantinople across Eurasia and North Africa. The wealth of Byzantium helped to fund the Crusades, one of the effects of which was to revitalize Europe (Laiou). Byzantine leaders were generally skilled diplomats, which helped them establish a series of treaties with their neighbours. These treaties extended the power of Byzantium and carried over into present-day alliances (Neumann). New scholarship suggests that the Byzantine Empire was as successful as the Roman Empire in shaping modern Europe (Angelov).

The rise of Islam during and after the Prophet Mohammed's life unified the region around religious beliefs and led to the development of agriculture to replace nomadic lifestyles. While the Islamic world was prospering with wealth, power, stability, and conquest, Europe was fragmenting and declining into an inauspicious feudal system. The Muslim world assumed patronage of most of the learning of the Western world, becoming home to the best of the world's arts, engineering, philosophy, and medicine. The Islamic Golden Age valued knowledge and was a vital advocate of preserving and transmitting earlier learning (Turner).

The Crusade invasions, in nine different waves from AD 1095 to 1291, added stress to the previously strong Islamic empire. As capitalism replaced feudalism in Europe, European merchants desired new markets for their products. This was one of the motivations for the Crusades (Riley-Smith). In addition, the Papacy was manoeuvring to increase its power. It endorsed the Crusades, using them as a way to gain political control over European kingdoms.

From the perspective of cultural development, the Crusades were important since they brought Islamic technology and scholarship back to Europe. They also required that European armies improve their methods of navigation, shipbuilding, food preservation, military building, and tactics (Asbridge). In many ways the Crusades also established the foundations of the modern nation-state and opened up much of the world to European exploration (Stark). They were the harbinger of future European conquest and colonisation.

The Romanesque style furthered the traditions of both the Roman and Byzantine Empires. The Catholic Church augmented its power and wealth during this period, and so it sponsored much of its art and architecture (Grant). Craft developments included not only architectural advances but also artistic changes in metal, enamel, and ivory work, detailed bronze and gold sculpture, illuminated manuscripts, stained glass, and embroidery (Toman). The churches of this era were taller and stronger than their predecessors because of new building styles such as the use of symmetrical planning, ardent decoration, and ratio in design (Banister).

Coinciding with the Romanesque movement was a rebirth of art, science, and culture with a great deal of social, political, and economic transformation. This intellectual revival in Europe during the High Middle Ages has been called the "Renaissance of the 12th century" (Benson). This intellectual reinvigoration of European culture was founded on a revival of Roman law and literature, including poetry, Greek philosophy and science, and Arabic additions to these traditions. During the Romanesque period the first European universities were established (Haskin viii). This early renaissance owed much to the Islamic Golden Age and the Byzantine Empire. Perhaps most importantly, it paved the way for the fifteenth-century Italian Renaissance and the seventeenth-century Scientific Revolution.

The Romanesque period in Europe was a southern movement, whereas the Gothic was largely northern and eastern. Given its historical placement, it forms the natural bridge between the Romanesque and the Renaissance (Charles). Like European art before it, the Gothic continued as an expression of Catholicism. Much of the art and architecture were designed to instruct illiterate audiences through biblical images (Gothic Art). Yet the Catholic Church was not the only patron of art. European urbanisation became a reality, oftentimes centring around the universities. A middle class arose whose new wealth enabled them occasionally to purchase art. Furthermore, as cities grew, trade guilds expanded their reach. These often welcomed artists and helped them towards literacy, accurate record keeping, and patronage (Cahill).

### 3.1.3 Historical and Cultural Environment from the Renaissance to the Industrial Revolution

Perhaps more than previous eras, the Renaissance helped revive Roman and Greek traditions in art, music, politics, culture, and society. Socially, urbanisation continued its earlier trajectories. Capitalism finally gained a firm upper hand over feudalism. Of great importance as well was European expansion. The Renaissance was the era when European ships sought out the New World. This exploration extended European power and represented a political shift from introspection to outward expression, which was also paralleled in the arts. Colonisation was instituted (Starn 122–4), made possible by advanced weaponry, navigation, and transportation, and driven by economic motives. Contact with Muslim traders taught European merchants different trading methods, including new standards of monetary exchange. The decimal system and algebra were imported into the merchant repertoire of Venetian spice traders, who were mediators between Europe and Arabia. There was also a rise in science, astronomy, and medical research (Morris).

While the Renaissance was still largely embedded in the Catholic Church, the Baroque Period took humanism to new heights and allowed for a transition away from religion (Friedell). Classical elements remained important for Baroque cultural achievements, while there was an important upswing in scientific research. The Baroque style is still occasionally seen in twentieth-century architecture . In the arts, it established a basis for the modern era, and is most often viewed as a necessary transition from the traditions of the medieval and Renaissance into the modern (Buci-Glucksmann).

The Baroque Period also coincided with an era in science and technology that required the application of logical reasoning. Known as the Scientific Revolution, European cultures witnessed unprecedented advances in knowledge and understanding. Where previous periods had made great advancements and hinted towards modern science, the Scientific Revolution was the turning point and the time when various sciences began to reject the prevailing doctrines from ancient Greece and the Middle Ages. A true foundation of modern science was established. Butterfield stated that the "revolution turned the authority in English not only of the Middle Ages but of the ancient world...it outshines everything since the rise of Christianity and reduces the Renaissance and Reformation to the rank of mere episodes" (viii).

After centuries of increased urbanisation, a change toward capitalism, and the crucial development of steam power, society was remade. In the eighteenth and nineteenth centuries, there were enormous and irreversible changes in industries like agriculture, mining, and manufacturing due to the rise of engines. Furthermore, the mechanisation of work and transportation, with its consequential displacement of human and animal power (Lorenzen), and the routinisation of production in the factory system where specialisation became the key, added to the social transformation of European life. These together made up the Industrial Revolution, which changed every aspect of daily life (More). The contemporary economic structure of work, and the difficulties involving global natural resource depletion and climate change, are direct modern consequences of such sweeping change (Weightman). The Industrial Revolution subsequently loosened the grip of all previous cultural traditions, allowing for changes in politics, art, and the human condition. Secularism became the dominant cultural mode of production as religion receded against the economic aims of capitalism. The benefits were many as well. With the revolution, life expectancy increased. Most human experience became firmly rooted in the cities that were themselves a result of the Industrial Revolution. Global horizons widened.

### 3.1.4 Historical and Cultural Environment – Conclusion

The historical and cultural environment of the period of antiquity can be summarised in terms of a number of significant factors. The most significant early trend is the development of an agrarian society in Mesopotamia and Egypt near river basins. This meant the stabilisation of human society in settled groups and away from hunting nomadism. As a result, small villages and cities collected into nation-states, which sometimes initiated the military conquest of surrounding areas. There was also the rise of cities, including Rome, which had over a million inhabitants. These cities arose not only because there was enough food for a large population but because farming required a relatively sophisticated political system to keep up irrigation systems, to store food for years of famine, to distribute food, etc. This era also saw substantial advances in medicine and learning, including the development of written alphabets. New forms of architecture were developed, which in turn allowed cities to grow. These larger cities helped to develop the kind of political and economic systems that still exist today.

What was most important was the linkage of certain kinds of technology that arose to support the agrarian lifestyle, for example irrigation systems in Mesopotamia which were later expanded on in Roman times through indoor plumbing and a system of aqueducts. This was the time in human civilisation when writing developed and made possible both the transmission of cultural knowledge and more precise methods of accounting and record keeping. Calendars and time keeping were developed as well as the complex legal systems required of stable societies and empires. All of these developments were in response to agrarian needs. In addition, these early civilisations, from Mesopotamia through Egypt and Greece to Rome, gave rise to an incipient science based around astronomy and medicine. Knowledge was passed through time from one civilisation to the next so that cultures could build on one another. This historical and cultural environment suggested the context within which ancient science and technology could further develop, thus it was important for the construction practises that will be discussed later.

The Byzantine Empire through the Gothic Age were defined by major changes in artistic and architectural styles as advances in building allowed for much taller, more elegant buildings and higher degrees of decoration. Increasing wealth allowed more resources to be put into art and not into survival. The age also saw the fall of Rome and the shift of learning to the East, to Constantinople and the rise of an insular culture in Western Europe. The Papacy grew in power and sent out the Crusades, which failed in their formal purpose of taking back the Holy Land but helped transform Western Europe. Revitalized by Arab learning and fed by new trade routes, Europe began to take over from the East in terms of wealth and political dominance.

The Gothic style is still seen today and certainly influenced other styles through to the eighteenth century, especially in terms of masonry. The emphasis on the human form in art and the human condition in literature continued well into the modern era and helped to secularise art and society as a whole. The historical and cultural environment of the Medieval periods was a change from that of more ancient civilisations. Trade and diplomacy advanced with the Byzantine Empire. The rise of Islam into an empire had important cultural consequences for the people under its sway and led to unique cultural expressions that later would influence Europe. The Crusades brought Europe into contact with Islamic society through religious and political hostility. This unified and strengthened Europe politically even as it ushered in the dominance of the Catholic Church, which would be of great significance for much of European building in the centuries after. New styles of art and architecture were kindled such as the Romanesque and the Gothic to give expression to the Church and its worldview. Greek and Roman science and art were reborn. All of these factors would have decisive consequences for later ages, beginning with the Renaissance.

The post-Medieval European world had a more rational trajectory. Religion continued to play a crucial cultural role in the lives of people, but there was more space for thought that eventually ushered in the radical transformation of the Industrial Revolution. Urbanisation became the trajectory for human society, replacing the previous foundation of agrarian existence. Capitalism became the new economic form. Fuelled by capitalism and fresh possibilities, Europe expanded through exploration and colonialism, seeking new products and markets. This was enhanced by the Industrial Revolution, which altered the way in which products were made and society was organised. From the Renaissance to the Industrial Age, the modern world in which we still live was born. The Renaissance revived the learning and humanism of the classical world. Science, math, and engineering became more important even as art and literature also flourished. Europe, which began colonising the world, also began to turn away from the Catholic Church. Protestantism began to rise, bringing about a different relationship between the individual and religion, even as other people turned away from religion as the driving force of their lives.

As science became more and more important, people began to be able to create machines that would have been unimaginable just a generation before. The development of steam power helped create almost every other form of machine and human and animal labour was mostly displaced. Production rose, cities grew, the world became something undreamed of – including the undreamed-of horror of pollution and climate change. These scientific advancements would in turn lead to the Industrial Revolution of the nineteenth century, which would fundamentally change the entire world. It would shift labour and production not only from humans and animals to machines and loosen the grip of tradition across all cultures, but would as well allow for further changes in politics, art, and the very philosophical concepts about the human condition. People would begin to live longer and have experiences in the cities that were a direct result of the Industrial Revolution, a much wider horizon than those in any previous society would have had the possibility even to imagine.

## 3.2 Knowledge and Scientific Environment

### 3.2.0 Introduction

The knowledge and scientific environment of each historical period facilitates problem solving, decision making, and developing the right skills and tools to get projects done. We may not think of ourselves as living in a world defined by science. Science seems like something that has to do with space exploration, chemistry experiments, and medical research. However, if we were to compare our own time to that of previous ages, we would come to a more complete understanding of the ways in which our everyday activities are defined by science. Even if we do not understand how something works, we assume that there is a rational, scientific explanation for it. For most of human history, in contrast, people relied not on scientific or mathematical explanations for the world around them but on religious or folk traditions. This was not, it is important to remember, because they were less intelligent than we are in the modern world. It was simply the case that people had not yet amassed enough knowledge.

Importantly, scientific knowledge did not increase steadily and unilaterally over time. Some eras saw great leaps in scientific knowledge while others witnessed only small advances, and other eras saw regression. In some periods science has been viewed as the enemy of religion or the state or both. In others it has been an arm of the state. For while science is about the search for truth, it is also directly related to the history and the culture of which it is a part. This section examines the role and development of science from ancient societies to the Industrial Revolution.

### 3.2.1 Knowledge and Scientific Environment from the Earliest Times to Classical Antiquity

The peoples of ancient Mesopotamia were seekers after knowledge. They kept detailed logs of the stars and other natural phenomena from 3500 BC on and developed the basis for modern mathematics (Hoffman). Babylonian astronomical observations were transmitted to other ancient civilisations, including the Greeks, the Indians, and the Muslims. They formed the foundational concepts and observations for subsequent scientific astronomy (Buccelati 35–47) and are still used today to aid scientists. Mesopotamian civilisation created the seeds of Western scientific endeavor. The Mesopotamians also developed practical technologies. One of their most important inventions was the wheel (Ancient Mesopotamia: Science & Inventions), which ever since has been the foundation of machine technology. Having founded the first agricultural society, the Mesopotamians enhanced farming technology to meet their needs. Methods of irrigation first cropped up in the area, including the dam, the canal, the reservoir, and the water pump. They invented a calendar on which their agriculture depended for its success. The Mesopotamian calendar included the concepts of days, the seven-day week, the lunar month, and the solar year (Scofield). For technological innovation, the achievements of the Mesopotamians were prolific. They were people of vast intelligence, creating ideas and objects that not only helped them, but have remained in use over the millennia and continue in their modern transformations to be an integral part of work and society.

The Egyptians followed the lead of the Mesopotamians in science and technology. One of their great contributions to human civilisation was the creation of the first alphabet around 1900 BC, which the Phoenicians would develop further. The concept of an alphabet spread to other key languages such as Greek, Latin, Arabic, and Hebrew. Alphabetic writing profoundly changed the way observations were recorded and transmitted since it used far fewer symbols (Jensen 256). The Egyptians also furthered knowledge about medicine. A surviving papyrus shows an understanding of major organs such as the heart with its major blood vessels along with the liver, kidneys, and bladder (Wilkins 240–4). The Egyptians also tried to understand how the brain and nerves worked, as well as playing a leading role in developing empirical scientific methodology.

For the Greeks, philosophy was an attempt to understand all aspects of the world in a rational way. Greek philosophers were seekers of truth and knowledge who used rationality and logic to pursue this aim. They were not scientists as understood in the modern sense, but their explorations in natural philosophy contributed to the later development of a scientific mindset. The Greeks considered many fields of investigation that would later turn into scientific disciplines. Like the Mesopotamians, they had a keen interest in the sky and its objects. They progressed in the science of astronomy and fine-tuned the previous calender system to make it more reliable for the regulation of farming work (Thurston 21). Great progress was made in medicine through various sources such as Greek healers, herb collectors, midwives, drug sellers, gymnastic trainers, physicians, and temple healers (Lloyd 38–9). Hippocrates founded the ethics of medical practise and laid the groundwork for all subsequent Western practises of medicine. Later in the Hellenistic period, Galen would advance medical observation through dissections. While Galen relied on Hippocrates, he challenged him as well. This shows the dynamic forward thrust of Greek science towards improvement over tradition rather than strict adherence to it. The Greeks also developed the fields of botany and zoology. Theophrastus wrote the first texts classifying minerals, rocks, animals, and plants. There can be no doubt that modern thought and science owe a great deal to the ancient Greeks.

In the areas of science and knowledge, the Romans were more consolidating than innovating. They relied primarily on previous Greek work, which they took and systematised. They likewise acquired knowledge from the regions that they conquered. Their impact on modern Western science was largely in transmitting these knowledge bases in a systematic way. For example, Lucretius passed on the Epicurean doctrine of atomism in his poem *On Nature*. Pliny the Elder collected information about plants, fossils, stones, resin, metallic alloys, and gems and recorded them along with his insightful comments. The mathematician, astronomer, and geographer Ptolemy lived under Roman rule in Egypt. He helped to systemise astronomy and created a connection between astronomical observations and astronomical theory (Goldstein

1–12). Greek physician Galen developed new theories of physiology by dissecting animals and wrote about the nervous system and blood vessels. Despite the fact that during the Roman Empire science continued to expand, the Latin texts that were written were largely compilations of work from the Greeks. New discoveries were rare for the Romans. So integral was Greek discovery to science that it was the language used for teaching and research, which hindered the spread of knowledge so much that the majority of Greek texts did not become available in Western Europe until the twelfth century.

### 3.2.2 Knowledge and Scientific Environment of the Medieval Period

Ironically, it was during the early Middle Ages – when scientific knowledge was in retreat – that science initiated a break with philosophy and became its own master (Saliba 32). The Byzantine Empire kept alive the discoveries of Greece and Rome, especially in the areas of science, mathematics, and medicine. They preserved the writings of Galen, Ptolemy, and Aristotle, and religious scholars like Aquinas and Buridan added extensive commentaries. While these were religious men, they were also dedicated to the spirit of early scientific inquiry. Byzantine scholars pursued advances in mathematical knowledge by interacting with Greek and Arabic sources. There was a similar cross-pollination between Europe and the Near East in fields such as zoology and astronomy (Saliba).

The Islamic Golden Age was vital in the development of social knowledge and science (Falagas, Zarkadoulia and Samonis 1581–6). During the whole of this period there were important developments in law, literature, technology, sociology, philosophy, navigation, agriculture, industry, and economics. In addition to specific inventions and discoveries, Muslim scientists made key advances in using the scientific method itself, including quantitative, empirical, and experimental research (Durant 162–86). Al-Haytham pioneered experimental physics and biology with his work in optics using the scientific method (Durant 53–5). Many Greek texts were translated into Arabic during this period, which was important for Muslim science but also for the preservation of the Western scientific tradition when it was later returned to Europe through translations. The Islamic world created important institutions. It helped develop the concept of the modern public library, where people wishing to educate themselves could check out manuscripts. The Arabs designed the library system of cataloguing (Françoise 988–91). The library became a centre for scientific discussion. Perhaps most importantly, the medieval Islamic world also invented the modern university and its system of diplomas and form of professorial instruction and lecturing, which later spread to Europe.

The Crusades were instrumental to Europe scientifically, since through extensive contact with the Arabic world during the Islamic Golden Age the mathematics, medicine, and social institutions of the Arabic world were discovered by Europeans. Algebra and optics became known in the West. Older Western traditions were reintroduced through the acquisition and translation of Arabic texts that preserved Greek and Roman science. This was also a time when military and naval technology experienced tremendous growth given the conditions of warfare that drove the Crusades.

Scholars now often call the twelfth century a European renaissance. The knowledge contained in classical texts was rediscovered in new Latin translations from Arabic texts. Aristotelian influence predominated together with the wisdom and learning of other ancient writers. The European university system was established alongside monasteries as centres for the propagation of knowledge. Scholars like Robert Grosseteste, Albertus Magnus, and Roger Bacon wrote about natural science to a growing audience. While Christianity did not recede as a dogmatic cultural system, it was not entirely determinative. Scholars could explore natural phenomena with an openness to past views, although often the learning acquired was purely rational rather than experimental, and was fused with a biblical worldview. In other words, the renaissance of the twelfth century played an integral part in transmitting scientific methodology within a predominantly religious environment that required thinkers to harmonise science with religion.

By the late Middle Ages, the pursuit of knowledge under the guise of science was still intertwined with Christianity. Though they placed God at the centre of their universe, Christian scholars were deeply curious about the way the world worked. Nicole Oresme, for example, pursued a quite rigorous examination of the world without recourse to theological explanations. Unfortunately, disease and famine plagued Europe for many years during this period, which cut short the expansion of knowledge and scholarship until the later Renaissance.

### 3.2.3 Knowledge and Scientific Environment from the Renaissance to the Industrial Revolution

The Renaissance brought science to the centre of society in a way that had not previously been done. It was most important in terms of scientific progress because of the development of the scientific method itself. Using empirical evidence through sensory observations and measurement, science and mathematics were integrated. This movement towards the full scientific method led to advancements in biology, astronomy, and physics.

The Renaissance was a time when humanism sprouted alongside traditional religion, often placing the two in dynamic tension. Scholars translated Greek texts into modern European languages. Some figures such as Pope Pius II tried to blend Christianity and science, while at other times scientific knowledge was suppressed when it varied with Catholic doctrine. Galileo Galilei was at the forefront of empiricism, stressing the importance of geometry for human understandings of nature. He demonstrated the willingness of Renaissance thinkers to challenge received tradition when he rejected some of the teachings of Aristotle on which the ecclesiastical system of Aquinas was based (Singer 217). After the crises of the Late Middle Ages, the Renaissance saw revitalized efforts in science. Many of the theories and discoveries of the time had enormous impact which has lasted to the present day.

The seventeenth-century Scientific Revolution was brought about by a shift in attitude. It involved a new form of rationalism that refused to warrant any received wisdom from prior historical periods and rejected all kinds of idealism or procedures in science that were not based on empirical research. Whereas the earlier times had shown glimpses into the application of the rational scientific method, the Scientific Revolution embraced it fully and completely to develop a new picture of the universe. Descartes set deductive reasoning on firm ground. Bacon's text on experience-based inductive reasoning became the standard for the scientific method. Isaac Newton applied Bacon's method to demonstrate the laws of motion, gravitation, and thermodynamics. These men provided models for the scientific process that would lead to a more mechanistic interpretation of the world based on natural laws. They were emulated by other sciences, including management and natural philosophy.

In terms of advances and inventions, this was a period of incredible foment. The Scientific Revolution proved the concept of the heliocentric solar system. The microscope made possible investigations into an invisible world not seen before. Logarithmic scales, mechanical calculators, and barometers were invented and used. The accuracy of the telescope was vastly improved by Hadley (King 77). Fluids, pressures, and vacuums came under better scrutiny. Numerous other inventions and insights pushed Western civilisation towards unprecedented scientific accumulation and a vastly enriched knowledge of the natural world that shaped the human worldview. These new technologies laid the foundation for the Industrial Revolution.

The Industrial Revolution was an outgrowth of the Scientific Revolution and its technological child. It was characterized by new energies, new machines, and the process of mechanisation of labour. It began in the eighteenth century when the first factories were built. The textile industry was the first to be fully mechanized. The landscape of England, and then other European nations, was transformed by the advent of the railroad, new roads, and canals. Steam and coal were harnessed to provide power. All of transportation and work was modified by these developments. Science and the scientific method considered to gain society-wide acceptance through the labours of academics.

Charles Babbage created the first basic computer in 1822, but his development of modern managerial methods was at least as important. He invented equipment to monitor workers' output; those who were the most efficient got a bonus. Babbage was inducted into management through the role of supervising his invention, and he took a particular interest in labour division in manufacturing. As an inventor, he created equipment to monitor workers' output, which was then used to generate a profit-sharing system involving workers being paid a bonus from company profits. Charles Sanders Peirce furthered the scientific method when he joined inductive and deductive reasoning in a complementary fashion. Peirce helped found modern statistics as well as inventing the idea of blind and controlled randomized experiments (Management).

### 3.2.4 Knowledge and Scientific Environment – Conclusion

From an analytical perspective, the knowledge of this early agrarian period in human civilisation shows a definite trajectory towards science and scientific application. Astronomy was one of the first sciences and developed in conjunction with writing and mathematics, both in Egypt and Mesopotamia. This early endeavour demonstrates the human longing to understand nature. Observation of the influence of stars and other heavenly phenomena led to the development and later improvement of the calendar, which was a practical application of astronomy to the organisation of agrarian life. In other words, it demonstrated both a scientific curiosity about the world and the capacity to make observations relevant through direct application. The Mesopotamians developed irrigation and the wheel along these lines. Medical knowledge showed increasing sophistication, from the early exploratory texts of Mesopotamia and Egypt to the later, more scientific views of Galen in the Roman period. The body was analysed, dissected, and written about with a view to human control over the processes of disease. A similar movement happened in natural sciences like botany and mineralogy, where the properties and utilities of natural objects were described and classified. These explorations moved away from a purely religious perspective into the realm of empirical knowledge and its application. Human civilisation was no longer content to suffer the consequences of fate or the whims of higher powers. In this early stage, thinkers strove to uncover nature's secrets and to manipulate that knowledge to bring greater control into human lives. Philosophy itself as a method or way of thinking was invented for the West in Greece. It signified the impulse towards rationality and analysis. Yet in none of these early civilisations was science freed from philosophy. Natural science was a part of metaphysics. No final truths about the laws of nature were achieved and wrested from the corruption of earlier superstitions and myths.

From Byzantium to the late Middle Ages, the fate of science was uneven. After the fall of Rome, the knowledge of the West receded to Constantinople, where it was saved for centuries. Much of the science and knowledge of the medieval period was based on preserving and reclaiming its ancient equivalents. This happened through dynamic exchange between various civilisations, as for example when the Crusaders were brought into contact with the Islamic world. During the Crusades, there was substantial mixing of Arab and European science and wisdom. Greek texts were translated into Arabic, and then translated back into Greek when the original texts were lost. Principles of math and medicine developed in the Arab world were injected into European science and the Arab and European societies enriched each other over the centuries.

There was a brief florescence of scientific knowledge in the twelfth century as Europeans began to revive Greek learning. On the whole, the scientific spirit was kept alive but did not advance tremendously. Reason could not quite break free from religion. Yet important institutions were established for the perpetuation of knowledge, such as the university, the monastery, and the library. By the late Middle Ages, the pursuit of knowledge under the guise of science was still intertwined with the hand of the Catholic Church. Though they placed God at the centre of their universe, Christian scholars were deeply curious about the way the world worked. Nicole Oresme, for example, pursued a quite rigorous examination of the world without recourse to theological explanations. Unfortunately, disease and famine plagued Europe for many years during this period, which cut short the expansion of knowledge and scholarship until the later Renaissance.

The world since the Renaissance is a world of science. The Renaissance itself saw breakthroughs in science and technology. Again, it was not so much the specific inventions that occurred during these years, although they were themselves important. Rather, it was the whole ideology that changed during the Renaissance. People again turned outward to the world and began to try to understand it. Progress in science and knowledge exploded after the Scientific Revolution. The empirical method of research into nature was elevated to a new stature. Various forms of reasoning were granted new credibility and led to more experimental and empirical methods of investigation. In fact, the entire view of the universe changed as a result of important revisions of older erroneous worldviews, such as the switch from geocentrism to heliocentrism. Scientific tools such as the microscope and telescope transformed observation methods and enabled new insights not previously accessible to the naked eye. New forces and natural laws were discovered as science was codified and standardised in the new environment of openness. Religion began to lose its grip. With the arrival of the Industrial Revolution out of the Scientific Revolution, a whole new set of technologies became available that transformed knowledge. The first computer – used to run textile mills – was developed, as were modern methods of mathematics and statistics. Steam power began to run the world and the everyday lives of people were changed in ways that their parents could not have imagined.

Science did not – and still has not – replaced religion. But the increasing presence of technology in people's lives inclined them more and more to look for rational explanations for the phenomena around them. Scientists began to develop theories that explained some of the most important phenomena, such as gravitation. It is also important to note that scientific knowledge did not increase steadily and unilaterally over time. Some eras saw great leaps in scientific knowledge while other eras saw only small advances, and other eras saw regression. In some eras, science has been viewed as the enemy of the church or the state or both. In some eras, science has been an arm of the state. For while science is about the search for truth, it is also always about the history and the culture of which it was a part.

## 3.3 General Management

### 3.3.0 Introduction

General management is an area of expertise of project management and it represents the organisational and interpersonal skills to get projects done. It involves planning, organising, staffing, executing, and controlling what an organisation does. It is the skill which determines how resources are allocated and optimized and is the foundation of project management skills.

This section shows how general management skills developed into Taylor's *Scientific Management* at the end of Industrial Revolution. Not only did it lead to the general management skills of the twentieth century, it also led to the two forefathers of twentieth century project management, Henry Gantt and Henri Fayol, formulating project management tools and the core elements of knowledge for contemporary project management. These management tools and core elements finally evolved into the project management body of knowledge. However, before that occurred, general management skills took responsibility for guiding and handling the project activities of each historical period.

Throughout history, the skill of general management has consisted in the details of everyday life. As discussed in the previous section, the knowledge environment of each historical period facilitated problem solving, decision making, and the development of the right skills and tools to get projects done. With respect to building construction projects, general management is the skill of handling the wishes of the patrons, maintaining financial control of the project, dealing with the army of workers on the construction sites, managing the logistics of building materials, ensuring the appropriate use of construction machinery, etc. This section examines the role and development of general management skills from ancient societies to the Industrial Revolution.

### 3.3.1 General Management from the Earliest Times to Classical Antiquity

The organisational behaviour of the Sumerian priests and the leadership of Hammurabi are the primary sources for understanding ancient Mesopotamian management style. Their writings, codes, and norms were used not only as a means to manage the people, but as a means of managing the gods (George). Sumerian priests employed writing and accounting principles to record business transactions and to keep track of the property of church and state. These leaders devised managerial controls by requiring priests to provide written accountings (e.g., receipts) of donations given to local agencies. In addition, administrative techniques must have been impressive since the Mesopotamian empires covered a large area (Snell 32). Hammurabi exemplifies the notable management techniques of Mesopotamian times. His code of law indicates a high level of social order, with rules and punishments for various behaviours. It codifies a patriarchal and hierarchical class system with clear social divisions between upperclass nobles, free merchant and builder classes, and slaves (Saggs).

*The Duties of the Vizier* was the first text on management which set out the goals of management and the tasks of the manager of ancient Egypt. It describes what the Egyptian vizier did, how he was expected to behave, how he was appointed, and his position in relation to other officers (Witzel 3). By 2500 BC the country enjoyed trade, peace, and prosperity. The massive pyramid tombs were built as lasting public monuments. In order to undertake such ambitious projects as pyramid building on a pragmatic level, the leadership of ancient Egypt needed to develop and implement management structures for planning, organizing, and controlling development and decision-making (Erman). It appears that approximately 20,000 workers were required. These workers would be divided into crews and subdivided into gangs, each of which in turn was divided into five tribes. Each tribe consisted of about 200 men (Lehner 224). This subdivision gave those in charge greater ability to monitor activity and maintain control. The Egyptians used writing, education, and moral philosophy to create an organised and productive society (Menu). Procedures were put in place for submitting written requests, and a staff of consultants was devised to help make decisions (Erman). Religious and political functions were described on papyrus and communicated through the system (Ruiz 129).

Many of the management principles, tenets of social organisation, leadership styles, and motivational theories utilised in modern societies are underpinned by Greek ideas. Socrates provided the definition of management as a distinct skill from technical experience or knowledge. Socrates was the first public figure to document the importance of delegating authority. Plato and Aristotle later developed Socrates' theory of work delegation to include commentary regarding the direct relationship between the specialisation of work and the division of labour with efficient work practise (Wren 19). Plato's *Republic* describes an educational system in which select young men should be trained not only with specialisation and expertise in mind, but in such a way that they develop personalities and skills appropriate to leadership (Pindur and Rogers 59–77). The ancient Greeks were aware of and utilised some important management ideas and practises. As outlined in the previous chapter, they used music to enhance the productivity of repetitious tasks (Glotz). Greece also contributed a theory of leadership through Thucydides' treatise on the Peloponnesian Wars. His argument was that leadership was dangerous in the context of democracy without appropriate checks and balances (Warner 620). This notion of checks and balances was an important step beyond previous ideas and formed the basis for subsequent democratic principles of effective leadership. Greek philosophy in general gave management theory insights into human and group behaviour. It provided a stepping stone towards more rational and inquiry-based analyses into social organisation.

At its height in the first and second centuries AD, the Roman Empire encompassed 2.2 million square miles with a population of 60 million people. To manage this vast and populous area, the Romans utilised a combination of management strategies: a Republican form of government with checks and balances, a disciplined military, a system of delegation, a prioritisation of education, and a network of political alliances (The Roman Empire). The emperors provide specific examples of management styles. Diocletian, who divided the empire into provinces, dioceses, and regions through which a chain of command was developed, was a master delegator (Osigweh). Julius Caesar relied on alliance building to achieve leadership and maintain power (Abbott 385). In the public domain, the Republican system of government balanced power among the executive, the legislative, and the judicial branches (The Roman Empire).

The Senate was an entirely new political body intended to eliminate the threat of tyranny by a single leader. These ideas were formative for later political arrangements in Europe.

### 3.3.2 General Management of the Medieval Period

Despite the fact that monotheistic Christianity was the official religion of the Byzantine Empire, society did not progress forward in thinking with regard to government or management during this time. Nonetheless, through writing and grammar this empire contributed significantly to the preservation and transmission of classical knowledge so that other societies could benefit from past systems (Anastos 410; Tatakes). Little was added to the history of management during this time (Cohen).

Muslim culture thrived during the eighth through thirteenth centuries in areas ranging from engineering and philosophy to artistry and trading (Kraemer; Turner). During this time, medieval Islam was open to humanistic notions of individualism, liberalism, religious freedom, and cross-cultural exchange (Hassan). The work of Al-Ghazali in particular had a significant influence on leadership and management (Chowdhry). Al-Ghazali was a Persian theologian, jurist, philosopher, cosmologist, psychologist, mystic, and scholar. His *Nasihat* (literally "Advice") was a collection of political writings which addressed issues relating to political authority. For instance, he commented on the role of communication as well as the personality traits which lead to effective leadership (Chowdhry). He contended that the line of communication to leadership should be known and repeatedly tested to ensure that leadership is engaging with the organisation as a whole. For Al-Ghazali, good leadership was a sacred duty and pleased God if executed correctly. In order to provide effective leadership, the leader must establish a model of right or moral conduct and be kept informed regarding any information that might affect his management of the empire. This reinforced the connection between moral conduct and effective management.

Although Crusade was largely a period of religious warfare and papal control, the unwritten code of knightly behaviour known as chivalry was decisive for leadership and management during this period. In connection to management, the historian Constantinou sees chivalry as a symbol for authority in management. He notes, "western usage contains two metaphors, both derived from the man and his horse – *chivalry and management*, the one from French *cheval*, 'a horse,' the other from Italian *maneggio*, 'the handling or training of a horse'" (Constaninou). At this time, knights were authoritative. They gathered at a round table, which has been called "the first management model." It entailed that men were chivalrous on the outside while demonstrating graciousness and respect towards one another when they met behind closed doors. The shape of the table suggested that there was no hierarchy or single leader. It was a model of equal partnership between the knights in their quest to slay the dragon of injustice (Manch and Henning 41). Eventually chivalry evolved courtesy books which provided guidance for behaviour that required respect for women and concern for the impoverished (Sweeney). The chivalric code of honour was the principal influence on management and behaviour during the Crusades in spite of the perpetual bloodshed. Moreover, in terms of management it was clearly a system that valued group communication. Chivalry in the model of the round table showed that the way in which a group approaches its social interaction will have an effect on the communication process itself.

During the twelfth-century Renaissance, revitalisation occurred in both political and intellectual realms (Sommerville). New institutions evolved like the university, imported from Islamic civilisation (Middle Ages). Work in agriculture and the trade crafts occurred primarily in homes, on farms, or in workshops next to homes or farms (History of Organization Work). In some cases, communities of houses worked together to create a "cottage industry" wherein a group of houses were built in a semicircle such that each house represented a particular step in the production cycle. These groups worked together, with no boss or commute, to create a final product in a clearly divided labour process.

The Gothic period was dominated by a resurgence in interest in the artistry of Roman master builders. From a management perspective, the Gothic cathedrals took decades to build and required substantial sponsorship from merchant interests. Accordingly, long-range planning was necessary along with a system of project governance. At times, examples of inefficiencies arose when the project would stop and then start again with a new manager who used different measurement standards and, therefore, caused new calculations and added cost and delay to the project (Lessons from History).

### 3.3.3 General management from the Renaissance to the Industrial Revolution

The European Renaissance from the fourteenth to the sixteenth centuries saw a rise in realism and rationality in political thought. This intellectual shift affected the political structure and management of the European people. It is evidenced clearly in the ideas of Niccolò Machiavelli, an Italian political theorist who saw self-interest as people's prime motivator. He adjusted political leadership away from Greek and Islamic moral ideas by redefining the ethics of a prince. While the prince must respect the liberty of his constituents, Machiavelli did not believe that the prince should always act ethically if it would lead to the disruption of his power. In fact, cruelty, miserliness, and deceit were advocated as good expedients at times if they solidified political power. In other words, Machiavelli placed the prince beyond morals and emphasized that his was to engage in war and other activities with the sole aim of retaining state power. Machiavelli also recommended fear rather than love as a means of maintaining control (George). He justified ruling by force instead of by law. Machiavelli's theory in *The Prince* reconfigures previous notions of virtue to justify immorality if done in the perpetuation of power (Anglo).

The Reformers John Calvin and Martin Luther were responsible for another significant shift in management around the same time. They reversed the notion that work was a necessary evil, promoting it instead as positive service to God. Diligence and joyful work habits became a way to glorify the divine. This approach was successful because it included the idea that God rewards such diligence with wealth. This work ethic contributed to the rise and flourishing of capitalism (Theopedia) when combined with individualism and reductionism. Protestants, particularly the Puritans, embraced other management-related ideas. Reductionism allowed work processes to be broken down into their smallest tasks to examine how they function. It pushed for the removal of unnecessary processes. Individualism created the ideology that people are real agents whose ideas matter and whose own self-management is efficacious. These changes towards a Protestant work ethic meant that work became a real purposive activity and not mere drudgery. These ideas were later incorporated into both the philosophy of seventeenth-century Newtonianism during the Scientific Revolution and the philosophy of liberalism, including the capitalist ideas of Adam Smith during the Industrial Revolution. Weaver has concluded that Frederick Taylor's Scientific Management was rooted in Puritanism (Weaver, APM 2).

Most historians recognize the Scientific Revolution as the period when humans began in earnest to seek answers to questions that for centuries had been answered monolithically by the Roman Catholic Church. The most prominent idea at this time was the need to question everything. Religious dogma, scientific knowledge, philosophy, and other disciplines were placed under scrutiny. Reason and knowledge became the two strongest tools in the search for truth. Because so much was now in doubt, humankind needed answers they could believe in. Furthermore, the laws of nature were believed to be discoverable through reason. Thus, to know how the world worked it had to be observed through the lens of reason. As a result, it was thought that everyone had the ability to make choices, obey laws, and adhere to moral standards (Scientific Revolution). Such rules of reasoning were nailed down as a model not only in the sciences but also in the field of management. It was from this point that the Industrial Revolution took off.

The eighteenth- and early nineteenth-century Industrial Revolution changed management practises irreversibly. Manual labour was replaced by machine-based manufacturing methods in factories that required new management procedures. Combined with the Protestant work ethic and the emphasis on reason, production entered a phase of routinisation and rationalisation. Processes were modified to maximize efficiency and to enable the use of steam power. The revolution in machines and infrastructure made train and ship transportation much faster and more efficient. Information could be exchanged more quickly due to the development of the telegraph. Industrialists rose in power, displacing the former nobility (Hudson 138–44). Their management practises were informed by the new literature contained in periodicals describing various technologies. Adam Smith wrote *The Wealth of Nations*, which founded the doctrine of laissez-faire management. His discussion of the division of labour led to the development of ideas of work simplification, greater productivity, and time studies in manufacturing (Mejia 20). Indeed, management theory technically came into being in 1899, when Frederick Taylor came forth with a new management style by which he sought to increase the productivity of labourers offloading steel at Bethlehem Steel (Stewart). Taylor believed and proved that he could improve productivity through increased wages based on the productivity of the worker (Weaver). In 1911 he published *The Principles of Scientific Management*, which turned out to be the starting point for modern organisation and has been a method of motivation for administrators of managerial technique. Because in the late nineteenth century ownership of business became distinct from its control, there was a need for professional managers, and Taylor's principles of management were those most in favour (Warner and Witzel 264).

### 3.3.4 General Management – Conclusion

In terms of management, therefore, this ancient agrarian period saw the progressive growth of social organisation into bureaucratic administration and lawful communities. The Sumerian priests used writing for economic management and accountability. Hammurabi's code and other such legal codes defined a class structure through which rewards and punishments were meted out. A whole system was arranged that verbalised the social structure into clear segments and responsibilities. Nothing was left to chance. The workforce was regulated and granted rights and responsibilities through such managerial controls backed by law. In ancient Egypt systems of writing were used to plan and organize large projects. There were procedures and consulting staffs for project management in addition to the ground-level personnel who would have directly supervised workers.

The Greek viewpoint warranted democratic leadership for the first time, but added to it the important notion of checks and balances to power, so that leadership and management were spread between separate entities rather than centrally located in a single person. It highlighted the need for specialised training through education for the skills required in leadership and in other work fields. The Greeks also designated management as a separate field from technical knowledge, understood the notion of authority delegation, applied the Socratic method to problem-solving, and clearly grasped work specialisation and the division of labour.

The Romans solidified the practise of power division and balance by inventing the republican senate. They used education, a well-disciplined army, and a highly efficient system of roads and transportation to control their provinces. Delegation of authority and alliance building were taken to new levels. Roman administration was it cornerstone. Many of these managerial practises became staples for later management.

Generally speaking, management did not experience many advances between the Roman and the Renaissance periods. The Byzantine Empire contributed nothing but the transmission of early management practises and texts. The Islamic Empire added important thoughts on lines of communication with leadership that kept cohesion within the entire corporate structure. Like the Greeks, the correct training and personality types for leaders, and the right moral conduct as an example, were attached strongly to good management. In addition, the university was started for training legal scholars so that the notion of credentialed leadership arose and carried on in

Europe during and after the twelfth century. Management at this time was deemed a responsibility handed down from God in both Islamic and Christian contexts. The code of chivalry in the Dark Ages developed out of notions of equal leadership and responsibility. It promoted a style of management that was not hierarchical, but a partnership based on mutual respect, open communication, and concern for common moral goals. A decentralised process of work production was typical of the twelfth century, in which cottage industries were the dominant form of production for both agricultural and skilled craftwork. This community organisation and division of labour went on without strict leadership from the top. More like chivalry, it was a participatory practise of interlocking partnership without a strong hierarchy. The Gothic period thrived due to sponsorship from the church and the merchant class, who arranged long-term project management that was often beset with difficulties due to the change in builders over time.

During the Renaissance and Reformation, some important new ideas for management came to the forefront. Notable individuals during this era, such as Niccolò Machiavelli, John Calvin, and Martin Luther had an effect on the management and leadership of the particular societies in which they lived. Indeed, they promulgated to their respective congregations the need to support their churches and the need to glorify God through working diligently and joyfully. One was that power was the ultimate motive for leadership, and anything expedient for its maintenance, even if it was traditionally unjust or not virtuous, was acceptable. This theory challenged previous notions of the leader as a moral exemplar. No longer was leadership acquired or justified on the basis of good moral education and wisdom, but solely as a result of good manipulative skills and the use of fear or violent tactics. Not much later, the Reformation transformed concepts of work and provided the moral basis for the growth of capitalism. At the same time, individualism asserted itself so that people began to see themselves not as the pawns of fate but as true agents capable of changing the world through their work. Processes began to be subject to scrutiny as well, as in reductionism, which picked apart a process into its elements and analysed what was unnecessary and how it worked. Out of this developed scientific rules for reasoning that began to see application in the field of management.

These blossomed in the Industrial Revolution. In the mid-eighteenth and nineteenth centuries, the Industrial Revolution brought significant changes to the agricultural, manufacturing, mining, transportation, and power. The technology of mechanisation forced new management strategies that stressed efficiency, time schedules, specialised division of labour, standardisation, routinisation, and quality control procedures. Rational theories of increased productivity were formulated. Resource allocation and price setting became new issues for discussion. The discipline of cost accounting emerged. All ran on the basis of a laissez-faire capitalist market within which these management ideas were embedded. Significant individuals during this time period included Adam Smith, the father of economics, and John Stuart Mill. Both Smith and Mill as economists provided several theses as to how to make the process of production more efficient. Additionally, individuals such as Robert Owen and Frederick Taylor demonstrate that the approach to management by different individuals may differ as everyone has their own personal will to work hard and succeed.

## 3.4 Construction Technology

### 3.4.0 Introduction

Construction technology represents the techniques and tools of each period that were employed to execute the projects. It represents the knowledge of the application areas, which is building construction in this research study. The right cultural environment provides the need for sophisticated project activities and as such for advanced construction techniques and tools. The right knowledge makes such techniques and tools possible.

From Mesopotamia to the Industrial Revolution, the progress of humankind in the realm of construction and architecture starts out, as all children do, with tentative steps, followed by assured steps, and ending with a sprint. All innovations in construction are built on the shoulders of those who have come before and the knowledge they had achieved in service to their religion and culture. The guiding hands of production have been religion, culture, and war alternately, but the end result has been progress that continues today. The foundations of all of these innovations, however, were the simple lever, pulley, and screw coupled with imagination and knowledge. From these humble beginnings great cities throughout Western civilisation have been built. This section examines the role and development of construction techniques and tools from ancient societies to the Industrial Revolution.

### 3.4.1 Construction Technology from the Earliest Times to Classical Antiquity

Mesopotamian construction technology began with mathematical knowledge. Mathematics was a tool used by necessity in architectural and construction designs (Boyer), although these designs stemmed largely from religious and social concerns. The need for advanced construction and design was predicated on the shift towards sedentary agriculture. Dwellings and temples only required the use of mud-brick, which was a natural fit for the material of choice due to the resources available (wood was sparse) and the climate (Darby). Though built only of tar (bitumen) and mud-bricks, which required only baking in the sun (Bilkadi), Mesopotamian structures cannot be considered entirely simple, since their temples were designed and made with architectural features like columns, domes, and arches (Darby).

The complexity of the ziggurat – Mesopotamia's great contribution to world architecture – was possible through the innovation of tunnel or barrel vaulting, which arranged bricks in a circular configuration along a determined line (Roth). These ziggurats, located in well-governed centres of urban congestion, were the great examples of Mesopotamian public works (Faiella). Mesopotamian construction technology evolved to meet the demand for such stepped buildings. As more permanent buildings were created, mathematics was used to create geometric forms and patterns on the interior of the temples (Boyer). The urban areas of city-states required civil engineering to provide water systems. Out of this need for artificially channelled water came the wheel and the water pump. The Archimedes screw, the earliest known pump, was used in Babylon at about the third century BC (Dalley and Olson). The wheel was invented during the fifth millennium BC and used in industrial and manufacturing applications before it was transferred to transportation (Sax, Meeks and Collon). Such technology was not only impressive, it had a profound impact on all later eras since it formed the crucial element for further machines (Yenne and Grosser).

Existing concurrently with the Mesopotamians, Egyptian construction technology evolved the techniques needed to build the towering pyramids that still exist today. With only stone, wood, and cooper for use as tools, it is believed that workers employed a system of wooden levers to detach the blocks and then cut the granite with copper saws (Lehner). The invention of surveying tools allowed the Egyptians to align the pyramids precisely against astronomical points (Shaw), making them the most accurately surveyed stone structures in the world (Coppens). Plumb bobs, the water level, the A-frame level, measuring ropes, and sighting instruments were all used in the creation of the various canals and pyramids (Root). These innovations were made possible through an understanding of isosceles triangles, further emphasising the essential usefulness of mathematics and its developmental role in the field of construction (Patel). Egyptian materials evolved to become more sophisticated. Stone replaced mud-brick, which had been used previously for tomb construction in the first and second dynasties (Edward). Stone was introduced in the construction of a private monument for Imhotep (Edwards). The two primary types of stone used in the pyramids were limestone and granite. A labour force of thousands was required for this task and for the transportation of the heavy blocks over often hundreds of miles (Coppens). The use of ramps was an obvious component in pyramid building and is one of the enduring Egyptian contributions to construction as a whole. Operating without cranes or scaffolding, the ramp was an essential technology for moving stone blocks vertically. There may have been as many as five different styles of ramp – linear, staircase, spiral, zigzag, and interior ramps (Heizer). Evidence for all these types has been found, though it is not always clear which type was used for pyramids where such evidence does not exist. What is important is that in relation to construction technology, the ramp was the Egyptian solution for upward building. It eclipsed the Mesopotamian ramps and allowed the building of much steeper structures.

Information about ancient Greek architecture exists mainly in surviving temples. These remain in large number, including examples not only from the Hellenistic period, but also the Roman period, which borrowed heavily from the Greeks. Abandoning the mud-brick building typical of Mesopotamia and even sometimes ancient Egypt, the Greeks used stone to build monument walls that supported the first tiled roofs known in architectural history. The innovation of tiled roof building spread rapidly and even reached western Asia Minor. Although these roofs were labour intensive and costly, the benefit in fire resistance made them essential to temple construction (Wikander 285–90). The most recognizable and persistent feature of Greek architecture is the column. There were three types: Doric, Ionian, and Corinthian (Benson). Simple machines were also born in ancient Greece through Archimedes in the third century BC (Ostdiek). These five machines – the lever, pulley, screw, winch, and wedge – existed as significant technologies in Greek construction (Koloski-Ostrow). They functioned by changing the direction and degree of force. Along with wheels, watermills, wheelbarrows, and inclined planes, these tools made work easier (Singer, Holmyard and Hall). The mechanical advantage gained through the increase of output to input force made loads easier to move and increased overall production (Anderson).

The most impressive machine to come out of this boom was the complex crane. The crane changed building technology by allowing large stones to be hoisted and erected with greater facility and without the need for built-up earthen ramps. The other great machine the Greeks invented was the watermill, the first use of hydropower in building processes. It operated using a water wheel or turbine to power some mechanical processes (Wilson). Like the crane, this machine facilitated construction and reduced the manpower necessary for temple construction.

The Roman Empire borrowed and built on the work completed by the ancient Greeks. Their most important and enduring additions to construction technology were concrete material, the arch, and the concrete dome. The evolution away from mud-brick towards stone continued with the Romans and their use of concrete, which were made of quicklime, pozzolanic ash, and pumice aggregate. These materials together spawned a revolution that liberated builders from the traditional constraints of stone or brick (Lancaster). Concrete hardened quickly and did not suffer the internal strains of earlier materials (Robertson). Working with concrete allowed the Roman builders to create new aesthetic designs. As the empire expanded, so too did its access to materials, including chalk and sand. The mortar in walls was sometimes mixed with crushed pottery, and concrete was lightened with pumice (MacDonald). Imported materials, however, were only used by the most affluent citizens. Romans themselves preferred locally available items like stone, wood, ceramics, and terracotta (MacDonald). They categorised stone into usable types and had a sophisticated understanding of stone varieties and their brittleness, durability, and porous nature (Robinson). For example, marble was used decoratively, lime and sandstone were applied for pedestrian low-wear areas, and basaltic lava or granites would be used in areas subject to increased stress (Moropoulou, Bakolas and Anagnostopoulou).

The Roman arch revolutionised construction not only aesthetically but from the standpoint of architectural structure. It was such a magnificent architectural form that it was used in both interiors and exteriors to provide support (Mark and Hutchinson). The first temple to be built using concrete was the Pantheon, which married this innovative material with a decorative classical Greek structure (Terenzio 280–85). The advanced achievement in the Pantheon was its hemispherical concrete dome, which showcased Roman architectural skill. It was during the Roman Empire and its technological advancements that art and structure began to blend.

The engineer Vitruvius wrote his classic text on Roman architecture and its composition. In it he described increasingly populated cities that needed temples, civic buildings, domestic buildings, pavements, water supplies, and aqueducts. These formed the motive for Roman building. These broad categories were also all conceived through the science of the time (geometry, mensuration, astronomy, sundials) and the machines available for use in building (siege engines, water mills, drainage machines, pneumatics, etc.) (Vitruvius).

### 3.4.2 Construction Technology of the Medieval Period

As with previous traditions, the Byzantine Empire combined the work of empires before it with its own religious impulse. Constantinople took on the architectural and construction mentality of its Hellenized, eastern neighbours (Van Milligan). The marriage of form and function introduced by the Romans found a home in the brickwork of the Byzantines (Hakim). Sculpted bricks were formed and aligned to produce bands of ornamentation showcasing Persian aesthetics in church walls (Hakim). In addition, the dome was a characteristic feature of Byzantine architecture.

The Hagia Sophia was built using ramps, levels, levers, pulleys, and winches. In its vaulting and domes, its builders demonstrated knowledge of the mathematics of angles and arches (Ousterhout). The major advance here was in the discovery and use of pendentives to create the dome support. This innovation made it possible to support a circular domed superstructure on a square base composed of four masonry arches (Vanderpool). In addition, the Byzantines adopted the technique of buttressing used in Roman saunas (Balance). They used buttresses as internal abutments that continue above the roofs of the side aisles. These propped up the main vaults. This was not a tremendous innovation, but it demonstrated the transmission of past construction technology.

Co-opting and adding to the Byzantine use of domes and arches, Islamic architects constructed large and heavy mosques using the same sorts of mechanical tools such as cranes, ramps, levels, and wheels. The most famous is the Dome of the Rock in Jerusalem. Fundamentally octagonal, the wooden dome is mounted on an elevated drum comprised of sixteen piers and columns, making a circle. This circle is surrounded by an octagonal arcade of twenty-four piers and columns. This construction outlined the progression and expansion that Islam made to the established construction of domes and arches (Kostof).

Islamic mosques usually consisted of columns and covered arched walkways along with a small niche and fountain placed in an open courtyard. Islamic construction transformed existing towers into minarets, or built them where they did not exist, usually at a building's corners. Minarets were a crucial addition to architectural style and function. Another important addition was on the interior, with both the often exquisitely carved *minbar*, or pulpit, and the domed section over the *mihrab* that was typically ornamented with tiles. This architecture used the same materials as previous eras, including marble, stone, brick, composites, tar, and metal. The most important

Islamic contribution to construction was perhaps the skilled trades and craftsmen, who perfected decorative techniques in sculpting, metallurgy, and other material artwork (Ousterhout). Many Islamic buildings are artistic masterpieces.

During the Crusades, religion shaped warfare as church-inspired Europeans teamed up with the Byzantines to oust Islamic forces from the Holy Land. Construction technologies progressed out of this dual influence of religion and war. Castles were introduced into the building lexicon. Such fortresses were built to withstand attack. The realities of warfare guided the design, producing buildings with high, thick walls capable of enduring attack for long periods. Canals or moats were dug around castles for strategic purposes (Ellenblum).

In fact, construction on the whole in the Crusades became strategic. Along with fortress-style building forms, war machines were invented utilizing ropes, tension, torque, and force for martial applications (Erlich). The Byzantine fortresses were large and imposing, able to house many people. This contrasted with the small garrisons of the Europeans, who had far less manpower for building (Smail). As Crusaders returned home to their castles, they brought back the influences of Byzantine architecture. One of these was the use of round towers, a structure preferable to the usual Roman boxed construction because it offered a better field of view and provided greater opportunity for resistance (Williams). The heavy structure and design of castles instituted a change in cranes, ramps, pulleys, and winches, as well as greater productivity in stone masonry (Williams).

At the same time as the staid and militaristic construction during the Crusades, the Romanesque period returned centrality to religious demands. Yet the building of the Crusades left its imprint. The new Romanesque cathedrals were built heavy and strong with a dark and gloomy interior like the castles. Beauty was less a part of construction, perhaps as a type of reminiscence about the recent wars (Edson). With the Romanesque, which borrowed much from ancient Rome, there was a shift in thinking about construction through a heightened focus on the design and use of interior space (Carlsson). Romanesque architecture looked to the designs of the Roman Empire for its structures. It sought harmonious proportions while using groin or stone barrel vaults, small windows, thick and heavy walls and pillars, decorative interior and exterior blind arches, rounded arches as roof supports, and decorative painting (Sacred Destinations). The heavy stone construction of stone vault ceilings required arches and improved buttress support employed through feudal labour and not the skilled artisans of prior times (Castles Architecture).

Following the Romanesque period, Gothic architecture used construction technology to emphasise a different sensibility of height and light. It designed structures based on vast spaces with an influx of light to create the impression of reverence (Branner). Achieving Gothic architecture meant maturing the design process to include small-scale modelling to test the stability of a proposed plan (Branner). Flying buttresses, rib vaults, and pointed arches solved the issue of creating tall structures while preserving light (Wilson). It was a time of experimentation that achieved great success in new structures. Gothic design conceived the flying buttress as a way to put support on the outside of a building so that the interior space could show the presence of God through increased light (Turnbull). The previous heavy strength of Romanesque cathedrals gave way to more graceful spires created through external buttressing that applied a stronger counteracting force towards the cathedral wall and counteracted the tendency of walls to bulge out from lateral pressure (Macaulay). With the skeleton of the building carrying all of the weight, there was no longer a need to construct intermediary curtain walls. Builders could experiment with pillars, ribs, and glass on the interior (Arch). Other innovative designs entered the scene, such as the sexpartite design (Erdogmas, Boothby and Smith).

Previous Roman arches and domes were sturdy and simple. The pointed arches of Gothic cathedrals replaced these Roman predecessors. The pointed arch allowed the construction of taller and more complex buildings, which included ribbed arched vaults that spanned large spaces (Vanderpool). Brought over from Islamic architecture, the pointed arches were an added dimension that helped defined the Gothic style and increase interior light. Further Islamic influence came in the use of decorative carved stone screens (common in earlier mosques) and window openings with pierced stone (Warren). The demand for monuments and cathedrals bathed in light spurred technology forward (Branner). The only major development in machine technology was the treadwheel. This represented a further evolution of the crane, although it was more a revival than an innovation. A big wooden wheel revolved around a shaft with a walkway for two people who manipulated the compass and clasp arms (Matthies). Like other cranes before it, it facilitated lifting heavy materials and could be used to build taller structures.

### 3.4.3 Construction Technology from the Renaissance to the Industrial Revolution

The Renaissance combined architectural technology with renewed vigour in the classical Greco-Roman design features of harmony and symmetry (Milo). Construction technology included the reversible hoist, a mobile crane on rollers with a hoist, a lifting device with pincers, a bell-lifting device with a counterweight, screw-operated lifting devices, and pile drivers. The energy used to operate these machines came from human and animal labour, although there were cases when hydraulic and steam power was used and wind power was investigated (Institute and Museum of the History of Science).With the cultural rebirth and advancements in art, particularly painting and sculpture, the construction of buildings advanced materially to allow for ornamentation. Throughout the Renaissance, arches, domes, and columns were all present as reminders of the past and its influence on both proportion and design applied to a variety of Christian structures (Ackerman). Domes were prevalent in church construction (Betts) and old Greek and Roman forms were utilised in the palaces of Florence and Rome, as well as trickling down to street level to create an aesthetic that blanketed an entire city-state (Partridge). The old triumphal arch was revived as well. Columns were used primarily for aesthetic rather than supportive purposes, illustrating the key emphasis in the Renaissance on ornamentation (Walker). There was no real structural revolution other than development of the dome. Brunelleschi found a new way to build a dome using a concentric method of construction rather than scaffolding. At Florence Cathedral, he built the first double-shelled dome.

Rooted in the early seventeenth century, Baroque style represented an esoteric move towards higher aspirations and superiority all while showing the power and might of the Catholic Church (Hersey). The architecture strived to show movement through utilisation of curvature in building and went away from the straight line models of the Renaissance with spiral shaped columns signalling its stylistic break. Different modes of craftsmanship were needed and so construction technology witnessed another shift in the evolution of mastery over materials, development of tools, and mastery of those tools (Hersey). Risalits were used in building facades that required a change in support planning and material strength along with any potential design elements (Cohen). The aesthetic was one in which everyone was to appear bigger and richer and so colonnades were decorated with straight beams to give an impression of more room. Builders and designers made use of convex and concave shapes, giving new opportunities in room design (Cohen).

Baroque construction practises contain methods used to increase masonry mortar setting time, employment of unique mechanical devices, along with innovative techniques in brick manufacture and laying using lime, plaster and freestone (Marconi). The use of ropes, pulleys, winches, levers, ramps, and other predecessors in construction technology had not changed much. What changed in the Baroque age was the connection between architecture and building technology, with technology belonging to engineers (Cohen). Culture during the Baroque period was one of rigid social structure with global changes in finance and commerce. The wealthy exerted their power through building (Houston and Snell).

The Industrial Revolution was a time when the nature of manufacturing was, in a word, revolutionised and mass production became a reality (Schivelbusch). Easier transport routes made the acquisition of materials faster and less costly (Evans). The ease of acquisition without the addition of a price gouge also revolutionised the construction industry (Schivelbusch).The critical technological advancement concerning construction was the harnessing of energy to power machines that took less of a toll on human and animal labour (Greenburg). Machines did the work of hand tools and could replace muscle power with steam power. Productivity began a steep climb.

From Britain the Industrial Revolution spread gradually throughout Europe and to the United States (Greenburg).The new methods increased the amount of goods produced and decreased the cost. Cities grew rapidly, and the demand for city construction and new methods of creating buildings that housed many people necessitated new engineering modalities (Houston and Snell). The perfection of the steam engine was instrumental in supplying the power to anything from clockwork to steam-powered cranes and steam shovels that were used extensively for the excavation of building sites without the need for large groups of labourers (Stuart). These advances changed the way construction was done in that without the proper machinery, the construction does not happen.

From Britain the Industrial Revolution spread gradually throughout Europe and to the United States. Indeed, the Industrial Revolution came gradually. However, when measured against the centuries people had worked entirely by hand, it happened in a short span of time (Greenburg).

Other major technological advances in construction include electricity, canal building, iron and brass smelting, steel production, oil and petroleum production, agricultural innovations such as the threshing machine, metal tools for hand and machine-originated building projects, reinforced concrete, steamships, the assembly line model for large factories, and many other smaller yet important inventions (Landow). Machine-made goods also changed building materials since metal was widely available, lumber could be milled more efficiently, and glass could be readily produced. Paints were mass-produced, and brought to market in a timely fashion. Steel, iron, and brass were available in large quantities for city construction. The Crystal Palace, erected in London in 1851, was a highly visible example of iron and glass prefabricated construction.

Roads were easier to build due to mechanised labour, like the steam shovel. The ability to create advanced transportation networks and increase communication across large distances (telephone, telegraph) enabled nation-building to happen on an unprecedented scale. Many things changed the world in this time of energy and commerce explosion, from materials, methods, and engineering practises to mathematics (Asif). The ability to have any material for any project through the advent of mass production and transportation impacted construction greatly.

### 3.4.4 Construction Technology – Conclusion

The time between Mesopotamia and the Roman Empire accounts for thousands of years, but the technological innovations are still helping to shape our world today. Analysing this first era of construction technology, one finds a definite movement in materials used from the basic mud-brick and tar of Mesopotamia through the granite and limestone pyramids of Egypt and the marble stone temples of Greece to the revolutionary concrete in Roman building. In each civilisation, geometry was important in knowing how to design the structures. In addition, all the monumental building were raised out of the needs of the populace, whether agrarian or urban, and their particular religious and political contexts. In other words, architectural technology responded to the needs of society.

Within the cultures of Mesopotamia the greatest leap lay in the discovery of mathematics, which made it possible to create more sophisticated dwellings. With the invention of agriculture, humankind stopped being hunter-gatherers that wandered across the globe and instead became sedentary. The transition from Mesopotamia to ancient Egypt also revealed a gradual evolution in construction materials and tools. Structurally, the pyramids of ancient Egyptian and Mesopotamian ziggurats were complex but largely uniform. They utilised barrel vaulting, and the Egyptians added corbel vaulting. The use of construction know-how in an age without the advent of iron or methods of efficient long-range transportation is truly astounding. The levels of technical expertise inherent in creating the inclines and stone blocks of the pyramids while taking into account astronomical positions, shows a level of sophistication in knowledge that encompassed materials, pulleys and transport system, as well as engineering. In Mesopotamia and Egypt one sees good surveying equipment, primarily physical labour, and primitive tools responsible for creating, shifting, and lifting materials up ramps.

Greek temples were simple structures that utilised stone columns and lintels supported structures in a large scale using simple machines consisting of pulleys and wedges, in addition to larger machines like the crane and the water wheel, which reduced the necessary workforce and gave priority to a smaller number of skilled labourers. Greeks columns became the predominant architectural form, with the advantage and innovation of supported tile roofs. City-states grew as did their populations and the need for civic projects became inevitable. Water pumps were created along with watermills which showed that humans were looking to outside energy sources to provide power – in this case hydropower. When the Roman Empire took over, it built upon the impressive knowledge of the cultures that had come before it, but it made a huge architectural leap with the invention of the arch. The arch was a crucial advance since it could distribute more weight. Advances in material production also caused subsequent advancements in architecture when concrete was invented. Being able to create material of varying weight made it possible to create more sophisticated and aesthetically pleasing architecture like the dome, which would act as an inspiration and catalyst for building in the future era.

The medieval periods saw many important changes in construction technology, even though overall it did not feature radical transformation. No significant changes in materials occurred in medieval times. The Byzantines preserved the Roman tradition and specialised in brick and masonry domes, integrating beautifully with the new use of pendentive technology to construct a dome on a foundation of a quadruple-arched square. Islamic architecture gave the world the minaret, the domed *mihrab* with ornate ceramic tile workmanship around it, the *minbar*, and the open courtyard surrounded by an arched walkway. The military fortress of thick, tall impenetrable walls and rounded turrets was perfected during the Crusades. This dark style lacked a real aesthetic drive and was mirrored in Romanesque cathedrals. In reaction to this, the Gothic style used the treadwheel for construction and build tall, light-filled cathedrals with pointed arches, ribbed vaults, and most importantly, the innovative flying buttress.

From an aesthetic standpoint only the change from Byzantine to Gothic can seem overwhelmingly different, but the inspiration for it all goes back to religion. The Byzantines represented the marriage of Western architectural achievements with neighbouring countries and cultures. Utilising dome structures for their own religious buildings as well as incorporating brick building with an ornamental twist, they showed the evolution from staid buildings to more beautiful and artistic buildings was well under way. Each culture adds to the previous achievements in terms of technique and tools. The golden age of Islam founds a cornucopia of societies to create compelling architecture. Along with levers, pulleys, and screws, there were the additions of the winch and pulley in ancient Greece and Rome followed by cranes, ramps, levels and wheels. Construction was an intricate system and the end result was a marriage of form and function.

The change in construction and aesthetics that showed up during the times of the Crusades in Europe is attributed to war. Two of the largest factors in shaping society are religion and war and when the two come together, adding to the ornamentation of architecture does not seem like the priority. That is not to say that cultures did not influence one another. Crusaders brought back what they had seen in the Holy Land to the feudal castles they inhabited. While thick walls that can stand attack are the most important features in a castle, Byzantine and Islamic architecture influenced builders to make round towers like those they had seen in the Holy Land that offered sweeping views of terrain. Persian rugs, acquired during the wars and brought back, became the art that decorated and insulated the walls. With the Crusades running into the Romanesque period there is a change in looking at the interior of a dwelling as something different than what it had been previously.

With the Crusades over and architecture wanting to stretch past its prison of fortresses it had been boxed into during the Crusades and into the Romanesque period, the Gothic period was a directly opposite reaction to what had come before it. It was also a time of pure experimentation when the decree of the Catholic Church to erect large buildings that would let in the presence of God through light was made; technology was forced to catch up. Building on the vaults and buttresses that were present in earlier cultures like the Byzantines, architects were able to create rib skeletons that did not need the structural support of before due to exterior buttresses, they were able to create cathedrals bathed in light. This was as different from what had come before as was possible in terms of design and aesthetics.

The era from the Renaissance to the Industrial Revolution witnessed dramatic changes. Steam power began in the Renaissance but was perfected in the Industrial Revolution. Neither the Renaissance nor the Baroque periods, which were predominantly aesthetic movements in terms of architectural ingenuity, altered previous methods, materials, or techniques that much, although they emphasized various forms of craftsmanship. With the Industrial Revolution, the aesthetic of building changed and the entire process of design and construction was altered in unprecedented ways. The Renaissance was a rebirth of science and curiosity harkening back to the ancient Greeks and Romans which influenced the art and design of this time. Inventions came fast with a number of machines created that would take away the need for 100 percent of the energy to come from human and animal. There were explorations into different means of energy, including wind and with this marriage of architecture, art, and technology the Renaissance created its own aesthetic. Using the classical designs of the Greeks and Romans, the Renaissance builders did not improve upon them much, but with their knowledge of structural support and materials, the elements of classical design could take on a purely ornamental, not structural role. Coupled with the art of the time, a street-level makeover of city-states spread across Europe and exists still today. Cultures shifted and commerce and financial classes became more solidified which found the rich showing their power for power's sake in the Baroque Period. This was a time where building became about esoteric higher ideals and so architects were shunted off to the design side while builders busied themselves with the engineering side of things.

Once the Industrial Revolution came along, however, construction and building exploded on a scale never before witnessed in the history of humankind. Together with steam power, the advent of factories meant that mass production was officially a reality. Metal tools could be made to do the job of hand tools, transportation and manufacturing were no longer a boondoggle meant that increased cost. Cities exploded in growth and demanded quick construction and building to grow with it which was possible through the Industrial Revolution. Metal, and any kind, was finally available to anyone and able to be shipped anywhere thanks to the manufacturing companies. This was also coupled with a number of other inventions like electricity and locomotive. The world was suddenly much smaller and yet growing much faster because of the foundations laid down through the thousands of years of human history. The growth of technology from the Industrial Revolution has been exponential with the time between inventions growing smaller and smaller making innovations the rule rather than the exception. What that means for construction technology is continued evolution.

## 3.5 Master Builder Tradition

### 3.5.0 Introduction

The master builder tradition represents the knowledge of the application areas in each period, the set of accepted practises and professional traditions of building construction. Those of us living in the modern world probably have never spent a lot of time thinking about this tradition. We understand that the way in which people learn the craft of constructing buildings works in much the same way as it has for centuries. It is basically an apprenticeship system, in which younger workers learn from those who are experienced. As they acquire more and better skills, they also become more and more independent, allowed to work first on simple projects on their own and then increasingly complex projects until they become their own masters and in turn take on their own students.

This system predates the Middle Ages. It has its roots at least as far back as Babylonian times. This section examines the history of the master builder tradition from the ancient world through to modern times, focusing on both how this tradition helped to train artisans who could pass on their skills from one generation to the next (improving their work's quality as they went) as well as on the ways in which the master builder tradition helped create safe buildings. The tradition developed at least as much for the public good as for the good of the craft traditions. This section examines the role and development of the master builder tradition from ancient societies to the Industrial Revolution.

### 3.5.1 Master Builder Tradition from the Earliest Times to Classical Antiquity

In Mesopotamia, the first code of law, the Code of Hammurabi, referred to design and construction as a simple process. The code forbade builders to use faulty design or improper construction techniques (Beard 13). It is likely as a result of such strict laws that a specialised class of craftsmen emerged who guaranteed the quality of their structures. To achieve such quality a regime for training builders probably began, although there is no evidence for any sort of guilds or trade organisations in the historical data. Certainly the royal palaces of Assyria and Babylon, or the temples of Sumer, would not have been built without strict regulation, a skilled labour force, and the most knowledgeable managers available at the time. What is known is that skilled brick builders had high status in Babylon. They began to use bronze and iron tools, which allowed them to build larger and stronger buildings. These builders, who developed skills through experience and likely passed those skills down through the generations, were central to the rise of Mesopotamian urban centres (Jackson 5).

The Egyptian master builder combined the roles of architect, engineer, and builder in one person. The clearest historical example was the polymath Imhotep, who served King Djoser in the third dynasty. Imhotep designed Djoser's funerary pyramid, the largest structure ever built made completely using stone (Kemp 159). It is presumed that Imhotep both designed and supervised the building. Manetho, an Egyptian historian, claimed that he developed a means of stone dressing buildings. For many years, scholars assumed that hundreds of thousands of slaves built the stone pyramids. However, they now generally believe that the workers numbered only about 20,000 and were paid to work when farming was done for the year. It is unclear how skilled this labour force was. Sophisticated engineering and organisation were required, but the labourers themselves were likely semi-skilled and not involved in design decisions (Merolla). Certainly experienced foremen were necessary to guide the actual building process on the pyramids under the direction of the design and engineering plan of the master builder. The Egyptian builders created huge constructions of fairly good quality in this way.

While the Egyptians used massive amounts of unskilled and semi-skilled labour to implement their designs, the Greek builders had simple machine technology and cranes that reduced the work force necessary. In addition, Greek master builders created workshops in which they gathered skilled stonemasons and improved their skills. For example, different masons were assigned to different types of jobs. This division of labour allowed the masons to specialise in certain kinds of carving, and with specialisation their masonry skills increased (Jackson 5). The Greek master builder was an *architekon*. He united the tasks of design and supervision of the actual building at the site. These classical builders were concerned with many of the same issues as today's builders, such as finishing on time and the cost of materials (Weaver 5). In other words, their role was comprehensive during the process, encompassing design decision, administrative duties, and direct participation in engineering.

The Roman master builder was an *architectus*. In the first century BC, the architect Vitruvius wrote about the *architectus* that "his personal service consists in craftsmanship and theory (*fabrica et ratiocinatione*). Craftsmanship is continued and familiar practice, which is carried out by the hands in such material as is necessary for the purpose of a design." In other words, the architect of a construction project had to be versed in the actual process of building. He was not separate from the craft. His role was not simply as an abstract designer unfamiliar with the real skill of engineering and building on the site. Vitruvius warned the *architectus* against reliance on theory abstracted from craft and the manual skill of building (Granger 7). Vitruvius's skill as an engineer and architect enabled him to develop designs, techniques, styles, and processes that served for centuries as the authority on building and design. While not scientific, his text created the model for architectural guidebooks.

### 3.5.2 Master Builder Tradition of the Medieval Period

The Byzantines used workshops as apprentice training schools. From this it can be assumed that a strong tradition of craftsmanship was in place, perhaps organised in an early type of guild. Byzantine artisans were so skilled that Islamic architects used their labour to create the decorative mosaics for the Dome of the Rock and the Great Mosque of Damascus (Byzantine Legacy). The ultimate goal of these training schools was to produce qualified craftsmen who would work through the ranks from apprentice to journeyman and master mason. The master mason himself was not arrested in development. He would hone his skills through increasing experience and by studying existing structures (Ousterhoust 52). The role of the Byzantine master builder was dictated by church leaders to the extent that the church determined every detail of the building, including construction methods (Ousterhout 3–7). Until the sixth century, the Byzantines used the terms *mechanikos*, meaning architect, and *mechanopois*, meaning engineer. There seems to be for the first time a separation here between designer and implementer. Within the legal codes of the Middle Byzantine era, a manager acted as the conduit from the client to the workers. This implies that the architect was not a manager either and had a limited administrative role, unlike in Greek and Roman times. This is confirmed in the records of a public works project in which a government official who was not an architect is appointed to oversee the construction with a master builder under his command (Ousterhout 43–8).

Islamic architects were able to pick and choose from a range of earlier styles, which allowed them substantial creativity as they incorporated previous architectural forms into their structures (Banister 571). Islamic architects improved the construction methods of the dome, allowing it to be seamlessly attached to the rest of a building.

They also crafted buildings that were less susceptible to earthquakes. The description of Islamic buildings must include the techniques used by masons for climate control in the hot and dry Middle East. They were basic techniques for the most part, such as small window openings in thick walls. However, the development of window scoops was sophisticated, resulting in a mastery of technique by Islamic builders.

During the Crusade, architectural knowledge was passed from one master builder to the next by word of mouth within the structure of master builders' lodges. Sometimes architectural designs were written and transcribed. One example was Abbot Suger's *Liber de Rebus in Administratione Sua Gestis*. There is no evidence that imported labour was involved, and many of these castles are in isolated and difficult places away from towns because of the need for safety. The skill required to build the structures would have been tremendous, given the challenging lay of the land, often slanting on elevated hills, and given considerations of military strategy that included defence against attack and siege. The builders learned quickly to change from wood and earth building to stone building. They adapted innovations from the Byzantine Empire. Thus, the master builders are seen as engaged in a dynamic dialogue with their own contemporary architecture and the military needs for which they were constructing.

In the Romanesque period, the Catholic Church became increasingly important as a patron of public building (Jackson 6). For its skilled workmen, it looked to the guilds. In a more organised and certain form, the movement that began with Byzantine apprentice training schools led in Romanesque building to the formation of true trade guilds, in which a lifetime's progression within a certain trade guaranteed job stability and led to the advancement of craft skills. Such craft guilds increased throughout Europe from approximately AD 1100 to 1426, although there were "free" cities without guilds. The pooling of labour and production gave the trade guilds a monopoly on power. There were even instances of struggles between greater guilds and the lesser artisan guilds. They were something like unions and allowed for the concentration of labour and production. Out of them came master artisans (Guild). The guilds allowed craftsmen to organise their trade and written contracts have survived, particularly in relation to ecclesiastical buildings. The role of architect was usually one with that of master mason, or *Magister lathomorum* (The Medieval Builder).

The archetypal Gothic structure was a cathedral designed by builders, craftsmen, and architects. With technology accommodating new designs, masons came to prominence again in the construction of massive cathedrals, working the stones to be laid, mixing the lime and sand, and using a level and plumb line to make sure that the foundation stayed level (Arch 9–17). The unskilled feudal workers of the Romanesque age gave way to skilled labourers and craftsmen once again who knew their trade and materials (What Is Civil Engineering).The construction of a Gothic cathedral was a massive building effort, involving scores of labourers, skilled craftsmen, cutting-edge machinery, specialized tools, and incredible engineering design. Supervising the whole feat were the master builders (Macaulay). A Dominican monk named Albertus Magnus (Albert the Great) probably had a significant impact on Gothic building. Documents describing a number of buildings mention the "Albertian manner" or

"Albertus system." The original plans for Amiens Cathedral in Cologne came from Albertus Magnus. His name is mentioned as the first clerk of the works in Cologne and in the Chronicles of Cologne and the book *Life of Albert the Great* (The Masonic Trowel). These texts all refer to a master architect, designer, and planner of great skill who may have influenced Gothic construction.

### 3.5.3 Master Builder Tradition from the Renaissance to the Industrial Revolution

The idea of the master builder underwent another transformation during the Renaissance (Jackson 7). Fillippo Brunnelleschi represented the traditional position that a master builder encompassed the roles of both designer and engineer/craftsman. He had been a clock maker and sculptor prior to becoming an architect, and so knew something about the importance of the craft process. In his view and practise, the person who designed the structure should supervise its building and should know something of the building process on the ground. Opposed to this was the new view of Leon Battista Alberti, who was a precursor to the modern architect as a pure designer. He argued that he could direct any master craftsman without himself getting involved in the construction process. He made plans that others worked from, thus for the first time separating design and construction into completely different concepts (Jackson 7). Alberti's façade for Florence's Santa Maria Novella was the first known project for which the designer was not the same person as the builder (Loulakis 47). Alberti inspired others to distinguish the art of architectural design from the science of engineering and the construction of building (Loulakis 47).

In the Baroque age, merchants influenced the building process through their sponsorship. What changed most, however, was the connection between architecture and building technology, with technology belonging to engineers (Cohen). Throughout the Baroque period, architect and master builder were regarded as the same. He was responsible for the design and construction and had total authority on the building site (Davis 108). Sir Christopher Wren was a master builder of the Baroque tradition. He was both a designer and a builder. He was given precisely these forms of responsibility and authority when he was commissioned for the rebuilding of St. Paul's Cathedral. Wren both designed the new cathedral and worked with a team to manage the actual construction on site. He was given the freedom to make design alterations throughout the process. The city and church authorities trusted him to participate fully in a hands-on way in the engineering and building of the project.

The separation of design and construction was completed during the Industrial Revolution, prompted by the fact that architecture became more and more theoretical with the increase in mathematical knowledge and material sciences. The changes that mass production and mechanisation brought to construction also had an influence. General contractors emerged to coordinate the work of different types of artisans (Jackson 7). This meant that the designer was no longer required to supervise the building on site. This role was taken over by the general contractor. Architects became design specialists. They still designed buildings and some, such as E. E. Viollet-le-Duc, wrote guidebooks for building design (Ramroth 8–12), but they did not organize the engineering nor oversee the craftsmen. This distinction between design professionals and building professionals was given institutional expression with the founding of the Royal Institute of British Architects in 1835, followed by the American Institute of Architects in 1857 and the Associated General Contractors of America in 1887 (Loulakis 48).

### 3.5.1 Master Builder Tradition – Conclusion

From the proto-classical societies of Mesopotamia through the Roman Empire, the concept of the master builder was being developed. At first the concept was a loose one and was focused as much on ensuring public safety as the increase and perpetuation of skills. Buildings were built primarily of mud-brick in Mesopotamia since this was the most common material. Greek and Roman builders shifted to stone, which was a more permanent material and began to add new decorative elements. In all of these societies, one person was essentially in charge of the design and construction of a building, although of course workers would be hired as needed to complete the work. Builders of this time had to face some of the same problems that modern builders do such as finding quality materials, difficult clients, and finishing jobs on time.

Greek and Roman architects both added important architectural details, creating more massive buildings that also contained graceful elements such as columns. The increasingly beautiful stone work of these empires required masons to have increasingly complex skills and so formed ateliers where they could pass on their skills to younger workers.

From the Byzantine to the Gothic era architecture changed in design substantially as buildings became taller and more elaborate. Windows were added to buildings (although window glass had first been used in Rome) and different kinds of stone work were required to support the weight of buildings. Solid stone walls are easier to construct than are walls that have windows in them since glass cannot be load-bearing. The cathedrals and churches that were lightened by these windows were touched by the divine, according to contemporary observers. The new kinds of masonry required new skills by master builders.

These master builders were still in charge of the entire project, from design to construction. They chose materials, hired workers, corrected mistakes as the buildings grew around them. The great buildings of this era often took generations to construct and master builders often passed down a project to their son, who in turn turned over the project to their sons.

Other buildings took a different direction as they served as fortifications. Crusaders needed strong castles to retreat to. They brought back these architectural ideas to Europe at the end of each Crusade along with Islamic elements. A number of buildings remain from this era, including Hagia Sophia and a number of European cathedrals. The buildings of this era were the vision of a single designer/builder but they were also the product of the work of dozens, sometimes hundreds of different artisans who had learned their crafts within guilds.

These guilds not only helped people learn trades but created monopolies that ensured only some people could train in each profession. This tended to keep wages higher. This was a distinct advantage for those in the guild since it allowed them to earn a living wage. However, for those without a family member or sponsor in the guild found it difficult to enter the profession.

Building from the Renaissance to the Industrial Revolution changed from the pre-modern to the modern world. The Renaissance brought about a rededication to the pursuit of science and engineering. Materials such as concrete that had been developed in the classical world but had fallen out of use were revived. The improvement in both knowledge and technology helped destroy the idea of the master builder even as it improved the safety of buildings and increased the variety of building types. As architecture required more and more years of study to understand the range of what was becoming possible. The same was true of the builder who working with an ever increasing number of different types of materials. There was simply too little time for one man to learn enough to be both architect and builder. The Renaissance and its successive eras, including especially the Industrial Revolution, forced specialisation of labour into many fields, and building was one of them.

For thousands of years the ancient master builder had been the most prominent professional responsible for construction. His status started to decline during the Renaissance, when artists such as Alberti, who believed that art of architecture was distinct from the science of engineering and the craft of building, began to be commissioned for buildings. Over the following 400 years, the master builder virtually disappeared. By the 1900s, the ancient tradition of the master builder had been fully replaced by architects and general contractors. This may be considered to have been to the detriment of society. As a result, architects may be said not to know how a building is really constructed; and builders are not fully aware of design.

## 3.6 Analysis of Building Projects

### 3.6.0 Introduction

The twenty building projects discussed in chapter 2 represent the project activities of the periods discussed and provide supporting examples for the historical evidence. They represent the application of the areas of expertise to project activities. Undoubtedly building construction is a dynamic field for historical research. Much can be learned about social organisation, management skills, technology, and aesthetics through investigating the various forms and histories of important buildings. Starting with the great ziggurat monuments in Mesopotamia, the human desire to build large-scale structures is an historical constant. In terms of labour, massive amounts of muscle and toil went into creating great brick and stone buildings that still stand today. The pyramids were built without the aid of cranes or train transportation, while later domes were erected without scaffolding using new hoisting mechanisms. In Roman times the army supplied labour, and later during the construction of the great European cathedrals skilled craftsmen from the guilds carried out the work. It was not until the end of the nineteenth century that large construction management teams replaced these guilds. So the history of project activities says something about society and its methods of management.

Technology and materials have also advanced over the centuries. From brick and stone to cement, iron, and glass, what is used to build has changed. Stronger materials have been employed than in earlier times, signifying scientific progress if not always elegance. The Romans perfected the cement arch, while the Greeks refined the marble column. Fortresses improved walls and, more recently, iron was used to build suspension bridges, glass palaces, and towers. All these changes were made possible by developments in materials. However, perhaps most importantly, technical changes in construction techniques and tools have shaped the field of building construction. This section will explore many of these changes through a summary investigation into the construction history of these twenty important buildings.

### 3.6.1 Analysis of Building Projects from the Earliest Times to the Classical Antiquity

The Great Ziggurat of Ur (ca. 2100 BC) was a pyramid-like structure atop which a temple once stood. Like other ziggurats, its core was built of sun-dried bricks of two kinds surrounded by a thick eight-foot layer of burnt bricks (Klein and Klein 34). This construction made it strong, durable, and time-resistant. It was probably built by intensive labour gangs of peasants and slaves (McIntosh 83). On top was a priestly shrine, now gone, that was likely 100 feet above ground. The shrine was dedicated to the worship of the moon god Nanna-Sin. Besides the building's immense size, it is important architecturally for its ingenious drainage system.

The Chaldeans knew that bricks swell in rain and could burst the walls. Therefore, they pierced the walls with drainage ducts through which interior moisture could pass out. This innovation worked in conjunction with reed matting and bitumen used as mortar to waterproof buildings (McIntosh 237). At every seven courses of stone, a layer of reed matting was laid and weep-holes and drainage shafts were placed, thus preserving the ziggurat from water damage.

Tower of Babel (ca. 600 BC) is an example of the failure of project management by communication breakdowns stems from the biblical text. There is evidence that the structure was finished, but this idea of project mismanagement is important in signalling the length the project took to come to fruition, its constant rebuilding and renovation, and the labour force used to build it, which would have consisted largely of conquered slaves from various lands who would have spoken different languages. Thus, the project would have been difficult in terms of the project managers' ability to communicate with those who did not speak Babylonian but were the actual labour force. Confusion on the worksite is imaginable.

The Hanging Gardens of Babylon (ca 600 BC) were a tiered structure built on stone foundations with brickwork above and layers of reeds and bitumen, a building with thick lower walls, foundations, and vaulted chambers to support a tiered superstructure. What makes the Hanging Gardens significant is in their use of irrigation to create an artificial environment. Construction of this type depended on a hydraulic technology for capturing, raising, and distributing water. The tiered Hanging Gardens is the first known building that was constructed with such an engineered system for water-lifting we call the Archimedes screw.

The Great Pyramid at Giza (2580–2560 BC) is a royal tomb. Its slope is more extreme than the ziggurat, it has no platforms, and at the top it tapers to a point. Furthermore, it was not equipped with stairs or ramps for climbing. The walls, piers, and roofs of the Giza pyramid are made of red granite and its passages and outer casing of polished Turah limestone. Its structure consists of massive stone blocks (Lehner 67). The pharaohs employed a regular work force of skilled masons and craftsmen that was "undoubtedly occupied full-time during the span of construction," probably augmented with peasant labour (Kostof 77). Lehner estimates a workforce of 25,000 of stone haulers and setters on shift every three months (Lehner 224). The workshops would have used massive amounts of fuel from the countryside. The greatest mystery is how such a massive structure was constructed without the use of cranes and pulleys. The most likely method was "some system involving a ramp or ramps" that were built up as work progressed (Lehner 209).

The Parthenon (490–432 BC) sits on the naturally fortified Athens acropolis. The temple was made of marble quarried outside the city, and the marble roof tiles were supported by cypress timbers that spanned the *cella*. Vast materials such as bronze, ivory, gold, cypress wood and human resources such as carpenters, bronze-casters, masons, dyers, embossers engaged in the project. It is laid out on geometrical measurements. The remarkable feature is its *entasis*, a swelling at the midpoints of the columns. The columns are thicker and closer together in the middle, tilt inwardly at the top, and are tapered upward harmonically. This curvature is a refinement of the temple platform (Rhodes 76). The pediments are what distinguished the Parthenon as unique and superior to other similar temples. These were designed by Pheidias, but carved by skilled workmen (Belozerskaya and Lapatin 74). Marble was quarried from Mt. Pentelikon for the pediments. This involved building roads and rolling the blocks down, then carting them to Athens and hoisting them up to sculpture workshops on the Acropolis (Palagia 7). They were chiselled from single blocks or pieced together. Stonemasons trimmed the statues after they were hoisted.

The Rhine Bridge (55 BC) near Coblenz was a legendary example of a wooden bridge built in service of empire. Its method involved pile driving thick timber piles, fastened two feet apart, obliquely (in direction of current) into the river at right angles to the bank. Forty feet downriver, the same was done. These piles were joined by two foot wide beams fitted into the spaces between the two piles of the pair. A diagonal tie was arranged between pile pairs. The upper pair was kept at right distance from the lower pair by iron braces. For protection against floating attack, an additional pile was driven in front of each pair. Then planks were laid over the structure, allowing passage over the river. Most remarkable was that the whole bridge was completed in ten days, demonstrating Roman building speed.

The Roman Colosseum (75–81 AD) has a foundation of twelve meter deep ring of concrete and stone blocks. It has eighty arches around it with two annular corridors at ground level and three storeys of stairs to different levels of seats. The main load-bearing skeleton was of dressed stone masonry throughout, travertine externally and tufa internally; concrete was limited to the vaults and upper internal walls and, to minimize the thrust of the uppermost tier of seating against the unsupported outer wall of the attic, the seating was of timber. The joining surfaces of stone were cut and mortared. The construction site was divided into four quadrants for simultaneous construction (Ward-Perkins 94). It utilised a massive force of slaves and the skilled labour of craftsmen working for the guilds (Taylor 137). The logistics were worked out beforehand, with efficient management, pre-fired bricks, pre-slaked quicklime, and a complex overlapping of crews working circumferentially. The Romans used cranes to lever and hoist stone blocks. Many cranes operated simultaneously and on multiple levels. Scaffolding and formwork was only brought in for vaulting. At this stage the cranes would be removed and timber formwork and scaffolding introduced. This is an important engineering development besides concrete in the history of building construction. (Taylor 156)

Pantheon (118–126 AD) is brick-faced concrete. The shafts of the porch façade are of gray granite, while the four inner columns are of reddish granite. All its original capitals and bases are of marble. The porch pavement is of marble and granite blocks. The original roof was perhaps framed in timber. It had a barrel-vaulted entranceway to the rotunda, framed by white marble pilasters. Its outer wall was probably covered in plaster. Under the dome, the colourful granite circles and squares of the convex ground for drainage, form the best surviving example of an inlaid marble floor from ancient Rome (Stamper 198). It was the largest vaulted concrete dome ever built. The dome was built by pouring successive rings of concrete against a hemispherical dome of wood upon which the huge wooden forms for the coffers were first positioned. As the concrete was poured a grid of ribs was gradually built up between the coffer forms, strengthening the dome by virtue of their thickness. (MacDonald 110) In a structural sense, their principal connecting vaults were conceived in exactly the same way as a Roman bridge or aqueduct, with each vault providing a counteracting force to the lateral thrust of the adjacent vaults" (Stamper 197). Its style was so successful – a portico with an unscreened rotunda – that it had an inestimable impact on later architecture. The dome had obvious later influence on the Byzantium Hagia Sophia and the Renaissance Florence Baptistery and St. Peter's.

### 3.6.2 Analysis of Building Projects of the Medieval Period

Hagia Sophia (532–34 AD) were design and built under the direction of Anthemius of Tralles and Isidore of Miletus, both "distinguished mathematical physicists" with extensive civil engineering experience. Where Hagia Sophia breaks new ground is in its use of pendentives. The transition of the square of the arches to the circular dome was made by these curving triangles, themselves buttressed by half-dome masonry. Each beehive shape would start at the corner junction of two supporting arches, but stop when level with the top of the arches, forming curving triangles (the pendentives) that met in a ring poised on top of a canopy formed by the pillars and the arches; on this ring the dome would rest, thrusting the weight back down on to the massive corner piers" (Nuttgens 143–4).

Grand Mosque of Damascus (706–715 AD) is the oldest congregational mosque in the Muslim world. It was built on an old Roman church (Hoag 22). The old site had four large towers at its corners and arcades around the edge which opened to a rectangular courtyard. Its layout was with three aisles parallel to the *qibla* wall with a raised transept. On the south façade, a *mihrab* was placed. A new two-storey arcade was built around the east, north, and west sides of the courtyard and covered with tiled roofs over wooden beams. Byzantine palatial architecture influenced its architectural style (Petersen 61–2). Damascus Mosque was influential in later Islamic architecture. The four towers of the precinct served as minarets for the first time in Islam. The features with lasting influence were: its three axial entrances, its transept, its alternation of piers and columns, its three deep sanctuary aisles, and its two-tiered arcades. This mosque was quite simply the model for all later congregational mosques because of its representation of a covered prayer hall adjacent to a courtyard surrounded by cloistered arcades. (Creswell 72)

Krak de Chevaliers (ca. 1144 AD) was a military advancement. Its walls were impregnable and its accommodations were well-supplied (Claster 263). Not only was it atop steep-side slopes and surrounded with double walls, a moat with drawbridge, and semi-circular towers, this Gothic-style fortress boasts an advance: the covered box machicolation. From these covered overhanging floor slots, missiles could be fired downward against scaling. The towers were connected by long vaulted passage "that enabled mounted knights to ride straight up into the impregnable heart of the fortress" (Billings 83). There was a cavernous undercroft for storage of five years supply of food. In addition to the imposing exterior was a pleasant interior. The project was a fusion of religious and military architecture, fortifications guided by religious design, construction, and function (Harrison 4). There was a monastic core (including knight's hall, dormitory, cloister and chapel) to the building with ribbed architecture, friezes, and bosses (Harrison 42). It had stylish charm and Gothic spirit as well as strength.

Pisa Cathedral (1063–1118 AD) consists of the cathedral itself, a baptistery, and a campanile. The original builder is generally believed to be Buscheto. The exterior is Tuscan marble in a hybrid Romanesque style. The cathedral has arcaded galleries, round-headed arches, a coffered ceiling over the nave, reused classical columns of granite or marble, and an ellipsoidal dome at crossing. On the interior, the decagonal white marble pulpit carved by Giovanni Pisano is one of the most impressive features. The cathedral was a combination of working labour and skilled master artisanship.

The baptistery building was not completed until the fourteenth century by the master builder, Diotisalvi. Its pulpit is hexagonal and was completed in 1260 by Nicola Pisano. A central fountain was designed in 1246 by Guido Bigarelli da Como. The Campanile is a warning tower. It is the work of Diotisalvi. The eighth story, with its bell, was added in the mid-fourteenth century by Tommaso di Andrea Pisano.

Notre-Dame of Paris (1163–1260 AD ) demonstrates a movement towards Gothic architecture, emphasizing luminosity and weightlessness. The flying buttress was the Gothic solution for thrust and compression of high walls. The cathedral's use of thin-wall construction made flying buttresses necessary to prevent collapse of the high nave vaults by supporting the wall on the outside (Jantzen 90). It displays the common Gothic twin towers on its façade. The project encompassed perhaps as many as four or five anonymous master builders. In terms of workforce, there must have been a robust army of craftsmen. Conservative estimates state 5,000 workers and several hundred craft masters from guilds. Stone was quarried outside of Paris, dressed on the spot, hoisted out of the pit by winches and levers, and loaded on long, two wheeled oxcarts (Temko 107). In addition to an onsite planning office, the whole site was a workshop. Although the master builders operated in a preindustrial age they had a variety of technical equipment at their disposal: the winch and the windlass, the inclined plane, the lever and the jack (Temko 140). Scaffolding, shoring, and centring were used by Gothic builders in conjunction with existing masonry or independent of it (Fitchen 17-18). The roof also provided space for the hoisting-gear needed to heave the stones of the vault into position (Nuttgens 162).

### 3.6.3 Analysis of Building Projects from the Renaissance to the Industrial Revolution

Dome Construction Florence Cathedral (1420–1436 AD) was proposed by Brunelleschi. He intended to build the dome without scaffolding. The methods used to erect the dome were revolutionary. It was the first dome undertaken without the use of centring. For one thing, he used herringbone masonry by which stones were laid sloping inwards, not horizontally. For another, the building procedure went in rings. A new ring was started only once the last ring was completed. Without scaffolding, there were eight teams of masons. They moved around the perimeter of the cupola (King 96). For safety, balcony was built inside the vault. The result was an incredible safety record, with only three recorded deaths for the duration of the project. Brunelleschi invented devices for the transportation upward and laterally of the sandstone beams and marble slabs. He invented a new kind of ox-driven hoist with a reversible gear that could raise heavy loads using less power and greater speed than ever previously. In addition, for lateral positioning of material he built a new kind of crane that operated once the stone reached the upper working level. All of this was radical innovation that contributed to the future of engineering. The cathedral has influenced architecture inestimably. It has to be seen as the "modern" building, which marked the end of the medieval period (Walker 77).

Façade of Santa Maria Novella (1456–1470 AD) was proposed by Alberti. He hid the sloping roofs of the aisles with two up-turned volutes which were the first examples of this architectural motif. The whole façade merges the lower Gothic elements with the upper new Renaissance elements (Orlandi 4). This triumphal arch facade is significant since it was the first time a designer had not participated in the construction. According to a dedication written to Cristoforo Landino by Fra Giovanni di Carlo, a friar at the church, Alberti designed the marble inlay on the façade, and this was executed by Giovanni di Bertino, a mason skilled in this art (Tavernor 99). Apparently Alberti was able to provide design models to the work site, then, but was not present for the actual building of the façade. This was a change in building methods.

St. Peter's Basilica (1506–1626 AD) was originally planned by Bramante. His structure was a Greek cross superimposed on a square with a central hemispherical dome supported on four massive pillars. After Bramante's death, the new architect Sangallo designed a new nave in harmony with the spatial grandeur of Bramante's choir. He strengthened the pillars, and built the nave vault and pendentives to support the proposed dome. Then Michelangelo Buonarroti was designated as architect in 1546. He created a bold, simple volume for the church that was to be covered by a hemi-spherical dome with prominently projected ribs. After Michelangelo, Giacomo della Porta gave the dome a more pointed profile. He accomplished the circular dome, which was made in two shells, internally brick shaped of orange-peel segments tied by ribs held with three iron chains (Nuttgens 185). The final architect of St. Peter's was Bernini who took the structure to completion in 1626 and turned to the square. Taking almost the entire sixteenth century and into the seventeenth century to complete, St. Peter's Basilica is the end product of the labours of many architects and builders.

St. Paul's Cathedral (1667–1711 AD) was designed by Christopher Wren. St. Paul's is significant in terms of the history of design. All parties agreed on a classical model, which was presented in 1670 (the First Model). This model was altered over time, contemplating a domed church on a traditional plan (the Great Model) versus a domed cross design with a large central space (the Greek Cross Model). The latter design was favoured and presented in a model in 1673. In 1675 a combination of the warrant and great model designs was approved. The sequence of schemes for St. Paul's demonstrates Wren's empirical, almost arbitrary approach to design (Soo 462). The foundation stone was laid in 1675 and across the years of building, forty-one contracts were entered into for mason's work, supplies of stone, bricks and bricklayers, carpenters, plumbers (Beard 28). Construction was constantly changing, but simultaneously limiting the design possibilities as the building went up. The church was complete in 1711. Its three-shell structure of brick cone within an inner masonry shell and outer timber shell is an impressive feat.

Menai Suspension Bridge (1819–1825 AD) was designed by Thomas Telford. He dominated British bridge building during this period. He followed the pattern of Derby and Pritchard's bridge, which was the first of its kind to use a single semicircular arch composed of five cast-iron ribs. The parts were assembled on this bridge not using bolts but through interlocking joints and wedges. Telford's distinction was to endow metal bridges with architectural grace (Kostof 599). He applied the principle of suspension to the huge span of 177 meters. It can be described as a roadbed hung from wrought-iron chains that are slung over towers and buried in rock at both ends. For rust-proofing, all the links were pre-treated in hot linseed oil before being dried in a stove. What anchored the roadbed were the massive masonry arches below. None of this was brand new; the techniques were already known. Telford's contribution was to approach this as an architectural problem, making it feasible on a large scale (Kostof 599).

Crystal Palace (June 1850–May 1851 AD) was designed by Joseph Paxton and constructed for the world exhibition in an age when mass production was beginning (Kostof 594). This was the new mechanical age. The building signalled social change. The main thing of material import was the increasing use of iron and glass. Iron was used to strengthen walls, floors, and domes. Plate glass developments in the 1840s made possible its complete glazing, no masonry was used. Several things are significant for the Crystal Palace. One, Joseph Paxton designed it on the model of the greenhouses. Two, it was designed with an internal skeleton of cast- and wrought-iron stanchions and beams. Iron structures created columns and framework for the five-aisled building. Three, it was prefabricated. This meant it could be disassembled, transported, and assembled from thousands of parts. Four, its erection depended upon railway transport and a sophisticated site organisation. As a result, the premanufacture and mechanisation of work site in the Crystal Palace project changed building practises. It led to the replacement of craft guilds by large contractors.

Eiffel Tower (1887–1889 AD) was designed by Eiffel for the 1889 World Exhibition in Paris. At the time, it was the world's tallest structure. Eiffel had extensive experience building arched wrought-iron bridges for railways and viaducts (Lemoine 192). It took about two years to complete. It was made out of prefabricated wrought-iron parts that were connected with bolts and rivets. What is impressive about the tower is the relation between strength and lightness. There are four piers and sixteen iron ribs, each of which rests on its own stone and concrete foundation. Given its height, wind was a major concern for its structural integrity and stability. Eiffel resolved this potential problem by providing diagonal framing within the structure, and by incorporating a system of windbreaks (Echols 229). The tower is full of space in a sort of open construction that allows wind to pass through it, thus minimizing wind resistance. The mathematical precision of the tower's components and the lightness of its lacy design made the tower a sophisticated product much ahead of its time (Echols 229).

### 3.6.4 Analysis of Building Projects – Conclusion

The history of construction from the Ur Ziggurat to the Roman Pantheon demonstrates a number of important aspects. In terms of working methods, most building during this period shows that the initiation of and payment for construction were arranged by kings or political leaders, while the labour force for the building came from slaves and agrarian peasants. The Tower of Babel indicates the possibility of communication breakdowns on site when foreign slaves were imported for work. It is certain that vast workshops were set up on the construction sites, perhaps best exemplified on the acropolis for the Parthenon and at the Colosseum. Here the craftsmen worked in a way not hitherto seen at earlier Middle Eastern buildings. In Roman times, construction was carried out under the orders of the emperor and the skilled labour came primarily from the military, although slaves must have been used as well. In the Colosseum, a particular method of circulating labour was employed in separate groups that enabled simultaneous construction of various areas of the building.

In terms of materials and technological processes, the great ziggurats and pyramids show the use of ramps for building upwards and a strong durable material (mud-brick or granite). In Roman times, one sees the invention of timber formwork and scaffolding for building vaults upwards, which replaced ramps. In the case of the ziggurats, a drainage system of reed and bitumen was embedded in the brick and the whole was rain-proofed, as later with the Colosseum, while the pyramids show no sign of such systems. An advance was made in the Hanging Gardens in the use of hidden hydraulic engineering within a terraced design to draw up water. The Giza Pyramid is distinguished by its use of quarrying and the transportation of large stones both over land and up into the building using levers and manual labour. The Parthenon replicates quarrying and transportation, but in this case it is of marble and granite columns. Mortar was used for the earliest buildings, but the Greek temple and Roman aqueducts use no mortar. They rely on weight and stone placement in arches and columns for their cohesion, or on iron cramps and dowels at the Colosseum. The Roman buildings are significant for the use of pulleys and hoists in construction, and their innovative techniques for spanning valleys using bridges on piers. They pioneered the use of concrete and the construction of supporting tiers of arches to counteract the effect of wind. These techniques received their greatest expression in the Roman Colosseum. Another advance was in building across water, as demonstrated by the Rhinebridge. A final notable development occurred with the Pantheon's dome construction. Here material was graded to be lighter as the building went upward. Timberwork was used to pour successive rings of concrete into ribs.

In terms of design, the Middle Eastern buildings are important for step-like forms and water systems. In Greek building, columns came into heavy use to support roof superstructures, as well as the frieze and the pediment. Rome added the vaulted dome and various forms of arches to the architectural palette. Decoratively, the Tower of Babel was painted, while the Parthenon was intricately carved and utilised *entasis* or swelling in the columns to ameliorate their appearance. The Greeks and Romans used more decorative materials in their designs than earlier, including bronze and marble.

In sum, in terms of materials, designs, and architectural techniques, great changes unquestionably occurred from the Ur Ziggurat to the Roman Pantheon. Especially important were the use of concrete and marble over stone and brick, and the employment of cranes and other time-saving and labour-reducing mechanisms to move large objects. The one area where there was little change was in the use of slaves and skilled craftsmen, although management techniques probably improved over the centuries.

Architecture made further strides during this period. The Hagia Sofia was the most impressive dome, although it was modelled on the Pantheon. Its novel use of pendentives made possible the placement of a circular dome on a set of square arches. Combined with the innovative double-shelled dome, this transformed basilica design. Islamic architecture took over the vaulted dome concept and placed it over the *mihrab*. Yet Islamic building did add new dimensions. At the Damascus Great Mosque, corner towers were erected to serve as minarets, which in Qairouan receive definitive Arabic form. This expanded the open courtyard tremendously, placing it next to a covered prayer hall and surrounded by arcaded walls. There was also a greater use of mosaic tiles for decorative purposes. This model was very different than the Christian basilica. In the Qairouan Mosque, prominence is also given to the teak pulpit. The fortress aspect of religious buildings gets its greatest expression at Krak de Chevaliers. Here the walls become impregnable, but the interior is not sacrificed.

A hybrid Romanesque architecture shows up in Pisa Cathedral. It is important for its classical columns combined with an ellipsoid dome and bronze doors, as well as its leaning campanile. Its fountains, coffered ceilings, and arcaded galleries prefigure the Renaissance. The baptistery of Pisa shaped later dome forms, most prominently at St. Peter's. Its style is quite different from the Hagia Sofia. While Pisa was built by many architects, like the mosques and unlike Hagia Sofia, it was important in terms of its building methods over the years, with clear shifts in its construction. Notre-Dame changed the form into the Gothic. It used the flying buttress, the rose window, the new cross-ribbed vault, and the two towers in front. The buttresses in particular were a crucial architectural advance for supporting nave vault walls from the outside through the diagonal distribution of weight.

Construction materials also changed during this final period. The domes of Florence Cathedral, St. Peter's, and St. Paul's were made of masonry. The Crystal Palace was constructed from the new iron and glass based on technological advances. Telford built the Menai suspension bridge using iron and interlocking joints. Eiffel built his tower using wrought-iron bolts and rivets. Clearly, materials had been revolutionized to enable different sorts of buildings.

Construction methods advanced tremendously as well. For one thing, competition came to construction in a new way. This began with the famous competitions for Florence Cathedral's bronze door and Brunelleschi's victory to build its dome. It continues through the competition for labour during the building of Wren's St. Paul's and up to Eiffel's company, which defeated 100 others for the building contract. A new era in selecting builders arrived, different than the older methods where the king or leader simply chose an architect. At Santa Maria Novella, Alberti was the first to design but not to build a building. Models and plans were sent to the worksite instead. Later with Wren at St. Paul's, competing models were debated and great freedom to change the design over time was granted so that it became almost arbitrary. Beyond this, Brunelleschi revolutionised building with his invention of ox-driven hoisting machines and by not using centring or scaffolding to build a dome, but working in circles around a platform. In more recent times, the Crystal Palace and the Eiffel Tower were created out of prefabricated pieces and using rapid train transportation. Mechanical derricks and elevators carried supplies upward. Guilds receded in the face of large material and building contractors. In sum, the way things were built changed radically.

Finally, construction design was transformed. Florence Cathedral had a unique double-skinned dome in which the interior and the exterior were totally different structures. It relied on a self-supporting skeleton, which had never been achieved before. St. Peter's and St. Paul's relied on older models and represented few architectural advances. Later, the Crystal Palace and the Eiffel Tower used iron skeletons for a less bulky building that was stronger than masonry. The tower used the rigid frame truss with iron ribs to distribute weight lightly onto piers and protect against wind. The Menai suspension bridge employed an iron chain suspension attached to masonry abutments in a wholly new principle of design. As a result of the material changes and new ideas about construction, building as a whole was transformed.

## 3.7 Summary

The analytical results of this chapter are now ready for discussion and synthesis in a substantial way that will make possible the formation of significant conclusions about the history of project management. The next chapter will concentrate on clarifying the links between the historical environment and the technology and management of building processes. The aim will be to use the data analysed in this chapter to draw out the implications of the interaction between the environment that fostered project activities and the actual process used by the master builders and those under them to achieve their results. Along the way, the significant shifts over time, both culturally and scientifically, will be seen to have caused corresponding shifts in construction and project management. Architectural projects responded to each new historical context in an evolutionary and creative way. Without an understanding of the influence of cultural and scientific forces on architectural projects, it would be unclear how these responses and transformations came about. This research will now turn to this synthetic investigation.

# Chapter 4

# History of Project Management

## 4.0 Introduction

This chapter will synthesise and discuss the research data presented and analysed in previous chapters to show how the cultural, scientific, and managerial realities of specific civilisations are relevant and directly linked to the construction technology and master builder project management of those civilisations.

The argument requires a synthetic view that integrates different kinds of historical facts. Connections must be drawn between cultural and scientific knowledge and the building process so that it becomes clearer precisely how they are related. How did the cultural and scientific background of each historical era make plausible the building and management skills for its great projects? How did the environment affect construction projects? Are there solid clues as to how construction applications came about as the result of historical conditions? How did the circumstances of each period influence the development of the areas of expertise and their arrangement in project activities?

Such questions will be asked and answered in this chapter. In order to arrive at significant findings, the history of project management prior to AD 1900 will be traced and detailed. The findings will establish the framework for the developmental synthesis of the evolutionary history of project management through the three main eras up to the 1900s, namely:

1. History of Project Management from the Earliest Times to Classical Antiquity
2. History of Project Management of the Medieval Periods
3. History of Project Management from the Renaissance to the Industrial Revolution

This chapter will demonstrate that project management has evolved over the ages; as culture, knowledge, and construction skills, tool and techniques evolved so did the purpose and construction of buildings. The following historical sections looks at the societal, the managerial, and the scientific changes, which took place prior to AD 1900. The impact of these changes on project management will then be evaluated. It is an attempt to provide clear, cogent, and significant insight about the history of project management from the earliest times to AD 1900 by the discussion of the findings at the end of each historical section to highlight their importance.

## 4.1 History of Project Management from the Earliest Times to the Classical Antiquity

### 4.1.1 Mesopotamia

#### 1. Construction Technology, Culture, and Science

The cultural environment was an essential underpinning of design and building in Mesopotamia. For one thing, the Mesopotamians developed a sedentary agricultural life involving animal domestication and crop cultivation in the plains. This meant that permanent structures were required for the arrangement of social life. It meant as well that urban administrative centres would develop around sites of leadership. These sites required civic building projects such as temples, law courts, and temples for public gods. Most important, perhaps, was religion. The ziggurats were built as the home to the gods, on top of which the priests administered the religious rites on behalf of the community. The Great Ziggurat of Ur (ca. 2100 BC) was conceived as the place where gods and human mediators met in the shrine dedicated to the moon god Nanna-Sin. Without the notion of meeting the gods halfway in the sky, the idea of the tall seven-tiered ziggurat would not have come about. The entire structure – a high stepped pyramid reaching towards heaven – was conceived on the basis of religious belief. Therefore, the cultural conditions that existed in Mesopotamia led to this architectural expression. The construction project was a response to imagined human religious needs.

A second cultural consideration is warfare. The Mesopotamian empires were continually engaged in wars of conquest or defence. After a defeat, their structures were sacked and destroyed. Based on this consideration, the impetus for fortifying important structures like temples and palace precincts is understandable. This is precisely what one sees in Nebuchadnezzar's Tower of Babel (ca. 600 BC). According to McIntosh, "the Etemenanki, the precinct containing the 'Tower of Babel,' was also fortified" (McIntosh 109). The need for defence, combined with the religious motivation, explains the height and solidity of the structure. It was also located within the city, around which were protective walls, not out in the unprotected plains.

The technology that built the ziggurats relied on several important scientific factors. The mud-brick material is explainable simply as being what was predominant in the region and easy to create using land and sun. Thus, it is an example of building using materials that are readily obtainable and close at hand. It needs no technological explanation.

However, why was there an alteration to the bricks through the addition of bitumen? This technological innovation in materials is not explainable by reference to something outside the construction industry. It was a direct response by innovative builders for a building product that would be stronger, more adhesive, and waterproof. The builders knew that simple mud-bricks swelled in rain. The added tar prevented this swelling, thus making the structures crack resistant. This is how the

Mesopotamian builders augmented their buildings through evolving materials. In addition, they realized that such mixed bricks required kiln baking to dry them rather than just sun. The innovation changed the shape of the brick, but it allowed the ziggurats to be built of a core of sun-dried bricks with an outer layer of fired bricks and ultimately produced a more durable material resistant to rain, flood, and time. Probably the underlying cultural rationale, in addition to this science, was for more permanence. Given the new sedentary lifestyle, more durable structures were needed.

In conjunction with this material change, another important application of general scientific understanding to specific construction technology was in water systems. Mesopotamian builders learned by experience that mud-brick buildings could be preserved more effectively through drainage systems. Science and technology had advanced Mesopotamian knowledge of irrigation systems, ploughing methods, and time-measuring systems as a cultural response to the new agrarian settled lifestyle. Techniques were quickly invented for storing, pumping, and moving water through channels. This direct application of farming technology had a huge impact on monumental construction. The Great Ziggurat of Ur had an ingenious system of interior drainage ducts that was made possible through irrigation technology. This innovation worked in conjunction with reed matting and bitumen used as mortar to waterproof buildings (McIntosh 237). In other words, one notices a general creative evolution of building based on the need for better materials and designs to prevent water damage.

Irrigation technology also made possible the Hanging Gardens of Babylon (ca. 600 BC). This tiered brick superstructure on a vaulted stone foundation was like a ziggurat with planted terraces. It required a hidden system of water delivery to eliminate the need for a large number of gardeners. In response, hydraulic technology for capturing, raising, and distributing water was applied. The technology likely involved Sennacherib's water-raising machine or some variation of it. The engineering technology was developed out of expertise in irrigation systems, aqueducts, and dams. The tiered Hanging Gardens was the first known building to be constructed with such an engineered system for water lifting.

Another factor was the use of ramps to build upwards. Ziggurats required ramps for transporting brick materials vertically. It is likely that the process was aided by the wheel, which the Mesopotamians invented first as a craft tool and then applied to their chariots. Wheel technology made possible later simple machines that the Mesopotamians did not invent. Thus, technology created outside the construction sphere was directly applied to the building process.

The construction technology of the Mesopotamians involved the use of primitive columns, domes, and arches to some extent. However, their most impressive engineering technology was tunnel or barrel vaulting. Such complicated architectural structures required the application of mathematics. The vault was a circular configuration along a determined line (Roth), but without prior understanding of geometry it would have been impossible to build. The Mesopotamian advances in science do not help to explain the development of this engineering technique, although they do indicate a scientific curiosity. The Mesopotamians observed astronomical phenomena and recorded data out of which they developed mathematical formulas. It was this type of numerical sophistication that must have given builders the notion of how to build barrel vaults.

Another important area is decoration. The ziggurats were painted, which implies both artistic and practical skills (Stiebing 283). Likely the temples and palaces were adorned with other types of decoration. This suggestion makes sense, since the Mesopotamians made advances in copper working, textile weaving, and glass making. That meant that a class of skilled artisans was in existence to respond to the architectural need for beauty and embellishment. The technology required for such decoration was available for use.

## 2. Master Builder, Labour, and Management

The labour for building the ziggurats, towers, palaces, and gardens of Mesopotamian cities was intense and vast, involving both semi-skilled peasant labour and slave labour. This is an estimation based on other historical evidence; there is no description of who the actual labourers were. It is known that there were skilled artisans doing decorative work in copper and glass, but it is not known how they were organized. The Code of Hammurabi seems to point to a special class of builders responsible for the design and construction of domestic buildings. They were liable for damage to the building and strict guidelines were applied to their practise. From this there likely developed some kind of traditional building society, or perhaps construction was just a type of family business.

The designers of the ziggurats, palaces, and gardens are entirely unknown, but they would have been familiar with the management techniques of the time. The king himself may have been responsible for the design, since he is shown on a stele conducting a construction process holding tools. More likely this was merely symbolic of his commissioning of the project. Whoever the builders and designers were, they would have had access to writing and legal codes. Writing had developed in the priesthood for record keeping concerning business transactions. The same system probably would have been used by the master builder to record administrative data related to building and for purposes of accountability and honest dealing. In other words, managerial control over building products, material resources, and labour would have been done partially through writing.

The designers and builders would also have understood their legal responsibilities to build safe and high-quality structures. The penalties in the Code of Hammurabi were severe if a builder caused the death of another through a building collapse. They constitute the first instance of building industry regulation. The designers and master builders were given a great deal of responsibility and would have been part of the noble class with a high status, as opposed to being freemen and slave labourers. Perhaps they came from high up in the military. In addition, given the well-regulated imperial governments in Mesopotamia, they would have been familiar with bureaucratic techniques. Their project management would have been well organized and lawful if the legal codes and political models are any indication.

The only challenge to this comes from the biblical account of the Tower of Babel, which implies a sudden disorganisation of building at the work site. It is possible, if slave labour was used extensively, that a communication breakdown between master builders and labourers could have resulted in a project management disaster. Additional support for this comes with the many renovations of large structures in Mesopotamia, which may signify the difficulty of completing projects. More likely these renovations were the result of the need to repair damage due to simple wear and tear on buildings or to warfare. The issue of communication was probably solved through translators. So the idea of poor project management is hard to sustain, although occasional confusion during a project was likely inevitable.

## 4.1.2 Ancient Egypt

### 1. Construction Technology, Culture, and Science

Like the ziggurats, the monumental pyramids of Egypt were created by a sedentary agricultural society that wanted lasting and permanent monuments. And like the ziggurats, they issued from royal and religious motives. These structures were not temples like the ziggurats, but they were religious funeral chambers, designed to house the dead pharaoh for journey to the next world. The complex Egyptian theory of and relationship with death led to the notion of mummification and entombment. The pyramids built for this purpose had chambers for tombs and valuable possessions for the crossover into the Egyptian afterlife. Their hidden passages, doorways, lack of stairs and platforms, and labyrinths were designed intentionally to discourage thieves. As to shape, it is not possible to know conclusively what the pyramidal geometry meant for society and religion; only the function of the structure is clear. This religious and royal background is important, nonetheless, in understanding the inspiration for such monuments.

The use of stone was a change from Mesopotamia, although some of the early pyramids were mud brick. The walls, piers, and roofs of the Great Pyramid at Giza (2580–2560 BC) were made of red granite and its passages and outer casing of polished Turah limestone. The whole structure consisted of massive stone blocks. Stone use can be understood from a religious or design perspective, not from a pragmatic perspective, since it required quarrying away from the site. Perhaps it was thought that granite, used for the chambers, was more durable or respectable than limestone. In any case, it was an evolution towards more dependable material structures.

The Egyptians possessed surveying and measuring tools of some sophistication. It is possible these were developed concurrently with astronomical studies and a greater knowledge of mathematics. Without question, these building instruments were developed in reliance on an understanding of isosceles triangles (Patel). This demonstrates the influence of mathematical knowledge on building technology.

The Egyptian technology for building vertically, as previously in Mesopotamia, was the use of ramps. In themselves these would have been an impressive engineering feat that required the skilled use of mathematics. They also show creative adaptation to different circumstances, since at least five different types of ramps are known to have been used. Along with ramps, the Egyptians compensated for the lack of pulleys and cranes by using levers and sheer manpower. These wooden poles were used to manoeuvre and adjust the large stones. Again, the technology was primitive but the result impressive. It demonstrates a lack of mechanical knowledge, presumably due to a dearth of more complicated mathematical schemes.

The Egyptians advanced beyond the Mesopotamians in another area: vaulting. They used the tunnel or barrel vault, as their Near Eastern counterparts did, but they added a new style called the corbel vault that creates arches using stones that jut out to support other stones. What this indicates is that Egyptian builders were not determined in their architectural structures by other civilisations or influences. Another example of this is the innovative cantilevered beams over the King's Chamber in the Giza pyramid. The pent roof distributes weight and stress in a new way. In other words, Egypt had skilful engineers who created new types of architectural supporting systems.

The other impressive technologies necessary for pyramid construction relate to quarrying and transportation. The granite procured was quarried in locations far removed from the actual site. The Egyptians did not have hardened copper tools, although they had saws and drills of soft copper. This meant granite had to be hammered away using stone hammers. Wedges of metal or soaked wood levers detached the blocks, which were then cut with saws. The process was unmechanised and labour intensive. It was technologically primitive, but impressive in terms of effort. The stones were loaded onto barges for transport down the Nile, sometimes hundreds of miles. These barges were unmotorised and human powered. Scholars believe they were transported over land through the manual pulling of sledges (by humans or cattle) across lubricated timber-baulked hauling tracks. This was an innovative system that did not use the wheel but the circular shape of logs instead.

## 2. Master Builder, Labour, and Management

The labour force required for monumental Egyptian construction projects involved tens of thousands of workers. Many would have been peasants, as in Mesopotamia, who worked for pay during the off-season from farming. The rest would have been slaves. These labourers functioned as stone haulers and setters. Many would have been skilled masons, while most others were there for pure muscle. There is no indication of organized labour in Egypt. Craft skill existed but was not that advanced.

The master builders are largely unknown except for Imhotep, who is known to have designed the stone pyramid of King Djoser in the third dynasty. They were probably noblemen educated in mathematics and astronomy. Their role encompassed all aspects of project management, from design, engineering, and building to administration. Those surrounding them may have risen through the ranks of the engineering class. They were skilled in management and planning, using alphabetic writing and papyrus to keep track of resources, materials, labour, and accounting as well as to correspond with royal and religious patrons. They submitted written requests using regulated procedures and consulted with a staff whose responsibility it was to make decisions. Communication was thus essential to the building process. In other words, Egyptian management operated on the basis of collective procedures that were highly organized and designed to make the best decisions possible.

### 4.1.3 Ancient Greece

### 1. Construction Technology, Culture, and Science

Greek temples were religiously motivated, as other ancient buildings were. They were also designed culturally to emphasize an inherited ancestral tradition of myths and heroes. The pediment on the Parthenon (490–432 BC), for example, includes immaculately carved representations of famous battle scenes between men and gods. The Parthenon as a whole was meant to symbolize the renewed power of Athens after the defeat of the Persians. The fact that it sits on the naturally fortified Acropolis is also significant in showing the blend of religious and military interests. It was from this cultural motivation – both religious and political – that many important Greek structures took their shape.

Greek science and philosophy were more advanced than previous civilisations, although it incorporated much of Egyptian and Babylonian wisdom. This was an agrarian society that developed larger urban city-states. Its seafaring prowess allowed expansion through conquest, which brought Greek civilisation into contact with the previous great cultures. Without such contact, it is not likely that the Greeks would have become as significant. This cultural background contributed much to Greek science and philosophy. The rational and analytical mind of the Greeks was evident in medical advancements, the development of natural history (zoology and botany), and the increased control over nature allowed by nuanced calendars. As such, this scientific background is important for an understanding of the new building technologies that allowed them to move beyond past civilisations.

The Greeks relied to a greater extent than previously on rational inquiry. Their investigations into astronomy and geometry created the context for builders to maximise mathematics in the making of monumental structures. As a result, buildings such as the Parthenon were laid out on geometrical measurements and constructed with precision using a mathematical ratio of 9:4. Although there are deviations, such as irregular spacing of columns and imprecise block widths (Carpenter 15), scholars tend to see these as aesthetic choices rather than flaws in calculation.

The Greeks built their monuments in stone, continuing the later Egyptian tradition. This stone also had to be quarried some distance from the work site and transported using ships and roads. The Parthenon required Pentelic marble quarried outside the city, along with cypress timber to support its marble roof tiles over the *cella*. Some of the granite obelisks for the columns for the Parthenon, quarried in Egypt, were lost at sea, leading some scholars to see the irregularities as the result of changed column height due to the loss. What is important is that ships and carts were the technology used, and this was made possible by the Greek sciences of navigation and geography in addition to ship-building skills, wheel technology, and the resourceful use of animal labour.

Stone columns were utilised to create a new structure that could support tiled roofs. This innovative structure, taken from nowhere else, rose in response to the need for fire-proofing and required an adequate method of weight support. Building such structures required heavy costs and labour; other mechanical techniques compensated by reducing labour and time. In addition to the structural advance, culture contributed new aesthetic design styles for columns (Doric, Ionic, and Corinthian). A remarkable new feature that appears at the Parthenon was *entasis*, a midpoint swelling of the columns, tapering and tilting at the top. This harmonic curvature is a refinement of the temple platform (Rhodes 76). It creates the aesthetic illusion of sagging horizontals. This is an application of mathematics to serve a cultural aesthetic.

Greek science also made possible the development of new machines. Archimedes and Heron designed and constructed winches, pulleys, screws, watermills, wedges, inclined planes, and other important time- and labour-saving devices using advanced mechanics and the mathematics of force, direction, and distance. Without such science, the tools could not have been invented. In addition, the crane was introduced for lifting stones. This advanced beyond the ramp technology used previously and was integral to the construction of the Parthenon. Loads were easier to move. The Greeks also experimented with hydro-power to build watermills for construction use. The results of scientific curiosity combined with rational methods of inquiry had powerful and lasting effects on the building industry.

## 2. Master Builder, Labour, and Management

Without question, Greek architecture demonstrates skilled labour to an advanced degree beyond the Egyptians and Mesopotamians. With the disappearance of ramps and the implementation of machines and cranes, there was a reduction in the workforce towards smaller groups of skilled labour with a higher degree of specialisation. Ateliers were formed at the work sites where the vast materials (bronze, ivory, gold, cypress wood) were spread out and human resources (carpenters, bronze casters, masons, dyers, embossers) engaged in the project. At these sites, skilled stonemasons were carefully divided into different labour groups. The effect of this development towards specialised skill is seen at the Parthenon. The pediments, made by superior craftsmanship, were designed by the master builder Pheidias but carved by skilled workmen (Belozerskaya and Lapatin 74). They were chiselled from single blocks or pieced together. Occasionally stonemasons trimmed the statues after they were hoisted. Individual carving methods can be discerned, but mostly they are uniform.

These skilled carvers implemented the designs en masse under the direct supervision of the master craftsman. It was a sort of mass production of statues and carvings, but all done under the watchful eye and final approval of Pheidias.

Overseeing each project was a master builder. In the case of the Parthenon this was the architect Iktinos, who was selected by Pericles after the previous architect was dismissed. Iktinos would have been influenced by the notions of leadership and management prevalent in Greek society. He was likely well educated as a leader. He and those following him might have had strict moral training to shape their character for leadership of the kind proposed by Socrates. He probably defined himself as a manager in addition to someone with technical knowledge and experience, rather than following Socrates in a separation of these disciplines. As a manager, however, he would have understood the delegation of authority, and the importance of labour division and specialisation for efficient project completion. When he encountered a problem, the rational method of working through different solutions would have been applied. His power was probably not absolute, since Greek theories of democratic political leadership understood that power should be kept in balance between different groups. In addition, a master builder like Iktinos would have had insights into worker motivation. He would have orchestrated construction with an eye towards finishing on time and saving cost in materials and labour.

### 4.1.4 Roman Empire

#### 1. Construction Technology, Culture, and Science

Roman technology developed in response to imperial expansion. Roads and bridges were necessary as military transportation and communication routes. Caesar's Rhine Bridge (55 BC) is a good example of a bridge used to cross into "barbarian" territory for conquest. It was built of timber in just 10 days across the river using pile-driving technology, and then destroyed. It indicates both the speed of Roman construction and the tremendous organisation necessary. In addition, it was used as a show of cultural and political strength, since it demonstrated that Roman power could overcome the Gauls' river god and pose a serious military threat of invasion.

Some buildings were religious and political, such as the Pantheon (118–126 AD), which served the several purposes of commemorating past emperors, providing a temple for the cult of the emperor, and housing an imperial audience hall. The Pantheon's great concrete dome was built to meet these motives, along with its magnificent inlaid marble floor. The image of imperial glory was intended to be reflected in the architecture. Other structures were spurred by practical concerns. The aqueducts such as those in Segovia or the Pont du Gard in France were the product of Roman cultural expansion, for they primarily served to supply water to town baths in the conquered provinces. These baths were sanitary and had an important social function within society; they also demonstrated Roman skill in irrigation and plumbing. Another building type was the amphitheatre, the most impressive example of which was the Roman Colosseum (75–81 AD). Here the building was inspired by the social need for shows and games. It is clear, therefore, that the Roman building program came from multiple cultural sources related to empire and society.

While the Romans borrowed strategically from previous science and technology, they did not make radical contributions beyond this. Their hoisting technologies, such as the crane, were adopted from the Greeks. Their knowledge of geometry, mensuration, astronomy, and sundials, as well as of machines like siege engines, water mills, and drainage devices, made possible their building program (Vitruvius). However, they were able to develop new major contributions to architecture.

The first of these was concrete, made of quicklime, ash, and pumice. Concrete was a radical advance beyond mud brick and pure stone building due to its strength, lowered internal strain, and flexibility. It developed due to experimentation with volcanic rock as well as from the necessity of finding quick materials for building as the army moved across the land. Interest in materials was evident in Pliny's system of natural history in which stones, gems, minerals, metals, and other natural objects were scrutinized. It is easy to see how this curiosity would have led to experimentation with new materials. In addition, its emphasis on utility shows the practical nature of the Roman mindset, which readily applied knowledge to practical uses. The Romans also had a sophisticated knowledge of various stones. While the main skeleton of the Colosseum was of cut and mortared travertine and tufa stone, the vaults and upper walls were concrete. The Pantheon's dome was also made of concrete, while other elements were of granite and marble. Concrete was thus a crucial addition to the material panoply of Roman building.

What makes the Pantheon important is how it showed construction technology at work. It was the largest vaulted concrete dome ever built, and required a masterful feat of engineering. The dome used volcanic Pozzolana mortar throughout, poured in concrete rings against a hemispherical timber-framed dome to build up a thick grid of ribs. This illustrated, among other elements, the Roman use of timber framework for dome construction, a method crucial for the creation of the arch. In the dome, the material was graded to be lighter as it progressed upwards. Such an innovative selective grading combined with the mortar strength, the foundation, the connecting vaults, and the carefully placed cavities in the drum made the dome possible. As an engineering feat based on concrete and structural knowledge, the dome influenced all of its successors, including the Hagia Sophia and St. Peter's.

The Roman arch revolutionized the aesthetic form and functional stability of architectural structures. It distributed weight in a new way that allowed larger buildings. This innovation replaced for the most part the column or post-and-lintel system. Columns became more decorative, as evident in the later Renaissance period. Just as important was that the arch made possible the concrete dome, since with greater stability such heavy structures could be supported down through the arched method of weight distribution. The arch was innovative as well when used in stacked layers to build aqueduct bridges or the arches around the Colosseum. This eliminated the need to build tall columns, replaced instead with shorter rows of progressively smaller arcades. This form would have a major influence on Islamic architecture.

## 2. Master Builder, Labour, and Management

The intensity of managing such a huge empire meant that the Romans developed management and leadership strategies that were applicable to site management. The organisation of labour for building projects would have followed the methods devised by the disciplined army and bureaucracy. In fact, many of the skilled workers came from the army. Taylor believes that there were trade guilds as well in urban centres that supplied skilled labour, in addition to slaves who were the brawn (Taylor 137). They were undoubtedly skilled just as the Greeks had been, familiar with their materials and skilled at masonry and in the new art of concrete. Skilled carpenters were essential for building the scaffolding and massive timber formwork required to lay concrete arches and domes.

The master builder would have been an expert at delegation, as Caesar and Diocletian were. There would have been a clear chain of command leading from the workers through the field engineers to the master builder himself. On the model of the division of empire into regions, the master builder would have divided the work area into clear sections to allow ongoing construction on multiple parts of the building at once while retaining overall control. This politically based model of organisation management was clear in the construction of the Colosseum, where work crews working on various levels, with and without cranes operated by humans and animals and in various quadrants at once, all coordinated their efforts to avoid interruption and disruption (Ward-Perkins 94). According to Taylor, the logistics were worked out beforehand, with efficient management, premade materials, and a complex overlapping of crews working circumferentially (Taylor). The work would have been patterned on the notion of alliances. At the level of decision making, a democratic process was probably in place whereby decisional power was shared between all important elements on the political model via the Senate. In this way the master builder's authority would have been balanced, as in Greek building, by other agents involved in the construction, such as managers and master engineers with more experience at ground level.

Yet as Vitruvius's comments make clear, the architect was selected on the basis not only of theoretical design (reason) but familiarity and practise with actual building. In other words, the Roman master builder was expected to possess the qualities of both designer and engineer or craft builder. These were separate, but both had to inhere in the person of the master to prevent the building of a shadow rather than a real structure.

### 4.1.5 From the Earliest Times to the Classical Antiquity – Conclusion

A basic scan of the notable achievements of ancient builders prior to the Middle Ages reveals some of the most significant structures in human history. Among these are the

Great Ziggurat of Ur, the Tower of Babylon, the Hanging Gardens, the Great Pyramid at Giza, the Parthenon, Caesar's Rhine Bridge, the Colosseum, and the Pantheon. These structures came out of the Mesopotamian, Egyptian, Greek, and Roman civilisations as enduring monuments which had irrepressible effects on the history of architecture. All of these structures have been analysed in this research project. Most of them are still standing today. None of them could have been completed without the separation of responsibilities and the advanced skills required for design, engineering, construction, and project management.

The conclusions reached in this research demonstrate that this era of project activities was foundational for all that followed. In it, the very concept of the master builder was created, along with the first surviving monuments that archaeology can still study. The history reveals the kinds of changes that took place in construction, management, and technology as a result of cultural and scientific pressures. What follows will sketch some of these important conclusions and evaluate the impact of these changes on project activities.

From the earliest time to classical antiquity, humans built upon the knowledge and traditions of the previous period. For the ancient Mesopotamians and Egyptians, it is impossible to know what these previous traditions were, since with these civilisations recorded history begins. It is clear with the Greek and Roman civilisations, however, that earlier knowledge from other cultures was sought out, accumulated, systematised, and applied. This intellectual growth produced many enhancements to life in general, and to project management and the construction of buildings specifically.

The basic elements of thinking and reasoning were developed by the earliest civilisations through the study of mathematics, written communication, law, medicine, production optimisation, astronomy, and science. For example, the Mesopotamians created a theory of disease epidemiology, while the Egyptians formed the first alphabet. Ancient Greece formulated the democratic principles of political organisation for use in the leadership of its city-states. The Roman Empire made great strides in the transportation of water for domestic and agricultural use. Many of these discoveries and achievements helped to produce both tangible and intangible infrastructures around which society organized itself, such as the concept of calendar time based on astronomy and mathematics. Without such intellectual advancements, building and organisational programs would not have been possible.

There were many other significant developments in ancient culture that influenced and extended the idea of labour and resource management. The Mesopotamians used written codes and laws to organise their society and economic system, applying these in addition to their understanding of the natural world and the gods who controlled it. Control was introduced through written codes used to manage daily relationships and business transactions. Ancient Egypt expanded management to include the planning and implementation of vast undertakings such as the pyramids. The Egyptians developed methods for planning, organising, and managing the decision-making process on such large projects. In ancient Greece, Socrates viewed management as distinct from technical mastery and documented the importance of delegation. Additionally, the ancient Greeks developed a democratic concept of leadership with checks and balances to limit the power of individual leaders.

The Roman Empire used managerial delegation and alliance formation, which provided the necessary social structure to manage a large and well-populated geographical space. By creating a chain of command, its leaders were able to create a vast transportation network, to develop a disciplined military, and to extend its government to include executive, legislative, and judicial branches. This evidence suggests that management and social organisation were thought out in ancient society, rather than being merely based on haphazard processes. Given this environment, project management could be expected to follow similar principles, since it was culturally rooted in other areas of life such as law, politics, communication, and economics.

Through the ages of early civilisation, construction techniques, tools, and materials likewise evolved. The Mesopotamians used mud-bricks to build homes and buildings with columns, domes, and arches. Later on they invented tar to reinforce the brick structures and provide waterproofing, which, combined with drainage systems, made their monuments and homes more durable. Such permanence was necessary given the change from a nomadic society to a sedentary agricultural society that lived in stable clusters. This facilitated the need for civil engineering and the use of the wheel and the pump for the transportation of water.

Around the same time, ancient Egypt contributed new construction methodologies such as quarrying and the ramp. Quarrying led to stone such as granite and limestone replacing mud bricks. The ramp allowed buildings to expand in height and mass. Egypt also introduced a distinction between craftsmen and engineers. With Roman builders, concrete was invented for stronger and faster building, which revolutionized construction. Within this trajectory it becomes clear how evolving technology responds to the needs of early human society. It shows further how changes in knowledge, social organisation, and managerial practises influenced the tools, technology, and materials used for construction.

In turn, the tools, technology, and materials available altered the role of the master builder, the project management, and the structures that were built. During these periods the master builder was the architect, the engineer, and the builder all in one role. Craftsmen worked with the master builder to improve and hone their skills. The master builder engineered tools to improve the transportation of materials to the work site. Additionally, the role of master builder was beginning to emphasise architectural skills over other skills. This was the beginning of the separation of architect from builder, but it was not complete.

The projects constructed during pre-medieval antiquity increased in size, purpose, and complexity from their respective previous ages. Mesopotamian culture began the evolution of construction with the development of ziggurats and bridges. The Egyptians created the pyramids as resting places for their kings. Ancient Greece created and mastered the use of columns as part of the support structure of its temples, which enabled the development of the pediment and the marble tiled roof, such as on the Parthenon. The Romans advanced building design and construction by improving on the column and by utilising and strengthening arches. These improvements enabled the building of wooden bridges and arcaded aqueducts over rivers and valleys, the construction of massive public buildings like the Colosseum, and the erection of the first concrete domes like that in the Pantheon. This progressive increase in the size, sophistication, and intricacy of construction projects reflects the progressive growth of architectural tools, materials, and technology.

Project management in the context of this research is defined as the successful use of material and human resources to construct a building. In the ancient world, project managers operated with limited tools to mine and shape materials, and limited technologies to transport and utilise those materials. Therefore projects spanned many lifetimes. Often the original purpose of the building changed as the leadership of the empires changed also. The design of the building altered as master builders retired or as new techniques and tools were created. The master builder was always responsible for the design and supervision of building construction. He created tools and machines to reduce the build time. He knew that his labour force would need to be replenished on a continual basis; therefore, he needed to orchestrate the transfer of learning and skills between the generations.

The role of master builder was crucial in society. His design and building work expressed the religious and national values of the civilisation. The ziggurat shrines, the pyramidal tombs, and the temples were all instantiations of the belief systems that guided daily life. In addition, there were more secular buildings such as palaces, assembly halls, amphitheatres, and gardens that expressed the cultural pride and ancestral heritage of each civilisation. All of them rose out of the aesthetic influences of their cultures and the deeply held worldviews associated with agrarian life or empire alike. As master builders perfected their arts, construction expanded from homes and religious structures to include infrastructures that facilitated the transportation of people, raw materials, and water. The creation of these infrastructures improved life for all. The master builder was the leader of this improvement and the director of cultural and national expression.

In summary, project management evolved over these early ages. As the ancient culture and knowledge environment changed, this had an effect on general management skills, construction tools, and techniques. From this evolution, the ancient professional tradition became prominent and nuanced in its project activities. Specifically, one sees that a maturing cultural environment gave rise to a civilisation that required certain types of project activities and the technology to achieve them. In addition, one finds that a maturing knowledge environment led to efficient management skills, the invention of more adequate tools by master builders, and the gradual sophistication of construction techniques. From this development of building, which was always related to culture and science, a professional tradition of master building was established in each civilisation. The master builders had tremendous responsibilities to design and construct monuments of cultural and national expression. On their work a coherent history of project management is founded.

## 4.2 History of Project Management of the Medieval Period

### 4.2.1 Byzantine Empire

#### 1. Construction Technology, Culture, and Science

Byzantine building was culturally determined by its new religion, but influenced by Roman and Eastern facets. The Byzantine Empire after Constantine was officially Christian. As a result, most of its greatest projects were churches like the Hagia Sophia (532–537 AD). This is perhaps the greatest example of early Christian architecture and set the tone for all later cathedral construction. It includes decorative architectural influences from Persia, although it is firmly based in the tradition of Roman domed temples such as the Pantheon. This Persian influence points towards the cultural fact of skilled Byzantine diplomacy and its economic centrality in the world of trade at the time. In fact, later the wealth of the empire would be used to fund the Crusades, which spawned new types of castles. Thus, culture was influential in multiple ways for architecture.

In Byzantine times there was a return to brick building. The technologies used were the same as the Romans, along with some of the traditional and important architectural forms like the vault and the buttress, which were extensive components of Byzantine building. This trend demonstrates an adherence to previous Greco-Roman traditions. This applies both to building and to the mathematics and science that were used to conceive of building design. Had the Byzantines not kept alive the older scientific and intellectual traditions – such as Aristotle, Galen, and Ptolemy – they would not have possessed the knowledge to build as they did.

However, the one exception to this reliance on past science was in the creation of a new method for dome construction. The pendentives used to raise a circular dome on a square of arches was made possible by an advance in the mathematics of angles and arches (Ousterhout). The transition between the square and the dome was made by curving triangles buttressed by masonry half-domes. At the time of construction, the master builders were uncertain that this new method would work. Yet it did, and a different way of supporting a dome down into the piers through curving triangles was invented. Out of this revolution came a new fusion of form: the marriage of a congregational basilica to a vaulted double-shell dome (Rodley 71).

The shortcomings of knowledge were clear at Hagia Sophia. Because this dome was erected under pressure of speed, the mortar did not bind properly. As a result of this structural weakness and an earthquake, the dome partially collapsed in 558 AD. This led to the first major reconstruction of the central dome from AD 558 to 562 (Mainstone 126). During this reconstruction, window openings were added around the bottom of the dome as an expedient for warding off cracking. The point is that Byzantine structures in some cases had limited stability due to the inadequate scientific knowledge of their builders.

## 2. Master Builder, Labour, and Management

The only significant contribution of Byzantine culture to theories of management came in preserving and transmitting ancient theories. Although their scribes made improvements to grammar and writing, it is unclear how these affected management. Nonetheless, a number of points can be made about labour organisation. The earliest form of European trade guilds developed in the Byzantine era. Training schools or workshops made it possible for apprentices to learn a trade and move up through experience (Ousterhout 52). While their organisation is not well known, they provided skilled masons for construction of the Hagia Sophia, probably working in competition against one another in large teams supervised by middle managers. They also provided skilled mosaicists for later mosques.

More is known about the master builder, who was called a *mechanikos*. It is assumed that this meant something like architect as distinct from the group of *mechanopois* who were engineers. This distinction is interesting, since for the first time there is a clear separation between design and engineering. The division should not be overstated, however, since at the Hagia Sophia the *mechanikos* was present on site and involved with construction management. In fact, for this church there were two master builders, Anthemius of Tralles and Isidore of Miletus, both "distinguished mathematical physicists" with extensive civil engineering experience (Freely and Cakmak 94). While they had the scientific knowledge to design and direct construction, they were not the overarching managers. The church had control over the building, including its design concept and construction methods. The church appointed a manager in an oversight role according to later Byzantine laws. This was a government official without connections to architecture who had the master builder under his command (Ousterhout 43–8). The manager was a liaison between the workers and the client and vice versa. As a result, the master builders were freed from administrative work as never before, although with the division of power between architect and engineer they also did not wield as much authority.

### 4.2.2 Islamic Golden Age

## 1. Construction Technology, Culture, and Science

The Islamic Golden Age spawned magnificent construction projects motivated by religion. Islam began its conquest of all the lands around the Arabian Peninsula during Mohammed's time. With each new territory conquered, mosques and palaces were built as the centre of urban administrative cities. It was important that the cities radiated out from the core of the mosque, illustrating the pivotal place of this building in Islamic culture. It was not only a place for prayer, but also a communal gathering location designed to encourage group identity. It evolved into the political centre of Islamic society. Like previous religious buildings, the mosque architecture of the

Islamic empire relied on the transformation from nomadic life to sedentary, agrarian life.

The pattern for the mosque began with Mohammed's model in Medina, Mosque Al-Masjid al-Nabawi (622–781 AD), which contained many of the important congregational elements such as an open courtyard, an assembly hall, a *mihrab*, and a *minbar*. But there was nothing ornate about Mohammed's crude building. Only the pattern of elements was important for later building, which would develop into the great constructions of the Islamic empire. These new buildings kept faithfully to the original features, although the decor, methods, materials, and scale changed dramatically.

Islamic building technology was taken from what was known. Cranes and other lifting and transporting machinery were commonly used. This is surprising to some extent, since Islamic culture made several important technological advances such as the streetlamp, the observation tube, surgical equipment, and waste disposal facilities. One would expect a similar level of ingenuity in the construction industry. However, they were fluent in the machine technologies of the day as a result of their strong heritage of technological breakthroughs. The design and implementation of building could not have succeeded without such a deep knowledge of science. Islamic culture strove for knowledge, establishing the university system for training lawyers and revolutionizing the library by introducing the library catalogue. It had also taken over many classical European texts and studied them for mathematics and natural philosophy. It was a culture that contributed to experimental physics, biology, and the scientific method (Durant 53–5; Lindberg 154–76). Given this scientific milieu, their construction prowess is not surprising.

The Islamic dome was adopted from Byzantine examples. It was a staple of Islamic construction. However, it was often given a new style of ornamentation using mosaic tiles. It was also expanded on at Jerusalem's Dome of the Rock, where an octagonal wooden dome was mounted on a drum of circular piers and columns. Thus, Islamic architects improved the construction methods of the dome by seamlessly attaching it to the rest of a building. In addition, they improved its strength so that it was resistant to earthquakes. These construction innovations represented the progress and expansion that Islam brought to the dome (Kostof). Additionally, the dome came to be placed over the *mihrab*, giving it a new emphasis. This stylistic innovation at the Great Mosque of Damascus (706–715 AD) was an instrumental contribution to future design.

It is possible as well that the minaret came from previous examples such as lighthouses or the bell towers on Christian churches. Whatever the derivation, Islamic architecture made the minaret a distinctive form. Sometimes it was just a single heavy tower, as at the mosque in Qairouan. More frequently, as at Damascus for the first time, four minarets were placed at each corner of the courtyard. There was an additional benefit to the minaret, since it could double as a watchtower during times of conflict. Thus it was an aspect of fortification during the militaristic campaigns of the Muslims and a defence later against the invading Crusaders.

The minaret combined in distinctive ways with other European forms like the pointed arch, the double-tiered arcade, and the dome to create a unique architectural style. This was made possible by the science and design technology available in Islamic culture. Islamic architects also adapted European building techniques for the desert climate, using smaller windows and thicker walls. With all of these culturally and environmentally produced construction technologies, the Islamic builders made enduring contributions to the evolution of construction.

## 2. Master Builder, Labour, and Management

The Islamic Golden Age was open to the humanistic notions of individualism, liberalism, religious freedom, and cross-cultural exchange (Hassan). These notions influenced the management philosophies used by master builders, and created the idea of importing skilled Byzantine artisans to work on mosques, particularly in the area of decoration and mosaics. In addition, they used quarried stone such as marble in their buildings, which required lots of labour and stonemasons. The elaborate teak wood *minbar* at Qairouan had to be crafted by men highly skilled in detailed woodwork. There was also the development of a unique geometrical decorative style in Islamic buildings, along with tiling, calligraphy, and garden designs. Their largest contribution to construction was perhaps the enduring legacy of the skilled trades and craftsmen who perfected these decorative techniques in sculpting, metallurgy, mosaics, wood, and other material artwork (Ousterhout).

The best picture we can get of the management style of Islamic master builders is in the work of Al-Ghazali, who wrote a crucial text on political leadership. In *Nasihat,* he stresses factors that were common to Islamic understandings of management and useful for project arrangement. First, he emphasised that communication channels should be open between the leader and the organisation, and repeatedly tested. Such openness would have meant a smoother flow of organised construction and less miscommunication. By comparison with the emperor, it would also mean that problems could be stopped before they happened if the master builder remained well informed of information that might affect decisions or the building process. Secondly, he stressed like the Greeks before him that the leader was a moral emblem. His personal behaviour must be above reproach so as to maintain the morale of the workers. This was underpinned by the religious notion that leadership was a sacred duty to be executed correctly. If he knew that his building and his duty were divinely sanctioned like this, the master builder would likely have made the utmost effort towards perfection and discipline. As a result of such a management philosophy, elegant mosques were built in the Islamic Golden Age.

## 4.2.3 Crusades

### 1. Construction Technology, Culture, and Science

Perhaps more than other ages, the Crusaders' construction technology was shaped by the culture and science of warfare. In Crusader castles like the Krak de Chevalier (ca. 1144 AD) one sees the absolute effect of the idea of defensive structures – buildings explicitly designed to withstand bombardment. Yet culturally, these structures were formed out of the impetus of economic expansion and religious ideas. The religious idea, sponsored by the growing Catholic Church, was to win back the Holy Land. This provided the overt ideology that led to castle construction in the East. The more subtle motive for this architecture was the decline of feudalism into an incipient merchant capitalism that thirsted for new markets to open. This involved a program of warfare against the powerful Islamic empire. Out of these historical foundations was born Crusader architecture.

Scientifically, it was an age in which knowledge was gleaned from the Byzantine and Islamic worlds and taken back to the West. The science (optics), math (algebra), and medicine brought back did little to affect architecture. Renewed trade between East and West introduced new goods like spices, diamonds, and oranges during this period. Little of this knowledge influenced castle building, though it had a somewhat greater impact on the related Romanesque cathedrals. Instead, military, naval, and political technologies were preeminent in informing fortress construction.

Abandoning aesthetics, castles sought simply to be best provided with thick, tall walls for the protection of those inside. They were designed with inner keeps that had storage and water supplies to outlast any siege. Strategic moats were dug where necessary around the walls. Tower design changed from the Roman box tower to the round tower to provide a better view of the surroundings. Often the sites were determined by natural fortifications such as hills where communication and surveillance were optimal. Such heavy and fortified structures would have required cranes, ramps, pulleys, and winches, as well as heavy stone masonry (Williams).

Krak de Chevaliers is a paramount example of a Crusader castle. It was a military advancement. Its walls were impregnable and its accommodations were well supplied (Claster 263). Not only was it atop steep-sided slopes and surrounded with double walls, a moat with a drawbridge, and semi-circular towers connected by long vaulted passageways, this fortress included an advance in defensive architecture: the covered box machicolation. From these covered overhanging floor slots, missiles could be fired downward against enemies scaling the walls without fear of retaliation. There was, finally, a cavernous undercroft designed for the storage of five years' supply of food. In other words, Krak de Chevaliers almost perfectly defines the type of fortified structure typical of Crusader architecture and technology.

While on the exterior there was little stress on aesthetic design, the castle's interior often betrayed a soft edge. Since families would accompany the knights, they might have taken up residence in the castles. In addition there were priests and other religious functionaries, along with government officials. As a result, Harrison can speak of a "fusion of religious and military architecture" (Harrison 4). There was a monastic core to the building, including a knights' hall, dormitory, cloister, and chapel. Aesthetics were expressed in ribbed architecture, friezes, and bosses (Harrison 42), providing stylistic charm within a strong and austere shell.

### 2. Master Builder, Labour, and Management

The labour for Crusader castles was most likely provided by knights of various traditions. Not much is known about their organisation in terms of building, since these were predominantly nobles from the military caste. They would have been strong and capable men of intelligence. The Byzantine Empire likely also supplied skilled craftsmen out of its early guilds, who would have travelled with the Crusading knights to supply the engineering and masonry on the gigantic fortresses. The skilled labour was evident primarily inside the castles. For example, the Gothic interior of Krak de Chevalier was ornately decorated. It was only in the heart of the castle, designed and built by skilled workers, that an aesthetic trend could be seen.

Master builders learned their trade apparently through word of mouth during this time. This transmission of design information occurred in master builders' lodges, which were the early equivalent of professional engineering and architectural societies. In addition, they had at their disposal texts such as Abbot Suger's *Liber de Rebus in Administratione Sua Gestis* that transmitted architectural designs.

Management techniques for master builders would have followed the basic philosophy of chivalry. This was founded on the idea of horse management, but its modulation for human interactions is found in the round table model, which meant respect for one another, gracious behaviour, and decentralised authority. There would have been a partnership mentality rather than a hierarchy or singular leadership. As such, the master builder might have been more ready to distribute work and authority around to many people in a democratic fashion. He would have understood as well the way in which social interaction styles affect group communication.

## 4.2.4 Romanesque

### 1. Construction Technology, Culture, and Science

The Romanesque architectural style coincided with the twelfth-century renaissance. One therefore expects to find evidence for cultural and scientific influences in construction technology. In cultural terms, the heavy, strong, and dark building that characterizes the Romanesque is reminiscent of Crusader castles. While Romanesque churches are religiously motivated, the style and motif take after the militaristic fortress. It is clear that influence has come back from the Crusades experience and combined with the new power of the Catholic Church to produce these monumental ecclesiastical structures. Perhaps sensing impending defeat at the hands of the

Muslims as well as the devastation of the plague, there is a sort of defensiveness to the thick Romanesque style that reflects cultural awareness.

In terms of science, the Romanesque style is built on rounded arches, barrel vaults, and apses. The exterior walls and pillars are thick and heavy. These were constructed on Roman models that sought harmonious proportions, as well as symmetrical planning and design ratios based on the classical and Arabic mathematics recovered from the Crusades. They clearly represent the intellectual revival that was going on during the High Middle Ages and centred on the newly established universities brought over from Islamic models. In these universities, classical and Islamic texts in all fields of science and literature were being consumed. Through the education system that trained master builders within the nobility, all this knowledge was applied to the field of construction.

Beautiful craftsmanship is also in evidence in the renewed emphasis on building interior spaces that were comfortable. Indoor plumbing advanced as never before. Blind arches were used decoratively, along with small windows, arched roof supports, and painting. Walls were covered with Persian tapestries as much for aesthetics as for insulation. Stained glass was advanced, as evident at Chartres Cathedral (thirteenth century). Attention was paid to interior furniture that used skilled wrought-iron workmanship. None of this is surprising given the cultural advances during this time in enamel and ivory work (from exposure to trade with the East during the Crusades) and the wealth of the renewed church, which could pour its resources into building programs. There were also advances in bronze and gold sculpture, embroidery, and the illumination of manuscripts (Toman). All this signifies a period of tremendous vitality for crafts, at least in the construction of interiors, which would be expected to contribute to the ardent decoration of Romanesque architecture. It was the gentle side of military architecture carried over from castle interiors.

Pisa Cathedral (1063–1118 AD) demonstrated both sides of early Romanesque architecture. The exterior was Tuscan marble. The cathedral had arcaded galleries, round-headed arches, a coffered ceiling over the nave, reused classical columns of granite or marble, and an ellipsoidal dome at the crossing. Around AD 1180 a bronze door with biblical scenes designed by Bonnano Pisano was installed. Inside, the decagonal white marble pulpit carved from AD 1302 to 1311 by Giovanni Pisano formed one of the most impressive features. The cathedral was clearly a synthesis of working labour and skilled artisanship.

## 2. Master Builder, Labour, and Management

The skilled labour was astute during the Romanesque period. All the previously mentioned ornamentation indicated a high level of craftsmanship. Perhaps many of the workers came out of the cottage industry style of organisation that had developed during the twelfth-century renaissance. This social arrangement of industry was like a collective workshop where families who lived adjacent to one another gathered in a specialised division of labour to make a particular product. This foreshadowed later

Industrial Revolution techniques. Each house represented a different step in the production process. There was no centralized authority and the work was divvied up among the members, each contributing their own set of skills to the final product. The advantages in efficiency were evident, as are the ways of apprenticing younger members slowly into the family trade.

The more probable model is that the skilled labour was taken from the guilds, whose power was on the rise throughout Europe after AD 1100. Artistic and trade guilds selected their members. Such pooled labour provided training, experience, a career trajectory, and security for the craftsman, who could eventually work through the stage of journeyman to master craftsman. This system allowed for the concentration of skilled labour and guaranteed quality controls. Non-members were excluded from building projects. It was an early form of labour union. At times these guilds had a monopoly on trade labour. Out of some system like this it is likely that the labour came to work on buildings like Pisa Cathedral.

The master builders themselves would have been influenced by knowledge generated in the intellectual revival at the universities. The Catholic Church was their principal patron. Pisa Cathedral was built over time by a number of master architects, including Buscheto, Diotisalvi, and Pisano, although not much is known about their experience or management techniques.

### 4.2.5 Gothic

#### 1. Construction Technology, Culture, and Science

The Gothic style was heavily influenced by the Roman Catholic tradition. Its decorative structures were pedagogical, telling stories from the Bible for absorption by the illiterate populace. This was a clear cultural aim of Gothic builders. The trade guilds continued during this period and helped bring their members to literacy and higher standards of record keeping. There was in addition a new cultural emphasis on the human form and condition. Gothic architecture implemented this cultural emphasis in the way its designs and statues portrayed the body. It signified the beginnings of artistic secularisation, thus heralding well in advance the Baroque and Industrial Revolution with their complete rejection of Christian architecture (Punter). Christian rationalists like Oresme, who investigated nature, helped further pave the ground for this later transformation.

Culture was also significant for Gothic building since it insisted on height and light-filled interiors. The aim was to increase the splendour to provoke religious reverence and awe within the sanctuary of the cathedral. While some of this came from the cultural power of the church, another reason for this emphasis came from city economics. With a more impressive structure, more pilgrims and tourists would come to the city. That meant that the merchants would grow wealthier. As a result, merchants started sponsoring church building. This fostered competition among towns to build the most attractive tall and light-filled churches. Thus, besides being the centre of town social networks, these structures brought in revenue. The cultural influence on architecture is evident here. As a result of striving for light, Gothic builders were forced to use new methods and technologies to achieve the necessary height and openness.

The pointed arch engineering that had been mastered first in Islamic building was one of these crucial Gothic elements which extended the capacities of European building. Another method employed for opening up interior light was the spanning ribbed vault. These experimental structures, erected using the revived technology of the treadwheel, were solutions to the question of height, enabling a tall structure while ensuring a suitable influx of light (Wilson). Perhaps the most important, however, was the flying buttress, a newly developed engineering structure designed to distributed weight laterally from the exterior to support the interior skeleton.

Accomplished with confusing complexity over a century, Notre Dame de Paris Cathedral (1163–1260 AD) is a good example of the movement towards Gothic architecture. It demonstrates the Gothic stress on luminosity and weightlessness. The flying buttress prevented the high nave vaults from collapsing and thus solved the problem of the thrust and compression of high walls, since the builders used thin-wall construction (Jantzen 90). The transverse distribution of weight through buttressed spokes created the possibility of increased height. Its pointed arches were employed alongside cross-ribbed vaults. Finally, Notre Dame displays the common Gothic twin towers and central rose window on its façade. It is exceeded in beautiful high stained glass at Chartres (Bony), but in other elements this cathedral is an exemplar of the progress of building technology.

## 2. Master Builder, Labour, and Management

The amount of labour used on Gothic cathedrals was large and required many skilled masons. In terms of work force, a robust army of at least 5,000 craftsmen and several hundred craft masters was employed from the guilds on Notre-Dame (Temko 107). Labour was needed for quarrying stone, dressing it, hoisting it, and loading it for transportation. Temko describes the Notre Dame site on the Ile-de-France as containing a planning office and a bustling workshop full of machines and skilled operators (Temko 140). Fitchen has shown how scaffolding, shoring, and centring were used by Gothic builders (Fitchen 17–8). In other words, there was plenty of skilled labour for the job, all organized in a rational way and with clear divisions of labour.

Due to the length of time the Gothic cathedral took to complete, often many master builders were involved. At Notre Dame, for example, it is estimated that there were four or five anonymous master builders. With each new builder, different standards, calculations, and designs took effect. Earlier work was altered, refined, or revised. At Notre Dame, for instance, the design was altered with the addition by the second builder of flying buttresses and chapels (Bruzelius). Therefore, planning was necessary to retain coherence and continuity in design, and to prevent additional costs and delays. There were inefficiencies and work occasionally stopped.

The design process matured to include small-scale modelling that tested the stability of a proposed design before it was built (Branner). This reflected the experimental and courageous nature of Gothic architecture, and foreshadowed the Baroque period when Wren's models became essential to the process.

### 4.2.6 The Medieval Period – Conclusion

The Middle Ages were likewise a time of significant evolution for the building industry. There is no dearth of monumental structures whose achievement was impressive both in terms of technology and project management. The Medieval period witnessed the construction of the Byzantine Hagia Sophia with its massive dome, the Islamic Grand Mosque of Damascus, the Crusader castle of the Krak des Chevaliers, the Romanesque Pisa Cathedral, and the Gothic Notre Dame de Paris. The discussion of these buildings has indicated beyond doubt that significant divisions of responsibility in terms of labour and project management, and advanced skills in design, engineering, and construction, were essential to their successful erection. As with the previous period, the cultural and scientific environment was an important shaping factor, both aesthetically and structurally. The line of development in construction project management is woven through the fabric of this history. What the Medieval period did in terms of building was to transmit previous knowledge and prepare for future knowledge. This was a crucial transitional period.

The Middle Ages marked the continued and even intensified use of religion as the basis for society. This period witnessed, among other important events, the beginning of the clash between Islam and Christianity. It also experienced the almost perpetual expansion and contraction of knowledge, science, law, and trade. All of these factors influenced society and influenced the design and construction of both public and private buildings.

Strategically located on the trade route between Europe and the East, the Byzantine Empire perpetuated much of the previous Roman Empire's leadership structure. Furthermore, Constantinople became the centre of knowledge once the Roman Empire and Rome itself had collapsed. Due to its location, its skilful diplomacy, and its cultural importance, the Byzantine Empire was able to wed the learning of Islamic culture with European knowledge. By and large, however, it was committed to Christianity and its architecture was driven to meet that need. Out of this came many great churches, the best known of which is the massive domed church of Hagia Sophia in modern Istanbul.

Shortly after the Byzantine Empire rose to prominence, the Islamic Golden Age flourished. It imposed unity on a previously fragmented politics in Africa and the Middle East, and established a society based on agriculture and committed to new religious principles. By nature, Islamic society was gripped with a search for knowledge. It was able to make significant contributions to art, engineering, philosophy, scientific method, and medicine. Some of these discoveries, such as those in optics and ocular biology, led to the development of the quadrant and sextant. It was from such an impetus that new social institutions appeared that were gathered around knowledge, such as the university and a new kind of library. All of these realities together demanded a type of architecture that would reflect the Islamic community and its expansion. The centre of the community was the mosque, and from this arose some of the most significant Islamic religious buildings in this period.

The Crusades of the eleventh century brought learning acquired from Islam to the West, albeit through the tragedy of war. They also increased the flow of trade, bringing new spices, gemstones, and foods to Europe. The pope and the Catholic Church emerged as the leaders of society and religion, unifying Europe under the banner of their moral, economic, and political power. The Crusades marked the beginning in Western architecture of a unique form, the religious fortress, in which religious and martial aims were merged.

The chain of history returned knowledge to Europe after the Dark Ages as the Crusaders came home, bringing with them the knowledge of Byzantium and the Islamic world. This included the preserved legacy of older Greek and Roman science and philosophy. In a way, light shone again on Europe as in the twelfth century it experienced an early form of renaissance. The renewed study of art, science, and culture instituted a change in architectural style and building materials. It increased the use of rounded arches and barrel vaults while reviving the decorative arts, particularly the use of metal, enamel, ivory, bronze, gold, stained glass, and embroidery, which were applied ornamentally to art and buildings. This was the Romanesque style, out of which emerged the impressive Pisa Cathedral.

The Gothic transition to the Renaissance was also initiated by the church. This new style counteracted the heaviness and darkness of previous cathedrals by striving for height and illumination. Intellectually this was a dark age, but the church used its architecture to inform the masses using artistically expressed stories. The search for designs full of light and reverential grandeur created structures such as the cathedral of Notre Dame de Paris.

Such was the cultural and scientific background for these movements in the Middle Ages. There was enough science combined with the preservation of tradition to create significant construction projects with all their varied activities. These projects required management techniques for the arrangement and supervision of labour, materials, and the construction process. There were several culturally important strains of thought regarding leadership and management during the Middle Ages.

During the Byzantine Empire religion was the focal point of individual and collective life, which was organized around the church. Yet the Byzantines are remembered for their ability to create powerful alliances through skilled diplomacy. This notion of alliances, taken from the Romans originally, and diplomacy was one strain. Islamic civilisation, focused on the humanistic notions of individualism, liberalism, religious freedom, and cross-cultural exchange, constituted another. Their art of management focused on keeping the lines of communication open and on establishing the leader as a moral exemplar whose conduct would be followed in the community. This was a return to the Socratic emphasis on the character of a leader. During the Crusades, management evolved into the code of behaviour for knights known as chivalry, which also stressed morality. It created the manners and mores of the society. The knights treated each other with respect and managed themselves as a group of equal partners. This attitude carried over to the Romanesque period as households combined to create cottage industries. Each neighbour was in charge of a specific process in the creation of a final product and they worked as a unified team without a formal leader. During the Gothic era cathedrals became the centre of town, where citizens gathered for religious services, town meetings, and markets. The size of the cathedrals created complex projects over many decades of construction. As a result, the Gothic period introduced the art of long-term planning and systematic project management.

The tools and techniques of construction grew more sophisticated as time progressed. Builders during the Byzantine Empire utilised ramps, levels, levers, pulleys, and winches as well as the mathematical concepts of angles and arches. These builders improved the supporting structure of domes and the use of buttresses. The Islamic Golden Age added new forms of the crane and decorative arts. Additionally, the Islamic community developed the craft of sculpting and the use of marble, composites, and metal as building materials. During the Crusades the predominant purpose of buildings was as protection against invaders, which required thick exterior and interior walls, round turrets, and the creation of moats. The need for security and the labour necessary to erect such sturdy castles brought about innovations in cranes, ramps, pulleys, and winches. Complementing these innovations were improvements in stonemasonry, including faster production and shorter construction times. The Romanesque period saw the creation of interior design, designating rooms for specific purposes. The comfort of residences became a focal point, with innovations in heating, cooling, plumbing, and running water. During the Gothic period builders began to study the use of height to create better lighting in cathedrals. This required certain key innovations like flying buttresses, rib vaults, and pointed arches. These structural devices created tall structures that maximised the availability of interior light. To construct their cathedrals Gothic builders returned to the treadmill, which allowed for control of the compass and clasp arms and provided more control of horizontal and vertical movements. As a result of all these innovations, their architects developed the habit of testing the stability of buildings first using small-scale models.

From the Byzantine Empire to the Gothic period, the repertoire of the master builder as architect expanded to include both functional and decorative design. The design process began to take into account the proposed use of the building, the impact of nature's elements on the building, and the residents' desire for comfort. In the Byzantine age, the master builders became the conduit for communications between the client, usually the church, and the workers, although the work was overseen by a government official and there was a distinction between architect and engineer. The master builder was becoming a project manager. During the Crusades, building management and knowledge of technology were transmitted by word of mouth in master builder guilds. Later, the master builders began to document their architectural designs and worked to educate each other on construction techniques and project management. During the Romanesque period, the workers began to organize themselves into guilds of specific crafts and trades, which created monopolies and managerial challenges for master builders.

In summary, the master builder continued as the master architect, designer, and planner while the structures they created became more complex. His role as project manager increased with this design complexity and with increased administrative demands. The selection of materials and design focused on strengthening the support structures of the building. In addition to supervising the specialised crafts and trades, the master builder added the role of educator to his list of responsibilities. The greater complexity of buildings also created the need for the master builder to develop skills in long-term planning.

On the whole, therefore, this period saw the evolution of project management towards greater maturity. Many of the older traditions were preserved and carried forward in the more complex designs demanded by changing historical and scientific realities. Construction tools and techniques developed to include greater use of cranes and treadwheels, which allowed buildings to grow in thickness and height. Some structural innovations were introduced including the flying buttress. Increasing sophistication was evident in the responsibilities of the master builder. Labour also became more organized in the Medieval period with the rise of the trade guilds. All of these factors contributed to the robust expansion of project activities and the refinement of project management.

## 4.3 History of Project Management from the Renaissance to the Industrial Revolution

### 4.3.1 Renaissance

#### 1. Construction Technology, Culture, and Science

Culturally, emerging capitalism, the spirit of exploration and enterprise, and the Catholic Church were the predominant influences on construction during the Renaissance. There was a new openness to the world, a delayed consequence of the Crusades combined with augmented shipbuilding that allowed travel. There was a general attitude of adventure, innovation, and challenge to tradition. Even as the ancient classics were being taught with vigour, the educated struck out to conquer new realms for Europe, demonstrating outward expression rather than introversion. This represented as well the new capitalistic spirit of entrepreneurs and businessmen who had wrested power from the old feudal nobility. As part of this endeavour, new buildings were conceived that shattered all preconceptions, such as the dome on Florence Cathedral (1420–1436 AD). The church asserted its power simultaneously and turned to build its own most impressive base with St. Peter's Cathedral (1506–1626 AD), intended to express and symbolize the eternal glory of Rome. Generally speaking, the building projects were inspired by the church, but the attitude needed to construct them was one of scientific openness and humanistic exploration. The glory went as much to men as to God.

The scientific experimentation of the Renaissance leads one to postulate innovative machinery and construction procedures. With the turn to empirical observation of natural processes, such as in Galileo's emphasis on geometry, and the stress on methodical inquiry to solve problems, one expects that a similar trend would have influenced building. In fact, this turns out to be true. Construction technology to create Renaissance architecture included the reversible hoist, a mobile crane on rollers with a hoist, a lifting device with pincers, a bell-lifting device with a counterweight, screw-operated lifting devices, and pile drivers, with all of the energy used to operate these machines taken from human and animal labour (Institute and Museum of the History of Science). The renewed interest in scientific principles also enabled engineers to harness hydraulic power for machinery (Institute and Museum of the History of Science).

However, the most enduring example of this scientific influence was Brunelleschi's ox-hoist crane, which was considered a marvel by other Renaissance scientists. This device was designed for the construction of the Florence Cathedral dome. Using the power of hitched oxen circling a post, it not only increased the lifting capacity for materials (like stone beams and marble slabs) using far less power, but included a reversible gear that sped up the hoisting process far beyond anything before. Brunelleschi also invented machines for lateral positioning of material. This was the radical innovation indicative of the Renaissance use of science that contributed to the future of engineering.

Brunelleschi's dome was substantial in another way. His proposed method of construction reflected the audacity of the Renaissance. He claimed that he could build the dome without scaffolding or centring, which had never been done. The revolutionary method he improvised used herringbone masonry, by which stones were laid sloping inward, and was accomplished with teams of masons moving around the perimeter in successive rings. In addition to this, the double-skinned dome he supervised was unique in its structural separation of the inner from the outer, which created a new style and enhanced its structural integrity (Gärtner 88). Its octagonal vault form stands without buttresses, struts, or transverse chains, supported only by a skeleton of ribs freed from wall supports. This style and technology signified the end of medieval building (Walker 77).

The Renaissance was a time of style. There was a renewed stress on classical and harmonic forms and ornamentation. The same kinds of arches, domes, and columns were used as a reflection of past proportion and design. Yet often they were simply aesthetic components of a structure, a mere homage to the classical world thought to be so perfect and beautiful. This was clear in Alberti's façade for Santa Maria Novella (1456–1470 AD). He shaped his design to mimic the Roman triumphal arch with a Greek pediment, and used columns for purely decorative purposes.

## 2. Master Builder, Labour, and Management

Perhaps the Renaissance was most notable for its varied contributions to the concept of project management. Several factors influenced project management during the Renaissance through to the seventeenth century. For one thing, algebra and the decimal method changed the way accounting was done (Morris). In addition, the skilled labour came from the guilds. Some of the building – for example, at Florence – was in fact controlled by wool and stonemason guilds. What is interesting is that the guilds, for the first time in project history, organised competitions to make design and building decisions. This reflected the new Renaissance attitude towards innovation and ingenuity of design and style. It further reflected the social context of capitalism that emphasized competition.

Other general trends in management may have had an impact on labour. The so-called Protestant work ethic turned hard work into a virtue. If the workers and builders adopted this attitude, they might have found themselves more motivated by higher goals to do a good job. In addition, there was a rising individualism that told people they were more active and influential in shaping their lives. Finally, the process of work moved towards further specification and efficiency with reductionism, which dissected the production process and eliminated wasteful elements. At the end of the day, there were still hard-working skilled labourers from the guilds who plied their trade honestly in pursuing the master builder's aims and designs.

It is possible that the master builders adopted the Machiavellian attitude of self-interest and power. Not applied for political purposes but to building, this makes sense in the Renaissance context where builders strove for reputation to distinguish themselves from others and thus acquire new building contracts as a reward. The Machiavellian emphasis on realism and expedients is relevant as well, since the moral aspect of the master builder faded while the concern for practical real-life problem solving heightened. The master builder was neither conceived of as an honourable or chivalrous knight nor as a moral political sage whose temperament and moral character defined his position. Rather, the master builder was renowned simply on the basis of the skills he brought to the job, although it is doubtful that he cared more about being feared or violent than about being admired and respected by his labour force, consultants, and assistants. In this sense, he fulfilled the Machiavellian ideal, free of moral judgment, if he could complete the project with excellence and thus win some form of power for himself. This may have been the motive behind much of Renaissance leadership and engineering.

St. Peter's required many different master builders over its centuries of construction, such as Bramante, Sangallo, Michelangelo, della Porta, and Bernini. All these builders worked independently but under church authority and with a church budget. The builders altered the design occasionally because it involved grafting a new, more magnificent domed structure onto an existing basilica, although Michelangelo in the end re-emphasized the original design.

The master builder Brunelleschi demonstrated much about the work of Renaissance master builders. He was hired to build the dome without previous architectural experience and on the strength of his design proposal, which won in a competition. This method itself looked forward to later procedures for bidding on construction jobs, although now no one would hire an inexperienced contractor. Brunelleschi was also granted freedom to be innovative. His management of new building processes was not discouraged but encouraged. The safety record on site was impressive despite the fact that no centre scaffolding was used. Crucially as well, Brunelleschi designed instruments for building. He was not only an architect but an inventor of machines. This was encompassed in his job description and reflected the general Renaissance mentality. Finally, Brunelleschi was part of the tradition. He believed fervently that the designer should also be the builder, involved in all aspects and phases of the work. He did not separate the role of architect from that of craftsman or engineer.

What is most clear in the Renaissance is the renewed concept of separating design from construction. This notion was present in the Byzantine age with the clear distinction between architect, manager, and engineer. It becomes more defined in this period with Alberti's rebellion against the master builder tradition. His participation in the construction of Santa Maria Novella was strictly on the design end. He sent his designs through a moderator to the work site where the engineers and builders worked. Alberti did not supervise the construction. His philosophy was that design was a specialised field that did not require the designer to be familiar with materials or working methods, which were better known by skilled craftsmen like master masons. In other words, he saw design as distinct from implementation. It is likely that his education had not been through the trade guilds but remained on the intellectual level. This was the version of the debate that most clearly presaged the changes in the Industrial Revolution, where Alberti's view triumphed over that represented by Brunelleschi.

### 4.3.2 Baroque

### 1. Construction Technology, Culture, and Science

Baroque architecture from the late seventeenth century onwards was fully determined by the cultural interests of the Christian churchs, whether Catholic or Anglican. It was an expressive form designed to counteract the Reformation view of simplicity. As part of the counter-Reformation, the Baroque was reactionary and wished to reassert the dominance of the church through the display of florid, dynamic, and powerful forms that would move its audience to recognize ecclesiastical power. To this end, it invented a style based on curves and emotionality, eliminating a more linear and transcendent style common in Roman predecessors which was meant to replicate harmony and peace. The Baroque wanted noise and dynamism.

Out of this cultural requirement, the unique form of the risalit was used to build façades. This changed design, support planning, and material strength (Cohen).

Room designs were altered to allow impressions of greater space and more curving shapes. The technology used to do this was not radically different, although some new mechanical devices might have been used along with innovative techniques in brick manufacture and laying (Marconi).

In addition, the Baroque both reflected and amplified the rigid social structure, which combined with global changes in finance and commerce to create a desire in the new rich to exert their power through building and to gain power using building (Houston and Snell). This was evident in Baroque palaces such as designer François Mansart's Château de Maisons (1642) near Paris.

During this period, European culture experienced the Scientific Revolution. This rational and empirical shift away from recognized authority had profound implications. The changes brought about in scientific methodology and modes of reasoning with Bacon and Descartes had a formative impact on Newtonian natural science. The laws of nature started to be explained, beginning with the mathematical formulation of the theories of gravity, motion, thermodynamics, and entropy. The development of algebra and logarithms alongside the establishment of heliocentrism and technological advances in calculators, microscopes, telescopes, and other tools allowed nature to be viewed, described, and understood in unprecedented ways.

Generally speaking, however, despite the Scientific Revolution that occurred at the same time, construction technologies did not change much in the Baroque period. This can be explained by a cultural lag. The scientific changes were so important that it took years to ingest their significance fully. As a result, the impact occurred later, during the Industrial Revolution. This is not to say that Baroque buildings did not reflect the historical conditions of the time. Christopher Wren's St. Paul's Cathedral (1667–1711 AD) clearly represented a logical Baroque worldview.

## 2. Master Builder, Labour, and Management

The emphasis on natural laws and moral standards during this time might have influenced management practises. More significant, however, was the logical and mathematical approach to knowledge and problems. This signified an analytical viewpoint trained to distinguish between things rather than to see them holistically. As a result, architecture and technology were separated. Technology continued to become associated with the role and expertise of engineers rather than designers (Cohen).

The new scientific methods had an impact on the master builder's role. This is clearly evident in the case of Sir Christopher Wren at St. Paul's in London. While he was considered an architect in the sense of design, he also encompassed the role of building supervisor, although this was primarily through the delegation of tasks. His principal role was design (Downes 15). He operated with a large staff of employees out of an office. That was where contracts were drawn up for a panoply of skilled labour, including masons, carpenters, bricklayers, plumbers, painters, carvers, and organ builders, and building materials like stone, lime, and sand (Beard 28). This was a substantial move towards the modern notion of architect, continuing the trend started in the Renaissance and forming a transition to the later industrial period.

The design process itself also mattered. Wren built numerous models of various plans over the years. These were subject to rejection or ratification by the vote of different parties, who debated factors like style and expense. Some have seen here an almost arbitrary process (Soo 462). What is important is that design was continually altered through the building process, affecting the unity of the building. Yet each new design was limited in possibility by its construction. With Wren, one sees a master builder primarily focused on design with a team of engineers in an office. On the jobsite were the skilled master craftsmen responsible for implementing the design under the leadership of the engineers. This moves substantially towards the modern notion of architect, continuing the trend started in the Renaissance and forming a transition to the later industrial period.

### 4.3.3 Industrial Revolution

### 1. Construction Technology, Culture, and Science

The cultural changes during the nineteenth-century Industrial Revolution were perhaps more than in any previous era forces for change in construction technology. The way things were built was irrevocably altered as a result of the wholesale societal changes that took place, spurred on by new forms of social organisation and scientific thought patterns. The critique of received authority which began in the Scientific Revolution came to fruition during the Industrial Revolution and its building programs. It is arguable that this was the most important era in the history of human work and building because of the realisation of new designs, new materials, and new practises made possible through mechanisation and mass production.

The two main cultural forces during this time were capitalism and urbanisation. Capitalism was linked with a global system of colonialism, made possible through Renaissance exploration. The Europeans had sailed all over the world and set up colonies and shipping networks, often violently and exploitatively, which had introduced new types of products, a new wealth, and a new political power into Europe. By nature, the capitalist system is expansionist. It seeks new markets and new ways to find cheap labour and transportation. During the Industrial Revolution capitalism underwent its greatest expansion and became the sole viable form of economic exchange in Europe. It also set up a conflict between labour and capital, a variation of the old conflict between peasants and nobility. Because it was based on a competitive "free" market, capitalism inherently sought labour-saving and time-saving devices by which it might increase efficiency and productivity. In other words, manufacturing and production processes were sped up through specialisation (division), automation, mechanisation, routinisation, and other alienating forms of production in which the human being was less a personality at work and more a replaceable cog in a much larger system.

This changed the way construction products were made. The concept of capitalism itself envisioned the mass production system and then made it a reality.

Furthermore, with the rise of the factory and the mechanisation of labour, farming began a decline and people flocked to the cities to find other types of work. Added to this there were advances in medicine which meant that population increased in urban areas, creating congestion and the rise of a new type of city. As a cultural force, urbanisation required new forms of uniform housing that demanded quick and cheap construction. They needed to be able to house numerous people as well. Thus, much of architecture was driven by the changing cultural needs.

The most important cultural factor remained capitalism. This shaped political ideas to allow all the radical changes to occur. Capitalism required the exploration and exploitation of natural resources for energy to fuel its projects and for new products to sell. It also required new transportation networks to get its products and materials moved around quickly and easily. This led to a demand for bridges, such as over the Menai Straits, canals, and railroads. The whole system of capitalism, based on competition between services and products, urbanisation, and the reorganisation of modes of production, was driven to create buildings for its new industries and employees. The new methods could be carried out easily. What was important was that the cultural context of these new socio-economic realities formed the groundwork of the Industrial Revolution and its building programs, expertise applications, and capacities.

Scientifically, it started with power. Science and the cultural change went hand in hand and it is hard to say which came first. Nevertheless, the science of the Industrial Revolution and prior to it created the technological skills and thought patterns that made possible new forms of work organisation and the single most important achievement, the steam engine.

Steam engines burnt large quantities of coal or wood rather than relying on human energy. They increased the output of machines to pull, lift, push, and move far in excess of any previous cranes or pulleys. Dirt could be moved by machines without hand shovels. Carts and animals were replaced by steam-powered locomotives that could carry more and move quickly. Human labour became more and more obsolete, except as it was necessary to manipulate machine-driven processes. The labour force was reduced. Productivity rose. The standard of living and expectations typically rose as well, although the way people made money changed. The cost of mass-produced goods went down because of greater efficiency and productivity.

These new forms of technology based on steam power required roads and canals, so the landscape changed. Machines were also used to build roads. Tracks were laid and bridges were built to allow machines to travel. All this meant that materials for building could be easily, cheaply, and quickly shipped from distance to the work site. Speed and ease were the keywords.

Within this context of massive cultural, scientific, and technological upheaval, construction was revolutionized in parallel ways, taking advantage of all the new motives and advances. One example of this was Thomas Telford's Menai Suspension

Bridge (1819–1825 AD), which reflected the cultural and scientific environment of the Industrial Revolution in several ways. In the first place, it was built of iron, a new material made possible by changes in mining and smelting. Iron building was not done prior to the Industrial Revolution. Secondly, its design used new mathematical principles. Telford's bridge formed a single semicircular arch composed of five cast-iron ribs. Most importantly, Telford applied the principle of suspension. The road was literally hung from iron chains that were linked to towers of anchored masonry. Such techniques were not possible earlier. Finally, Telford's bridge represented an expansion of the road and railway network that was essential to the Industrial Revolution. It was a symbol of the changing landscape and the acceleration of transportation caused by the steam engine.

A different kind of example comes at the Crystal Palace (June 1850–May 1851). Paxton's design illustrated several important aspects of social change and construction technology in the Industrial Revolution. Its use of plate glass and iron continued the change in materials, both of which were made possible by production advances in glass and iron factories. This was as important as the Roman invention of concrete. It challenged masonry because these materials were less expensive, thinner, and stronger for the construction of skeletons. All of the pieces of the Crystal Palace were prefabricated in factories, transported quickly by rail to the site, and assembled. This exemplified the factory system for the mass production of tools and material parts for building. As a cultural symbol this building was important too. It was disassembled and moved to another location. Never before in history had such a large structure been mobile in this way, nor had building been executed so quickly. These features signified the changing conditions of life.

A final example was the Eiffel Tower (1887–1889). Also built quickly given its grand scale, this wrought-iron tower was made out of thousands of prefabricated parts that were connected with bolts and rivets. Thus it represented industrial construction. Structurally its design applied another new principle, that of the rigid truss frame, which united stanchion and beam and made the load light going through the ribs into the piers. Its openness nullified the wind effect. These novel design ideas, guided by advanced mathematics, demonstrated the new capabilities of industrial building. Furthermore, the process of building advanced using machines such as steam-powered derricks and windlasses, with scaffolding, and utilised the elevator – a new technology – to lift materials upward. Aesthetically it was a horror to many, but this reflected what a great evolution had been occasioned in construction technology through cultural and scientific pressures.

## 2. Master Builder, Labour, and Management

In the Industrial Revolution, the professional designer and the professional construction manager received their definitive separation. The process leading to this had its founding in the Byzantine period. Then in the Renaissance the issue was clearly raised as a debate between the traditional master builder, who comprised multiple roles linked with design, craft, and building, and the pure designer. The Baroque period moved further in this direction with the separation of designer and engineer, the latter responsible for the actual technological process of building and craft supervision. Yet it was the final period in the 1800s where the two roles were severed entirely.

After this, their only interaction was communication, which took place efficiently through telegraphs, telephones, and improved systems of information delivery. The professional manager held ultimate responsibility for construction, while the designer's authority with respect to the client receded. On-site work done by subcontractors was managed by large general contractors who provided the supervising engineers. This change was a direct consequence of the arrangement of work in the Industrial Revolution, where specialisation was given new dimensions and management sped up to keep pace with the quickening of material manufacturing, steam-powered machine labour, and transportation systems. It also was necessitated by the increase in the mathematical and mechanical knowledge of structures. It became difficult if not impossible for one person to understand the complicated mathematics of design and materials, and to apply this within the field of craftsmanship and building. With increasing information through new media, it was also difficult to keep abreast of current technological advances.

All of these changes were evident in the three buildings discussed above. In the case of the Eiffel Tower, the new system of bidding out design contracts – one that harkened back to Renaissance competitions – is clear. Eiffel was not a single man but a design firm under his direction, and his company won the contract over 100 other bidders. With Telford, Paxton, and Eiffel, fresh designs using different materials were implemented based on new principles of mathematics and production. In each case, the site work was managed efficiently by the contractor, not by the architect. The contractor coordinated subcontracted labour in these buildings. The sites were organised with sophistication based on premanufactured materials and mechanisation of the worksite. Craft guilds vanished, replaced by contractors to improve productivity and uniformity. The designer made designs off-site and submitted them to the contractor. Architecture moved away from involvement with construction. The master builder tradition disappeared with this professionalised split.

The change to labour was in the reduction of the amount of manpower necessary given the ascendancy of the new machines and the mechanisation of all processes formerly requiring human and animal muscle. The work force reduced although the scale of the building projects increased. Labourers were required to possess increased specialisation, and may have been guided in their work practises by the Protestant notion of the intrinsic value of work. In addition, knowledgeable people were needed to run machines. The notion of the guild dissipated, transformed now into the industrial labour union that tried to negotiate wages against entrepreneurial capitalists who built to make money. Subcontractors and contractors managed their own labourers under the overarching eye of the general contractor. The architect, who was now a pure designer, played no role in the management of craft builders or engineers.

Much of the management thought during this time influenced the way labour was organised in the factory system. A great deal of scrutiny was applied towards increasing worker motivation and productivity through incentives. The division of labour into specialised tasks was amplified. Manufacturing processes were simplified and reduced, with their unnecessary elements eliminated. Production was standardized and submitted to quality-control procedures, increased surveillance, and monitoring. This entire culture was in the service of profit.

All of these management theories, driven by a social scientific thrust, combined to lay the groundwork for twentieth-century management techniques, epitomized by Taylor's *The Principles of Scientific Management* (1911), which extends beyond the time period of this investigation. They reflect the growing need in the Industrial Revolution for the creation of a professional class of managers. Many of the ideas would have been adopted by industrial contractors in their supervision of work processes, although only in an elementary form. As such the Industrial Revolution, both in its social and technological influences, prepared for later generations of project managers.

### 4.3.4 From the Renaissance to the Industrial Revolution – Conclusion

Drastic changes took place during the early modern period, culminating in the virtual overthrow of the master builder tradition and the revolution of mass production during the Industrial Revolution. Evidence for these changes has been presented in the research, analysis, and synthesis of the cultural, scientific, managerial, technological, and professional areas related to this historical period. The impact of these changes can now be evaluated. During this time Europe saw the construction of many notable buildings, including Florence Cathedral with its massive dome, the façade of the Santa Maria Novella, St. Peter's Basilica, St. Paul's Cathedral, and, with the origin of iron as a construction material, the Menai Suspension Bridge, the Crystal Palace, and the awe-inspiring Eiffel Tower. The completion of all of these projects represents the specific organisation and technology of the project management characteristic of early modern construction. They reflect the early modern cultural environment within which the project activities took place, the knowledge environment which facilitated problem solving, decision making, and the development of skills, the general management skills which determine resource allocation and optimisation, early modern construction techniques and execution, and the professional tradition that organized the labour and management of the projects.

The period between the Renaissance and the Industrial Revolution focused on the revival and improvement of Greek and Roman knowledge in science and mathematics. The acquisition and employment of new knowledge produced significant changes in how people worked, how and where they lived, and how quickly products such as building materials could be produced. Individuals in society began to question the theories of earlier generations, which lost their authoritative hold on society. They began to accumulate new knowledge through empirical evidence and the integration of science and mathematics. Sir Francis Bacon introduced the process of inductive reasoning, which required scholars to consider all the evidence. During the Scientific Revolution, new instruments of measurement, such as microscopes, barometers, and calculators, came into existence. Scholars began to understand the physical principles of natural phenomena such as gravitation, thermodynamics, and motion. From the Renaissance, which spawned this new empirical openness, through to the Scientific Revolution, the traditional worldview was challenged. This created an environment in which construction evolved.

Other important factors contributed to this change. During the Renaissance, feudalism was exchanged for an emerging capitalism that expanded its influence over the following centuries. The land-owning nobility lost power to the rising entrepreneurs and businessmen, who began to gear politics in their favour. The economic system of capitalism became the fundamental basis for organizing societies. This switch encouraged Europe to find fresh sources of raw materials and different markets into which to sell their increased output, leading to the expansion of trade and European colonisation of the world. Another important change was the movement towards secularisation during the Baroque period. Society began to question the answers given by the church. The Industrial Revolution was rooted in these two important changes and in the Scientific Revolution. It took advantage of science and secularisation for economic purposes by using new knowledge to create new machinery driven by steam power. This machinery reduced the need for human labour and increased the amount of output while decreasing the time it took to manufacture that output. The result was a system of highly regulated factories in which productivity and efficiency were implemented as never before possible. Their products were sent out across the new network of rails and canals, changing the visible landscape and altering societal structures, including buildings.

General management evolved at the same time as more sophisticated knowledge was acquired. During the Renaissance, the theory of management was greatly influenced by the writings of Niccolò Machiavelli and his emphasis on self-interest and power and motivating factors. He recommended that leaders control the emergence of self-interest through management by fear. The Protestant reformers simultaneously changed the attitude of individuals regarding labour. The Protestants and later the Puritans introduced a number of ideas including reductionism, individualism, and later the Protestant work ethic that resonated strongly in the spirit of modern management. Calvin and Luther believed that work was not a necessary evil but a way to serve God. In the Baroque period, rational secularism displaced the religious stranglehold on knowledge, and people began to use reasoning to figure out how processes worked and why certain rules were in place. Protestants ideas were later incorporated into both the philosophy of seventeenth-century Newtonianism during the Scientific Revolution and the eighteenth-century philosophy of liberalism, including Adam Smith's capitalism. This formed the foundation for Frederick Taylor's Scientific Management.

A greater emphasis on rationality led to the idea that everyone had the ability to make choices, obey laws, and adhere to moral standards. These ideas combined in the Industrial Revolution with analytical techniques geared towards improving factory management through motivation and rewards for productivity. Taylor's scientific management at this time focused on work simplification, time studies, resource allocation, production standardisation, work planning, cost accounting, quality control, and interchangeable parts; everything that makes up the current curriculum of an MBA program. Not only did scientific management lead to the general management skills of the twentieth century, it also led to the two forefathers of twentieth century project management, Henry Gantt and Henri Fayol, formulating their project management tools and the core elements of knowledge for contemporary project management. These finally evolved into the project management body of knowledge.

With the expanded duties of scientific management, leaders shifted from management by fear to a more civilised method of management by reason and morality. The social, cultural, and scientific milieu inspired important developments in construction technology. The Renaissance combined art and architecture with technology to produce new means of construction. This included many new machines such as the reversible hoist, a mobile crane on rollers, screw-operated lifting devices, and the various machines devised by Brunelleschi to build his impressive dome in Florence. At the same time, advances in the creation of power were taking place through the efforts of Renaissance inventors. Hydraulic and wind power were used for the first time since the faltering Greek efforts to power machinery. Because of these innovations, buildings could be constructed within the lifetime of the master builder, whereas previously structures had taken generations and multiple builders.

During the Baroque period design and construction were influenced by increased knowledge of the properties of raw materials and the development and mastery of new tools of production. The division of work between the architect and the engineer was becoming more apparent. Often buildings were designed by one man, but the building was done by engineers who oversaw teams of skilled craftsmen. The architect increasingly moved towards design and model building, as was the case with Wren. The engineer was increasingly seen as a master of technology. This furthered the cause of Alberti, who in the Renaissance had designed buildings without being involved in their actual construction.

The Industrial Revolution gave birth to steam power and mass production, leading to easier means of transporting raw materials to construction sites and new forms of energy to power machines. Tools and parts were fabricated in factories and made of metal. Urbanisation required that construction costs be lowered. An increase in the number of buildings needed created an increase in the buildings' capacity to house people. This increased production of housing at a lower cost could only take place with the integration of new tools, machines, and energy into the construction process.

The period from the Renaissance to the Industrial Revolution witnessed the segregation of master builder responsibilities into three specialized areas: design, engineering, and craft. The application of the new scientific findings to the process of constructing a building increased the need for a different person to create and execute each specialisation. One person could not perform all three tasks simultaneously as in previous eras. During the Baroque period the master builder was an archite was responsible for design, construction, and hiring others to do the constru The focus was on design, but management and on-site duties were still requ, including consultation with engineers and master craftsmen. During the Industrial Revolution, building design became more theoretical and the separation between design, engineering, and project management evolved still further. The role of the construction specialist emerged to coordinate the work of different types of artisans and manage the construction project. This role was performed by the general contractor or project manager – a new phenomenon spawned out of the context of the Industrial Revolution. By the 1900s the concept of a master builder had been completely replaced by the concept of a number of professionals who specialised in architecture, engineering, and construction project management. This specialisation had the advantage of allowing individuals to contribute their best skills and interests to the construction of a building.

Thus, building construction experienced new and important shifts going through the Renaissance into the Industrial Revolution. These transitions in project activities were culturally and scientifically dictated by important new social realities such as capitalism, secularism, urbanisation, and the Scientific Revolution. In response to these movements, the construction industry altered its management methods, its organisation, and its technologies. Decisions were made differently. Problems received new solutions. Materials changed to meet new demands. Different skills, tools, and techniques were necessary to meet the new exigencies. The execution of construction projects changed substantially from previous eras. As a result, the master builder tradition ended, with its duties divided between architect, engineer, and project manager in control of skilled craftsmen. This reflected the ongoing evolution of construction projects and made possible the modern notion of project management.

## 4.4 Summary

Based on this chapter's discussion and synthesis of the material, the research is now ready to draw significant conclusions about the history of project management up to AD 1900. The relationship between the historical circumstances formed by each era's cultural and scientific environment and the construction practises and technologies should now be clear. The historical data is supported by relevant examples of building projects within each historical period. By summarizing the findings to highlight their importance at the end of each historical periods, the chapter provide clear, cogent, and significant insight about the history of project management from the earliest times to AD 1900.

The hypothesis of this research has been confirmed in the present chapter. There are indeed significant connections between the broader context of each society and the building models and practises implemented through areas of expertise. In fact, these are determinative for the history of construction. Without the background influences, the building technology and management techniques used by the master builders, architects, engineers, and craftsmen would not have existed as they did. There is a mutual and dynamic interaction between cultural and scientific forces and building. These forces provided the motivation, tools, techniques, methods, and design impetus used in both construction technology and project management. Now the significant conclusion can be drawn with all these connections that will be found in the final chapter.

# Chapter 5

# Conclusion and Recommendation

## 5.1 Conclusion

The definition of project management employed in this research is *the application of knowledge, skills, tools and techniques to project activities to meet project requirements.* It is the very deliberate orchestration of the areas of expertise to complete a specific project. To investigate the history of project management is to gain an understanding of the historical development of the areas of expertise and their application to project activities.

This research identifies six research topics, based on the areas of project management expertise, to guide data collection and the research process. In the contribution to architecture, the research regards "building construction and engineering structures" as the application area of project management. This research study has followed the trajectory of architectural project management, based on its current definition, through twelve eras of architectural history. It has presented, analysed, and synthesised data from each era to show how the cultural and scientific background influenced the orchestration of each area of expertise to complete its specific projects.

Chapter 1 introduced the motivation for the current study, presented a research methodology, and justified its research hypothesis. Chapter 2 provided a detailed literature review conducted to supply the historical data on which the study is based. It followed twelve architectural time periods through the six topics of historical and cultural environment, knowledge and scientific environment, general management, construction technology, master builder tradition, and twenty building project examples.

Chapter 3 presented the data of the earlier chapter and added investigative analysis. Through a careful study of events and practises related to these research categories, the research will trace circumstances at different historical periods that affected the development of the areas of expertise and their application to project activities. As a continuation of the previous chapters, the goals are to recapitulate the historical data and extend its clarity and significance. The analytical presentation provided in chapter 2 was used to develop the interpretive synthesis of the history of project management in chapter 3. By understanding the historical development of the areas of expertise and their application to project activities in this way, the history of project management was revealed.

Chapter 4 was discussion and synthesis. It attempted to merge together the various strands of data to make clear the connections between the cultural/scientific trends and specific construction technologies, and between the management/leadership philosophies and specific labour and master builder practises in project management. It was integrative and followed the categories through the three major epochs of Western civilisation. The point was to try to explain the history of project management as it emerged out of specific cultural, scientific, social, and management-specific contexts. In other words, it presumed to show that the history of project construction tools and techniques and management skills did not happen in a vacuum, but was directly linked with developments and circumstances in other spheres of history. This chapter intended to provide a clear, cogent, and significant insight about the history of project management from the earliest times to AD 1900.

The literature and specific project examples have provided evidence to confirm the hypothesis that circumstances at each historical period affect the development of areas of expertise, such as management, materials, and technology, and their application to project activities. There are no situations in which this is not plausibly the case. Furthermore, the impact of the changes within each era on construction and management practises has been evaluated and made salient for the history of project management up to AD 1900.

The significance of this study rests in its ability to add insight to the existing body of knowledge concerning project management prior to AD 1900. It has attempted to formulate a template for investigation of the history of project management. Moreover, it is hoped that the research contained in this study is a significant contribution to the growth of project management as a discipline. The desire is to raise awareness of the project management profession and its place in history by outlining the key features of that history.

Indeed, to investigate the history of project management is itself to understand the historical development of the areas of expertise and their application to the project activities. The work reviewed in this research study has indicated that project management is as old as humankind and that even ancient history presents the development of different areas of expertise and their application to various project activities. The history of project management shows that it is a dynamic field, changing and evolving in creative and innovative ways to meet the demands of its context. There is nothing static about it. Without this constant development, the ideas we have about construction and the notions that inform project management would lack a solid historical foundation and risk falling into old errors easily avoided through such knowledge.

The investigation into the history of project management becomes clear as the research findings are examined through the organising process of the problem set that was proposed at the outset of the study, namely:

1. The cultural environment in which project activities were performed;
2. The knowledge environment which facilitated problem solving, decision making, and development of the right skills and tools to get the projects done;

3. The general management skills which determined how resources were allocated and optimized;
4. The construction techniques and tools used to execute the project;
5. The professional traditions, which includes the organisation of labour to manage the projects;
6. The project activities, which includes an examination of historically valuable buildings.

Project management has evolved alongside the cultural and knowledge environment. As general management skills, construction tools, and techniques evolved, so did the professional tradition and project activities. It has moved in stride with the fluid and changing cultural and knowledge environments. It has adopted and shared general management skills presented in other spheres, in some cases even inspiring them. It has existed in dynamic interaction with the fields of science, mathematics, economics, politics, and religion down through the centuries. Many of the technological advances in civilisation have come as a response to building projects that challenged the minds and abilities of skilled master builders, engineers, and craftsmen, encouraging them to find new ways to lift heavy materials or build more stable structures, or new ways to express religious worship or national pride. This great and winding path has been traced, dissected, and integrated into a series of important conclusions about the way history, technology, social organisation, and leadership interweave through time and context. A mature cultural environment gives rise to civilisation and leads to various project activities. A mature knowledge environment leads to efficient management skills and sophisticated construction techniques and tools. Mature management skills, construction techniques, and tools allow for a professional tradition. The application of these environments, knowledge, skills, techniques, tools, and traditions to project activities makes project management possible.

Perhaps most importantly, this study has shown in detail how project activities have arrived at where they are today, as the child of the Industrial Revolution and all that came before it. It explains the historical process by which the master builder came to be the designated designer of a structure and not its craftsman or engineer. Its evidence explains the historical and contextual origin of the split between project manager and general contractor. In essence, it tells the story of how contemporary project management became possible.

Previously building projects were erected over decades using thousands of labourers, primitive machines and tools, and hundreds of managers. Today building projects are erected in the span of a year or several years using less labour, more powerful machines, and more efficient management systems. Yet the history of this development shows that at all times great structures are possible, and technology, skills, and management are necessary. The ziggurats and pyramids of ancient days, the Greek temples, Roman amphitheatres, Islamic mosques, and Christian castles and cathedrals were marvels of building construction and used the culture, science, labour, management, and techniques that were historically and readily available.

The same may be said of the great era that moves from Renaissance innovation in dome building to the massive iron and glass towers and suspension bridges of the Industrial Revolution period. All these buildings reflect the glory of their patrons and the strengths and limitations of their science and chronology. Each is magnificent in its own way, and their combined legacies have had an enduring impact on all subsequent building.

This research study has tried to bring this history forward using the analytical category of project management. Various styles of planning, organisation, and construction have been shown to be useful throughout human history. In earlier times project management was not a science, although skilled master builders combined multiple roles that would be impossible today. Applied project management achieved its purpose haltingly without the complexities of today's management practises. Yet without those earlier activities, the field would not have evolved. We owe much to all these efforts from whose gradual evolution has developed the knowledge necessary to give birth to a more contemporary practise.

In the modern era project management was put on a scientific footing. This investigation has journeyed from the earliest times up to the turn of the twentieth century. It stopped just before the two forefathers of twentieth century project management, Henry Gantt and Henri Fayol, codified their project management tools and made lucid the core elements of the project management body of knowledge. As a result of this study, contemporary project management has been placed into perspective. Its significance can be more readily compared with that of earlier models. The conclusions of this study might also contribute to adding to this body of knowledge, having uncovered lost or forgotten aspects of project management that are absent from today's science. It is hoped in any case that, having shown that historical circumstances have inestimably affected the development of project expertise and applications over time, further research can be done to increase the precision and value of both historical and contemporary scientific understandings of project management.

## 5.2 Recommendation for Future Work

Based on the conclusions drawn in this study, the researcher recommends a further full-scale study of the history of project management. The researcher suggests the *areas of expertise* be categorised in further detail. The five areas should be broken down and further elaborated. The "Construction Technology" section of this research should be further disseminated into and investigated in terms of "Building Design and Technology" and "Construction Method and Technology." Besides exploring the cultural and scientific environments, the researcher suggests to investigate the economic environment of each historical period. The researcher will also conduct the investigation into the historical development of the project management of the twentieth century, in which the missing area of expertise of this research study, "Project Management Body of Knowledge (PMBOK)" will be discussed in detail.

### 5.2.1 Research Timeline

The researcher recommends four separate research studies of the history of project management of the following periods:
1. From the Earliest Times to the Classical Antiquity
2. The Medieval Period
3. From the Renaissance to the Industrial Revolution
4. The Twentieth century

### 5.2.2 Research Topics

The researcher also suggests the *areas of expertise* to be categorized in further detail and recommends study of the history of project management in the following topics:

1. Project Management Body of Knowledge (PMBOK)
   Since the historical development of the PMBOK is a twentieth-century event, it will be discussed in detail in the research study, "History of Project Management of the Twentieth Century"
2. Project Environments
   The research will focus on the following topics:
   - Historical and cultural environment
   - Knowledge and scientific environment
   - Geographical and economic environment
3. General Management
   The research will combine general management and interpersonal skills as one topic.
4. Interpersonal Skills *(refer to item 3)*
5. Knowledge of the Application Area
   In the contribution to architecture, the research will regard "building construction and engineering structures" as the application area. In particular, the research will focus on knowledge of the following topics:
   - Build design and technology
   - Construction method and technology
   - The master builder and design-build tradition
6. Application of the expertise areas to the project activities
   The research will employ building examples to demonstrate this topic

### 5.2.3 Research Questions

The constellation of questions that drives the historical investigation will be the following:

*What was the historical development of the following areas during the different specific historical periods selected for analysis?*

1. *PMBOK (of the twentieth century)*
2. *Historical and Cultural Environment*
3. *Knowledge and Scientific Environment*
4. *Geographical and Economic environment*
5. *General Management and Interpersonal Skills*
6. *Building Design and Technology*
7. *Construction Method and Technology*
8. *The Master Builder and Design-Build Tradition*
9. *The Analysis of Building Projects*

In the quest for credible answers to the research questions, the history of project management will be traced and detailed using these topics as directives. It is the application of these environments, knowledge, skills, techniques, tools, and traditions to project activities that makes project management possible.

# Bibliography


Aaboe, Asger. "Scientific Astronomy in Antiquity." *Philosophical Transactions of the Royal Society* 276.1257, 1974. Print.

Abbot, Francis Ellingwood. *Organic Scientific Philosophy: Scientific Theism*. Charleston, SC: BiblioBazaar, 2009. Print.

Abbott, Frank Frost. *A History and Description of Roman Political Institutions*. Boston: Ginn & Company, 1901. Print.

"Academy Papyrus to be Exhibited at the Metropolitan Museum of Art." *The New York Academy of Medicine* 27 May 2005. Web. 29 Mar. 2009. <http://www.nyam.org/news/2493.html>

Ackerman, J.S. "Architectural Practice in the Italian Renaissance." *Journal of the Society of Architectural Historians*, 1954. Print.

Adena, L. *The Enduring Legacy of the Byzantine Empire. CLIO History Journal*, 2008. Web. 27 Mar. 2009. <http://cliojournal.wikispaces.com/The+Enduring+Legacy+of+Byzantium>

Ages, A.T. *Gardner, H*. London: Wadsworth, 2003. Print.

"Albert the Great." *The Masonic Trowel*. Web. 26 Nov. 2009. <http://electroluminescent/Articles/General/about_individual_files/Albert_the_great/Albert_the_greatcoat>.

Alchermes, Joseph. "Spolia in Roman Cities of the Late Empire: Legislative Rationales and Architectural Reuse." Dumbarton Oaks Paper, 1994. Print.

Aldred, C. *Akhenaten: King of Egypt*. London: Thames and Hudson, 1991. Print.

Allen, Rob. "Variations of the Arch: Post-and lintel, Corbelled Arch, Arch, Vault, Cross-Vault Module." *Civilization Collection* 5 Apr. 2009. Web. 11 Aug. 2009. <http://contentdm.lib.byu.edu/u?/Civilization,776>

Altet, Xavier Barral I. *The Romanesque: Towns, Cathedrals and Monasteries*. Köln: Taschen, 1998. Print.

Anastos, Milton V. "The History of Byzantine Science. Report on the Dumbarton Oaks Symposium of 1961." Dumbarton Oaks Papers, 1962. Print.

"Ancient Greece: Culture and Society." UP. Web. 10 Aug. 2009. <http://www.ancientgreece.com/s/Culture/>

"Ancient Greece: Philosophy." *The Discovery Channel* 2009. Web. 10 Aug. 2009. <http://www.yourdiscovery.com/greece/philosophy/index.shtml?cc=US>

The Ancient Egypt Site. Web. 12 Aug. 2009. <http://www.ancient-egypt.org/>

"The Ancient Master Builder." Web. 7 Nov. 2009.
<http://www.masterbuilderfellowship.com/page5.html>

"Ancient Mesopotamia: Science & Inventions." *The Oriental Institute of the University of Chicago.* Web. 28 Mar 2009. <http://oi.uchicago.edu/OI/MUS/ED/TRC/MESO/science.html>

Anderson, James. "Anachronism in the Roman Architecture of Gaul: The Date of the Maison Carrée at Nîmes." *The Journal of the Society of Architectural Historians 60.1* (2001): 68–79. Print.

Anderson, Janeane. *Brunelleschi's Dome: How a Renaissance Genius Reinvented Architecture.* Vinculum (2007): 18–9. Print.

Anderson, William Ballantyne. *Physics for Technical Students: Mechanics and Heat.* New York: McGraw Hill, 1914. Print.

Angelov, D. "The Making of Byzantium." Harvard University 2001. Web. 25 Mar. 2009. <http://www.hks.harvard.edu/kokkalis/GSW1/GSW1/01%20Angelov.pdf>

Anglo, S. *Machiavelli: The First Century.* Oxford: Oxford UP, 2005. Print.

Anthony, David A. *The Horse, the Wheel, and Language: How Bronze-Age Riders from the Eurasian Steppes Shaped the Modern World.* Princeton: Princeton UP, 2007. Print.

Applied History Research Group-University of Calgary. "The Black Death." *The Islamic World to 1600,* 2009. Web. <http://www.ucalgary.ca/applied_history/tutor/islam/mongols/blackDeath.html>

"Architecture and the Medieval Builder." *Wikipedia.* Web. 26 Nov. 2009. <http://en.wikipedia.org/wiki/Architecture#The_medieval_builder >

Arch, J. "Structural Appraisal of the Florentine Gothic Construction System." *Journal of Architectural Engineering,* 2007. Print.

Artz, F.B. *The Mind of the Middle Ages.* Chicago: U of Chicago Press, 1980. Print.

Asbridge, T. *The Crusades: The Authoritative History of the War for the Holy Land.* Hopewell, NJ: Ecco Books, 2009. Print.

Asif, M., and Muneer, T. "Energy supply, its demand and security issues for developed and emerging economies." *Renewable and Sustainable Energy Reviews,* 2007. Print.

Atrisgerinko, V.A. *Origins of the Romanesque.* London: Lund, 2005. Print.

Ballance, Selina. "The Byzantine Churches of Trebizond." *Anatolian Studies,* 1960. Print.

Banister, F. *A History of Architecture on the Comparative Method.* London: Elsevier Science, 2001. Print.

Bard, K. A. *The Oxford Illustrated History of Ancient Egypt.* Oxford: Oxford UP, 2000. Print.

"Baroque Architecture." *Wikipedia.* Web. 11 Aug 2009. <http://en.wikipedia.org/wiki/Baroque_architecture>

Barrett, Matt. "The Byzantine Period." *History of Greece.* Web. 11 Aug. 2009. <http://www.ahistoryofgreece.com/byzantine.htm>

"Basilica of Santa Maria Novella." *Wikipedia.* Web. <http://equipartition/kiwi/Basilica_of_Santa_Maria_Novella>.

Beard, Geoffrey. *The Work of Christopher Wren.* Edinburgh: John Bartholomew, 1982. Print.

Beard, Jeffrey, Loulakis Michael, and Wundrum Edward. *Design-Build: Planning through Development.* New York: McGraw-Hill, 2001. Print.

Bellis, Mary. "Thomas Telford." *About: Inventors. New York Times,* 2007. Web. <http://inventors.about.com/od/tstartinventors/a/Thomas_Telford.htm>

Belozerskaya, Marina, and Kenneth Lapatin. *Ancient Greece: Art, Architecture, and History.* Los Angeles: J. Paul Getty Museum, 2004. Print.

Bennett, David. *The Creation of Bridges: From Vision to Reality.* London: Aurum Press, 1999. Print.

Benson, J.L. "Spiraly Fluted Columns in Greece." *Hesperia,* 1959. Print.

Benson, R. E. *Renaissance and Renewal in the Twelfth Century.* Cambridge: Harvard UP, 1982. Print.

Berg, Christopher. *Amazeing Art: Wonders of the Ancient World.* Mansfield: Quill Press, 2001. Print.

Betts, Richard A. "Structural Innovation and Structural Design in Renaissance Architecture." *Journal of the Society of Architectural Historians* 52.1, 1993. Print.

Bilkadi, Zayn. "Bitumen – A History." *Saudi Aramco World Magazine* 35.6, 1984. Print.

Billings, Malcolm. *The Crusades: Five Centuries of Holy Wars.* New York: Sterling Publishing, 1988. Print.

Bird, S. *The Essential Roman Baths.* London: Scala Publishers, 2007. Print.

Blickle, Peter. Unruhen in der ständischen Gesllschaft 1300–1800. *Enzyklopädie deutscher Geschichte, Bd. 1.* München: Oldenbourg, 1988. Print.

Boardman, J., Griffin, J. and Murray, O. *The Oxford History of Greece and the Hellenistic World.* Oxford: Oxford UP, 2001. Print.

Bonde, S., C. Maines, and Richards, R. "Soils and Foundations." In *Architectural Technology Up to the Scientific Revolution: The Art and Structure of Large-Scale Buildings,* edited by Robert Mark, 16–50. Cambridge, MA: MIT Press, 1993. Print.

Bonde, S., R. Mark, and E. C. Robison. "Walls and Other Vertical Elements." *Architectural Technology Up to the Scientific Revolution: The Art and Structure of Large-Scale Buildings,* ed. Robert Mark, 52–137. Cambridge, MA: MIT Press, 1993. Print.

Bowen, E. "Roman Commerce in the Early Empire." *The Classical Weekly* 14 May 1928: 201–6. Print.

Boyer, Carl B., and Merzbach, Uta. *A History of Mathematics.* New York: John Wiley & Sons, 1968. Print.

Branner, Robert. "Gothic Architecture." *Journal of the Society of Architectural Historians,* 1973. Print.

"Bridge Over the River Rhine 55 B.C." *Wikipedia.* Web. 26 Nov. 2009. <http://lessons-from-history/node/46>

Brotton, J. "Science and Philosophy." *The Renaissance: A Very Short Introduction.* Oxford: Oxford UP, 2006. Print.

Brown, David. *Mesopotamian Planetary Astronomy-Astrology.* Styx Press, 2000. Print.

Brown, Lieca. “Re-visiting Ancient Construction Methods. (Mesopotamian technique known as Geosynthetic Reinforced Soil)(Brief Article).” 1 February 2001. Point of Beginning: *Magazine for Surveying and Mapping Community.* Web. 20 Mar. 2009. <http://www.pobonline.com/Articles/Industry_News/d03a817cac0f6010VgnVCM100000f932a8c0____>

Browne, Edith. *Romanesque Architecture.* Oxford: Blackwell, 2005. Print.

Bruzelius, Caroline. “The Construction of Notre-Dame at Paris.” *The Art Bulletin* 69, Dec 1987. Print.

Buccellati, Giorgio. “Wisdom and Not: The Case of Mesopotamia.” *Journal of the American Oriental Society* 101.1 (1981). Print.

Buci-Glucksmann, C. *Baroque Reason: The Aesthetics of Modernity.* New York: Sage Publications, 1994. Print.

Burckhardt, Jacob. *The Civilization of the Renaissance in Italy.* 1878. Boisestate.Edu. Web. 4 Apr. 2009. <http://www.boisestate.edu/courses/hy309/docs/burckhardt/2-1.html>

Burnett, Charles. “The Coherence of the Arabic-Latin Translation Program in Toledo in the Twelfth Century.” *Science in Context* 14 (2001). Print.

Burney, Charles Allen. *From Village to Empire: An Introduction to Near Eastern Archaeology.* Oxford: Phaidon, 1977. Print.

Butterfield, Herbert. *The Origins of Modern Science, 1300–1800.* New York: Macmillan, 1957. Print.

“Byzantine Legacy.” *Wikipedia.* Web. 26 Nov. 2009. <http://equipartition/kiwi/Byzantine_architecture#Byzantine_legacy>

“Caesar’s Rhine Bridges.” *Wikipedia.* Web. 26 Nov. 2009. <http://equipartition/kiwi/Caesar’s_Rhine_bridges>

Cahill, T. *Mysteries of the Middle Ages: And the Beginnings of the Modern World.* New York: Anchor Press, 2008. Print.

Capra, Fritjof. *The Science of Leonardo; Inside the Mind of the Great Genius of the Renaissance.* New York: Doubleday, 2007. Print.

Carlsson, Bo. “The development and use of machine tools in historical perspective.” *Journal of Economic Behavior and Organization,* 1984. Print.

Carpenter, Rhys. *The Architects of the Parthenon.* Baltimore, MD: Penguin Books, 1970. Print.

Castleden, R. *The Mycenaeans.* New York: Routledge, 2005. Print.

Castles Architecture. “Romanesque Architecture.” Castles Architecture. March 2009. Web. 22 March 2009 <http://www.castles.me.uk/romanesque-architecture.htm>

Charles, V. A. *Gothic Art - Art of Century.* New York: Parkstone Press, 2008. Print.

Chatfield, Carl. “A short course in project management”. Microsoft. Web. <http://office.microsoft.com/en-us/project/HA102354821033.aspx>

Chaudry, M. *Fundamentals of Islamic Economic Systems.* Muslimtents.com, 2003. Web. 22 Mar. 2009. <http://www.muslimtents.com/shaufi/b16/b16_19.htm>

Cheam, Frederick. *Great Cathedrals.* New York: Golden Press, 1974. Print.

Childress, Diana. *Johannes Gutenberg and the Printing Press*, Minneapolis: Twenty-First Century Books, 2008. Print.

"The Chivalry Code." Web. 11 Dec. 2009. <http://www.essortment.com/all/chivalriccode_rxnf.htm>

Chowdhry, Sajjad. "Imam Ghazali on Leadership Ethics." *Dinar Standard*, 18 Jun. 2007. Web. 16 April 2009. <http://www.dinarstandard.com/management/AlGhazali061507.htm>

Claster, Jill N. *Sacred Violence: The European Crusades to the Middle East, 1095–1396*. Toronto: U of Toronto Press, 2009. Print.

Cleland, David I. and Gareis, Roland. *Global Project Management Handbook*. New York: McGraw-Hill Professional, 2006. Print.

Cleland, David I. and Lewis R. Ireland. *Project management: Strategic Design and Implementation*. New York: McGraw-Hill Professional, 2006. Print.

Cochrane, Charles Norris. *Thucydides and the Science of History*. Oxford: Oxford UP, 1929. Print.

"The Code of Chivalry." Web. 11 Dec. 2009. <http://www.baronage.co.uk/chivalry/chivalıa.html>

Cohen, Gary B. and Franz A.J. Szabo. *Embodiments of Power: Building Baroque Cities in Europe*. New York: Berghahn Books, 2008. Print.

Cohen, H. Floris. *The Emergence of Early Modern Science. The Scientific Revolution: A Historiographical Inquiry*. Chicago: U of Chicago Press, 1994. Print.

Colvin, Howard. *A Biographical Dictionary of British Architects: 1600–1840*. 3rd ed. New Haven: Yale UP, 1995. Print.

Conant, K. *Carolingian and Romanesque Architecture, 800–1200*. New Haven: Yale UP, 1992. Print.

Constable, Giles, Benson, Robert L., and Lanham, Carol D. *Renaissance and Renewal in the Twelfth Century*. Cambridge: Harvard UP, 1982. Print.

Contantinou, M. Costas. *States of Political Discourse: Words, Regimes, Seditions*. London: Routledge, 2004. Print

Coppens, Philip. *Socrates, That's the Question*. Feature Articles – Biographies, Philip Coppens.com. Web. 8 Jan 2009

Coppens, Philip. *The Great Pyramid: a Course in Project Management*. The New Pyramid Age, 2009. Web. 8 Jan. 2009. <http://www.philipcoppens.com/nap_art2.html>

Coulton, J.J. "Lifting in Early Greek Architecture." *The Journal of Hellenic Studies*. 1974. Print.

Cowen, Richard. Ancient Irrigation. Chapter 17. Department of Geology: U of California, 1999. Web. 8 Jan. 2009. <http://mygeologypage.ucdavis.edu/cowen/~GEL115/115CH17oldirrigation.html>

Creswell, K. A. C. *A Short Account of Early Muslim Architecture*. Rev. James W. Allan. Aldershot: Scolar Press, 1989. Print.

"The Crusades – Crusade Legacy." Experience Festival.com, 2009. Web. 2 Apr. 2009. <http://www.experiencefestival.com/a/The_Crusades_-_Crusade_legacy/id/1271304>

"Crusades." *The New Catholic Encyclopedia Vol. IV.* New York: McGraw-Hill Book Company, 1966. Print.

"Crusader History 1." *Stronghold Heaven.* Web. 26 Nov. 2009. <http://stronghold/crusader history/crusader3>

"Crusader History 3." *Stronghold Heaven.* Web. 26 Nov. 2009. <http://stronghold/crusader history/crusader3>

Cuff, Dana. *Architecture: The Story of Practice,* Boston: MIT Press, 1991. Print.

"Culture in the Baroque Era." Baroquelife.org, 2008. Web. 27 Mar. 2009. <http://www.baroquelife.org/index.php>

d'Alverny, Marie-Thérèse. "Translations and Translators" in Constable, Giles, Benson, Robert L., and Lanham, Carol D. (eds.) *Renaissance and Renewal in the Twelfth Century.* Cambridge: Harvard UP, 1982. Print.

Daileader, Philip. *The Late Middle Ages.* Audio/video course from The Teaching Company, 2007.

Dalby, Andrew. *Cato: On Farming.* Totnes: Prospect Books, 1998. Print.

Dalley, Stephanie and Olseon, John Peter. "Sennacherib, Archimedes, and the Water Screw: The Context of Invention in the Ancient World." *Technology and Culture* 44.1 (2003). Print.

Dalling, R. *The Story of Us Humans, From Atoms to Today's Civilization.* New York: iUniverse Press, 2006. Print.

Daniels, Peter and Bright, William. *The World's Writing Systems.* Oxford: Oxford UP, 1996. Print.

Dalby, Andrew. *Cato: On Farming,* Prospect Books, 1998. Print

Darby, Hamilton D. "The Oriental Institute of the University of Chicago: Teacher Resource Center, Ancient Mesopotamia: Architecture." Oriental Institute of the University of Chicago. Web. 20 Mar. 2009. <http://oi.uchicago.edu/OI/MUS/ED/TRC/MESO/architecture.html>

Davis, Howard. *The Culture of Building,* Oxford: Oxford UP, 2006. Print.

*"De architectura." Wikipedia.* Web. 12 Nov. 2000. <http://en.wikipedia.org/wiki/De_architectura#cite_note-0>

Degryse, P., Elsens, J. and Waelkens, M. "Study of Ancient Mortars from Sagalassos (Turkey) in View of Their Conservation." *Cement and Concrete Research* (2002): 1457–1463. Print.

Diamond, J. *Guns, Germs and Steel.* New York: W.W.Norton, 2005. Print.

Dinsmore Jr., H. Robert. "The Ancient Master Builders." Master builder. *Fellowship for the Built Environment.* Web. 26 Nov. 2009. <http://fellowshipping/page5.html>

Dinsmore, Paul C. *The Right Projects Done Right!* Chichester: John Wiley and Sons, 2005. Print.

Dlott, A. M. (2007) *Ancient Mesopotamia.* Classics Technology Center. Web. 30 Mar. 2009. <http://ablemedia.com/ctcweb/showcase/dlottmesopotamia1.html>

Dodson, A. *The Complete Royal Families of Ancient Egypt.* London: Thames and Hudson, 2004. Print.

Downes, Kerry. *Sir Christopher Wren: The Design of St. Paul's Cathedral.* London: Trefoil, 1988. Print.

Durant, Will. *The Age of Faith (The Story of Civilization, Volume 4).* London: Simon & Schuster, 1980. Print.

Earnshaw, R. A. *Digital Convergence: Libraries of the Future.* Berlin: Springer, 2007. Print.

Echols, Gordon. "Eiffel Tower." In *International Dictionary of Architects and Architecture,* ed. Randall J. Van Vynckt. *Volume 2: Architecture,* 227-29. Detroit: St. James Press, 1993. Print.

Edson, Armi. "Orders and Continuous Orders in Romanesque Architecture." *Journal of the Society of Architectural Historians* (1975). Print.

Edwards, I.E.S. *The Pyramids of Egypt.* Harmondsworth: Penguin, 1993. Print.

"Edwin Smith Papyrus." *Encyclopedia Britannica.* Web. 29 Mar 2009. <http://www.britannica.com/EBchecked/topic/179901/Edwin-Smith-papyrus>

Eisenstein, Elizabeth L. *The Printing Press as an Agent of Change.* Cambridge: Cambridge UP, 1980. Print.

Ellenblum, R. *Crusader Castles and Modern Histories.* Cambridge: Cambridge UP, 2007. Print.

Elton, H. *Warfare in Roman Europe, AD350–325.* Oxford: Oxford UP, 1996. Print.

Engammare, Max. *On Time, Punctuality, and Discipline in Early Modern Calvinism.* Cambridge: Cambridge UP, 2009. Print.

Erdogmas, Ece, Thomas Boothby, and Elizabeth Smith. "Structural Appraisal of the Florentine Gothic Construction System." *Journal of Architectural Engineering,* 2007. Print.

Erlande-Brandenburg, Alain. *The Cathedral: The Social and Architectural Dynamics of Construction.* Trans. Martin Thom. Cambridge: Cambridge UP, 1994. Print.

Erlich, M. "Crusaders' Castles – The Fourth Generation: Reflections on Frankish Castle-Building Policy During the 13th Century." *Journal of Medieval History,* 2003. Print.

Erman, Adolf. *Life in Ancient Egypt.* London: Macmillan,1984. Print.

Ettinghausen, Richard, Oleg Grabar, and Marilyn Jenkins-Madina. *Islamic Art and Architecture 650–1250.* New Haven: Yale UP, 2001. Print.

"The European Voyages of Exploration." The Applied History Research Group, 2001. Web. 5 Apr. 2009. <http://www.ucalgary.ca/applied_history/tutor/eurvoya/index.html>

Evans, Francis T. "Roads, Railways, and Canals: Technical Choices in 19th-Century Britain." *Technology and Culture,* 1981. Print.

Faiella, Graham. *The Technology of Mesopotamia.* New York: Rosen Publishing Group, 2006. Print.

Falagas, Matthew, Zarkadoulia, Effie, and Samonis, George. "Arab Science in the Golden Age (750–1258 C.E.) and Today" *The Faseb Journal* 20, 2006. Print.

Feldhay, R. *The Cambridge Companion to Galileo: The Use and Abuse of Mathematical Entities.* Cambridge: Cambridge UP, 1998. Print.

Fitchen, John. *The Construction of Gothic Cathedrals: A Study of Medieval Vault Erection.* Oxford: Clarendon Press, 1961. Print.

Fletcher, Sir Banister, and Cruikshank, Dan. *Sir Banister Fetcher's History of Architecture.* "4366-Crusades and the Knights of Malta." Web. 2 Aug. 2009. <http://Marianna/sstudios001.html>

Flower, H. E. *The Cambridge Companion to the Roman Republic.* Cambridge: Cambridge UP, 2003. Print.

Fordham. *Internet Medieval Sourcebook Project.* Web. 18 Jan. 2009. <http://www.fordham.edu/halsall/>

Foster, Benjamin R. and Foster, Polinger Karen. *Civilizations of Ancient Iraq.* Princeton, NJ: Princeton UP, 2009. Print.

Françoise, Micheau. "The Scientific Institutions in the Medieval Near East." *Encyclopedia of the History of Arabic Science* 3. London: Routledge, 1996. Print.

Frankfort, Henri. *The Art and Architecture of the Ancient Orient.* 5th ed. Pelican History of Art. New Haven: Yale UP, 1996. Print.

Freely, John and Cakmak, Ahmet S. *Byzantine Monuments of Istanbul.* Cambridge: Cambridge UP, 2004. Print.

Freeman, C. *Egypt, Greece, and Rome.* New York: Oxford UP, 1996. Print.

"Frederick Taylor, Early Century Management Consultant." *The Wall Street Journal,* June 13 1997. Web. 1 Aug. 2009. <http://www.cftech.com/BrainBank/TRIVIABITS/FredWTaylor.html>

Friedell, E. *A Cultural History of the Modern Age: Baroque, Rococo and Enlightenment.* New York: Transaction Publishers, 2009. Print.

Galileo Galilei. *Il Saggiatore* (*The Assayer,* 1623). In Stillman Drake (trans.) *Discoveries and Opinions of Galileo.* Garden City, NY: Doubleday, 1957. Print.

"The Gantt Chart History." Web. 8 Sep. 2009. <http://www.ganttchart.com/History.html>

Gärtner, Peter J. *Filippo Brunelleschi: 1377–1446.* Köln: Könemann, 1998. Print.

George, S. *The History of Management Thought.* Englewood Cliffs, NJ: Prentice Hall, 1972. Print.

Gilfillin, S.C. "Lead Poisoning and the Fall of Rome." *Journal of Occupational and Environmental Medicine* (1965): 53–60. Print.

Glotz, G. *Ancient Greece at Work.* New York: Alfred A. Knopf, 1926. Print.

Goldberg, Marilyn. "Greek Temples and Chinese Roofs." *American Journal of Archeology,* 1985. Print.

Goldstein, Bernard. "Saving the Phenomena: The Background to Ptolemy's Planetary Theory." *Journal for the History of Astronomy* 28, 1997. Print.

Goldsworthy, A. *The Complete Roman Army.* London: Thames and Hudson, 2003. Print.

Gorini, Rosanna. "Al-Haytham the Man of Experience. First Steps in the Science of Vision." *Journal of the International Society for the History of Islamic Medicine* 2.4, 2009. Print.

*Gothic Art*. Heilbrunn Timline of Art History, 2009. Web. 25 Mar. 2009. <http://www.metmuseum.org/toah/hd/mgot/hd_mgot.htm>

*Gothic Dreams – Appreciating a Cultural Legacy*. Earthlore Explorations, 2009. Web. 27 Mar. 2009. <http://elore.com/Gothic/introduction.htm>

Grafton, Anthony. *Leon Battista Alberti: Master Builder of the Italian Renaissance*. New York: Hill and Wang, 2000. Print.

Granger, F. *Vitruvius on Architecture*. Boston: Harvard UP, 1970. Print.

Grant, Edward. *The Foundations of Modern Science in the Middle Ages: Their Religious, Institutional, and Intellectual Contexts*. Cambridge: Cambridge UP, 1996. Print.

"The Great Pyramid of Giza." Web. 25 Nov. 2009. <http://lessons-from-history/node/44>

Greenburg, Dolores. "Energy, Power, and Perceptions of Social Change in the Early Nineteenth Century." *The American Historical Review*, 1990. Print.

Griffin, Jasper, John Boardman, and Oswyn Murray. *The Oxford History of Greece and the Hellenistic World*. Oxford: Oxford UP, 2001. Print.

Grimal, Nicolas. *A History of Ancient Egypt*. Oxford: Blackwell, 1992. Print.

Guerra, Francisco. "Maya Medicine." *Medical History* (1964): 31–43. Print.

"Guild in European History." *Wikipedia*. Web. 26 Nov. 2009. <http://en.wikipedia.org/wiki//guild#European_history>

Gutzwiller, K. *A Guide to Hellenistic Literature*. New York: Basil Blackwell, 2007. Print.

"The Hagia Sophia." *Wikipedia*. Web. 26 Nov. 2009. <http://wikipedia.org/wiki/Hagia_Sophia#Third_church_.28current_structure.29>

Hakim, Besim S. "Julian of Ascalon's Treatise of Construction and Design Rules from Sixth-Century Palestine." *Journal of the Society of Architectural Historians* (2001): 4–25. Print.

Hall, J. *A History of the Archaic Greek World*. New York: Wiley, 2007. Print.

Hall, Marcia B. *Renovation and Counter-Renovation: Vasari and Duke Cosimo in Sta Maria Novella and Sta Croce 1565–1577*. Oxford: Clarendon Press, 1979. Print.

Halson, J. *Bysantium: A History*. New York: Tempus, 2002. Print.

Hansen, M. *The Shotgun Method: The Demography of the Ancient Greek City-State Culture*. Kansas City: U of Missouri Press, 2006. Print.

Harris, J. *Constantinople: Capital of Byzantium*. London: Continuum Press, 2007. Print.

Harrison, F.L. and Dennis Lock. *Advanced Project Management: A Structured Approach*. Aldershot: Gower., 2004. Print.

Harrison, Peter. *Castles of God: Fortified Religious Buildings of the World*. Rochester, NY: Boydell Press, 2004. Print.

Harvey, William. *De Motu Cordis*. Cited in Debus, Allen. *Man and Nature in the Renaissance*. Cambridge: Cambridge UP, 1978. Print.

Haskins, Charles H. *The Renaissance of the Twelfth Century*. Cambridge: Harvard UP, 1927. Print.

Hassan, Ahmad. "Transfer of Islamic Technology to the West, Part III: Technology Transfer in the Chemical Industries." *History of Science and Technology in Islam.* Web. 30 Mar. 2009. <http://www.history-science-technology.com/Articles/articles%2072.htm>

Hauck, George. *The Aqueduct of Nemausus.* Jefferson, NC: McFarland, 1988. Print.

Heizer, Robert F. "Ancient Heavy Transport, Methods, and Achievements." *Science,* 1966 Print.

Heldman, Kim. *Project Management Jumpstart.* London: SYBEX, 2003. Print.

"Henry Laurence Gantt's legacy to management is the Gantt chart." Web. 1 Aug 2009. <http://www.ganttchart.com/History.html>

Hersey, George L. *Architecture and Geometry in the Age of the Baroque.* Chicago: U of Chicago Press, 2000. Print.

Hillenbrand, Robert. *Islamic Architecture: Form, Function and Meaning.* New York: Columbia UP, 1994. Print.

"The History of Management." Web. 1 July 2009 <http://faculty.cox.smu.edu/~rasberry/web/mn03370_honors/handouts/Management%20History.pdf>

"History of the Organization of Work: Organization of Work in Pre-industrial Times: Medieval Industry." *Britannica Online.* Web.<http://www.britannica.com/EBchecked/topic/1359490/history-of-the-organisation-of-work>

Hoag, John D. *Islamic Architecture.* Milan: Electa, 2004. Print.

Hodge, A. Trevor. "Aqueducts." In *Roman Public Buildings,* ed. Ian M. Barton, 127–49. Exeter: U of Exeter Press, 1989. Print.

Hoffman, Paul. *The Man Who Loved Only Numbers: The Story of Paul Erdös and the Search for Mathematical Truth.* New York: Hyperion, 1998. Print.

Hooker, R. *Rome: The Punic Wars.* Washington State University, 6 Jun. 1996. Web. 31 Mar. 2009. <http://www.wsu.edu/~dee/ROME/PUNICWAR.HTM>

Horace. (n.d.). *Epistulae* 2.1.156f.

Horstmanshoff, H, Stol, Marten, and Tilburg, Cornelis. *Magic and Rationality in Ancient Near Eastern and Graeco-Roman Medicine.* Netherlands: Brill, 2004. Print.

Houston, Rab and Snell, K.D.M. "Proto-Industrialization? Cottage Industry, Social Change, and Industrial Revolution." *The Historical Journal,* 1973. Print.

Hudson, Pat. *The Industrial Revolution.* Washington, DC: Library of Congress, 1992. Print.

Hughes, Donald J. and J.V. Thirgood. "Deforestation, Erosion, and Forest Management in Ancient Greece and Rome." *Journal of Forest History* (1982): 60–75. Print.

Internation Finance Corporation of the World Bank Group. "Bituminous Geomembrane Coletanche ES3." Technical Presentation. Washington, D.C.: The World Bank, 2005. Print.

"Internet Modern History Sourcebook: Industrial Revolution." Fordham.edu. Web. 12 Aug. 2009. <http://www.fordham.edu/halsall/mod/modsbook14.html>

Irwin, Robert. *The Arabian Night: A Companion.* Tauris Parke Paperbacks, 2003. Print.

"Islam and Islamic History in Arabia and the Middle East." Islamcity.com, 2001. Web. 28 Mar. 2009. <http://www.islamicity.com/mosque/ihame/Sec12.htm>

Ismāʿīl, Muhammad Kamal. *The Architecture of the Prophet's Holy Mosque al Madinah*. Ed. Salma Samar Damluji. London: Hazar, 1998. Print.

Jackson, Barbara. *Construction Management Jumpstart*. London: SYBEX, 2004. Print.

James, T. *The British Museum Concise Introduction to Ancient Egypt*. Ann Arbor: U of Michigan Press, 2005. Print.

Jantzen, Hans. *High Gothic: The Classic Cathedrals of Chartres, Reims, and Amiens*. Trans. James Palmes. Princeton, NJ: Princeton UP, 1962.

Jensen, Hans. *Sign, Symbol, and Script*. New York: G.P. Putman's Sons, 1969. Print.

"John Stuart Mill." *Encyclopedia Britannica Eleventh Edition*. Web. <www.britannica.com>

Kähler, Heinz. *Hagia Sophia*. Trans. Ellyn Childs. New York: Praeger, 1967. Print.

Kato, Shiro, Aoki, Takayoshi, Hidaka, Kenichiro, and Nakamura, H. "Finite-Element Modeling of the First and Second Domes of Hagia Sophia." *Hagia Sophia From the Age of Justinian to the Present*, eds. Robert Mark and Ahmet S. Cakmak, 103–31. Cambridge: Cambridge UP, 1992. Print.

Kemp, Barry J. *Ancient Egypt*. London: Routledge, 2005. Print.

Kennedy, H. *The Armies of the Calphs: Military and Society in the Early Islamic State*. New York: Routledge, 2001. Print.

Khaleefa, Omar. "Who Is the Founder of Psychophysics and Experimental Psychology?" *American Journal of Islamic Social Sciences* 16 (1999). Print.

King, Geoffrey. *The Traditional Architecture of Saudi Arabia*. London: I. B. Tauris, 1998. Print.

King, Henry. *The History of the Telescope*. New York: Dover Publications, 2003. Print.

King, Ross. *Brunelleschi's Dome: The Story of the Great Cathedral in Florence*. London: Chatto & Windus, 2000. Print.

Kinney, Dale. "Roman Architecture Spolia." *Proceedings of the American Philosophical Society* (2001): 138–161. Print.

Klein, H. Arthur and Klein, Mina C. *Great Structures of the World*. Cleveland: World Publishing, 1968. Print.

Klotz, Heinrich. *Filippo Brunelleschi: The Early Works and the Medieval Tradition*. New York: Rizzoli, 1990. Print.

Koloski-Ostrow, Anna Olga. "New Perspectives on Ancient Technology and Engineering in Greece and Rome." *Technology and Culture* (2008). Print.

König, Alice. "Knowledge and Power in Frontinus' *On aqueducts*." *Ordering Knowledge in the Roman Empire*, eds Jason König and Tim Whitmarsh, 177–205. Cambridge: Cambridge UP, 2007. Print.

Kostof, Spiro. *The Architect*. Oxford: Oxford UP, 1977. Print.

Kostof, S., Castillo, G., and Tobias, R. *A History of Architecture: Settings and Rituals*. New York: Oxford UP, 1995. Print.

Kraemer, J. *Humanism in the Renaissance of Islam*. London: Brill, 1992. Print.

Kreis, S. *Ancient Western Asia.* Historyguide, 26 Feb. 2006. Web. 31 Mar. 2009. <http://www.historyguide.org/ancient/lecture2b.html>

Kreis, Steven. "Lesson 2: Ancient Mesopotamia." *The History Channel,* 2006. Web. 10 Aug. 2009.

Lahanas, Michael. "Heron of Alexandria." Web. 2 Aug. 2009. <http://mahanas.de/Greeks/HeronAlexandria.htm>

Laiou, A. E. (2002). *The Economic History of Byzantium.* Dumbarton Oaks/Harvard University. Web. 29 Mar. 2009. <http://www.doaks.org/publications/doaks_online_publications/EHB.html>

Lancaster, Lynne C. *"Reconstructing the Restorations of the Colosseum after the Fire of 217."* Journal of Roman Archaeology 11 (1998): 146–174. Print.

Lancaster, Lynne. *Concrete Vaulted Construction in Imperial Rome. Innovations in Context.* Cambridge: Cambridge UP, 2005. Print.

Landels, J.G. *Engineering in the Ancient World.* London: Constable, 2000. Print.

Landow, George P. "The Industrial Revolution: A Timeline." 26 Jan. 2006. Web. 22 Mar. 2009.<http://inventors.about.com/gi/o.htm?zi=1/XJ/Ya&zTi=1&sdn=inventors&cdn=money&tm=62&f=10&tt=14&bt=0&bts=0&zu=http://www.victorianweb.org/technology/ir/irchron.html>

Lasseter, Roland. *All Ye Lands: World Cultures and Geography.* Hong Kong: Catholic Schools Textbook Project, 2002. Print.

Laughlin, Burgess. *The Aristotle Adventure, a Guide to the Greek, Arabic, and Latin Scholars Who Transmitted Aristotle's Logic to the Renaissance.* Flagstaff, AZ: Albert Hale, 1995. Print.

Lawrence, T. E. *Crusader Castles.* London: Michael Haag, 1986. Print.

Lebedel, Claude. *Les Croisades, Origines et Consequences.* Editions Ouest-France, 2006. Print.

"Lecture 26: The 12th Century Renaissance." *The History Guide.* Web. 12 Aug. 2009. <http://www.historyguide.org/ancient/lecture26b.html>

Lehner, Mark. *The Complete Pyramids.* New York: Thames and Hudson, 1997. Print.

Leick, Gwendolyn. *The Babylonians: An Introduction.* London: Routledge, 2003. Print.

*Leonardo da Vinci – Renaissance Man.* BBC, 2007. Web. 4 Apr. 2009. <http://www.bbc.co.uk/science/leonardo/>

"Lessons-from-history." Web. 5 Apr. 2009.<http://lessons-from-history.com/node/48>

Lewis, Archibald. *Nomads and Crusaders: AD 1000–1368.* Indiana UP, 1988. Print.

Lewis, Bernard *What Went Wrong.* Oxford: Oxford UP, 2002. Print.

Lilley, K. *Urban Life in the Middle Ages: 1000–1450.* New York: Macmillan, 2002. Print.

Lindberg, David. "The Theory of Pinhole Images from Antiquity to the Thirteenth Century." *Archive for History of the Exact Sciences* 5 (1968). Print.

Lindberg, David. *Science in the Middle Ages.* Chicago: U of Chicago Press, 1978. Print.

Lloyd, G. *Magic, Reason and Experience: Studies in the Origin and Development of Greek Science.* Cambridge: Cambridge UP, 1979. Print.

Löffler, Klemens. "Humanism." *The Catholic Encyclopedia VII.* New York: Robert Appleton Company, 1910. Print.

*Looking at the Renaissance.* Open University, 2007. Web. 5 Apr. 2009. <http://www.open.ac.uk/Arts/renaissance2/looking-text.htm>

Lorenzen, J. (2009). *Rehabilitating the Industrial Revolution.* Julielorenzen.net, 2009. Web. 4 Apr. 2009. <http://www.julielorenzen.net/berg.html>

Loulakis, Michael C. *Design-Build for the Public Sector.* Gaithersburg, MD: Aspen Publishers, 2003. Print.

Macaulay, David. *Cathedral: The Story of Its Construction.* New York: Houghton Mifflin, 1973. Print.

MacDonald, William. "Some Implications of Later Roman Construction." *Journal of the Society of Architectural Historians* (1958): 2–8. Print.

MacDonald, William Lloyd. *Pantheon: Design, Meaning, and Progeny.* Boston: Harvard UP, 1976. Print.

MacDonald, William L. *The Architecture of the Roman Empire: An Introductory Study.* Rev. ed. 2 vols. New Haven, CT: Yale UP, 1982. Print.

Machiavelli, Nicolò, ***The Prince.*** Trans. W. K. Marriott. 1908. Web. 8 Oct. 2009. < http://www.constitution.org/mac/prince17.htm.>

Marconi, N. "Know how to restore: construction techniques in Baroque Rome – practises, devices and 'secrets.'" *Structural Studies, Repairs and Maintenance of Heritage Architecture IX* . Wessex Institute Press, 2005. Print

Madden, T. *The New Concise History of the Crusades.* New York: Rowman and Littlefield, 2005. Print.

Mainstone, Rowland J. *Hagia Sophia: Architecture, Structure and Liturgy of Justinian's Great Church.* London: Thames and Hudson, 1988. Print.

Makdisi, George. "Scholasticism and Humanism in Classical Islam and the Christian West." *Journal of the American Oriental Society* 109.2) (1989). Print.

Maloney, W.J., and M.P. Maloney. "Pierre Fauchard: the Fauther of Modern Dentistry." New York University College of Dentistry, 2009. Web. 1 Aug. 2009. <http://www.ncbi.nlm.nih.gov/pubmed/19774867>

Man, John. *The Gutenberg Revolution: The Story of a Genius and an Invention that Changed the World.* London: Headline Review, 2002. Print.

"Management: Historical Perspectives" Answers. Web. 1 Feb 2010. <http://www.answers.com/topic/management-historical-perspectives>

Manch, Susan G., Joel F. Henning, and Marcia Pennington Shannon. *Maximizing Law Firm Profitability: Hiring, Training, and Developing.* New York: ALM Properties/Law Journal Press, 2006. Print.

Marconi, N. "Know How to Restore: Construction Techniques in Baroque Rome – Practices, Devices and 'secrets.'" *Structural Studies, Repairs and Maintenance of Heritage Architecture IX.* Southampton: Wessex Institute Press, 2005. Print.

Mark, R. and E.C. Robison. "Vaults and Domes." In *Architectural Technology Up to the Scientific Revolution: The Art and Structure of Large-Scale Buildings*, eds. Robert Mark and Ahmet S. Cakmak, 138–80. Cambridge, MA: MIT Press, 1993. Print.

Mark, Robert and Hutchinson, Paul. "On the Structure of the Roman Pantheon." *The Art Bulletin* (1986). Print.

Marsden, E.W. *Greek and Roman Artillery: Technical Treatises.* Oxford: Clarendon Press, 1971. Print.

"The Masonic Trowel." Web. 28 Mar. 2009. <http://www.themasonictrowel.com/>

Matthies, Andrea. "Medieval Treadwheels. Artists' Views of Building Construction." *Technology and Culture* 33.3, 1992. Print.

McIntosh, Jane R. *Ancient Mesopotamia: New Perspectives.* Santa Barbara, CA: ABC Clio, 2005. Print.

McNeill, Willam H. "In the Beginning." *A World History*, 4th ed. New York: Oxford UP, 1999. Print.

Mejia Gomez, Luis R., David B. Balkin, and Robert L. Cardy. *Management: People, Performance, Change*, 3rd ed. New York: McGraw-Hill, 2008. Print

"Menu." *Introduction to Egypt.* Web. 12 Aug. 2009. <http://www.ancientegypt.co.uk/writing/activity/main.html>

Merolla, Lisa. "3 Mysterious Builds: How Ancient Peoples Move Monoliths." *Popular Mechanics* 21 Aug. 2009. Web. 2 Oct. 2009. <popularmechanics.com/home_journal/workshop/4328400.html>

Meyer, Carol. "How Project Management Developed. Gantt Chart. Project Smart." Project Smart co.uk, 2009. Web. 9 June. 2009. <http://www.projectsmart.co.uk/how-project-management-developed.html>

"Middle Ages". *Encyclopedia Britannica.* Web. 29 Mar 2009. < http://www.britannica.com/EBchecked/topic/195896/history-of-Europe/276200/Christianity-Judaism-and-Islam >

Middleton, Robin and David Watkin. *Neoclassical and 19th Century Architecture.* New York: Abrams, 1980. Print.

Milani, Miriam. "Antiquities of Ancient Rome. Ancient Building Materials." March 2009. Web. 20 Mar. 2009. <http://www.mariamilani.com/ancient_rome/rome_building_materials.htm>

Miller, Keith. *Saint Peter's.* Cambridge: Harvard UP, 2007. Print.

Milo, Francesco. *The Story of Architecture.* New York: Peter Bedrick Books, 1999. Print.

Molleson, Theya and Dawn Hodgson. "The Human Remains from Woolley's Excavations at Ur." *Iraq* (2003): 91–129. Print.

Moorey, P.R.S. *Ancient Mesopotamian Materials and Industries: The Archaeological Evidence.* New York: Oxford UP, 1999. Print.

More, C. *Understanding the Industrial Revolution.* New York: Routledge, 2000. Print.

Morelon, Regis. *General Survey of Islamic Astronomy*, Encyclopedia of the History of Arabic Science, Vol. 1. Routledge, 1996. Print.

Moropoulou, A., A. Bakolas, and S. Anagnostopoulou."Composite Materials in Ancient Structures." *Cement and Concrete Composites* (2005): 295–300. Print.

Morris, N. *Everyday Life in the Renaissance*. New York: McRae Books, 2008. Print.

Mumford, L. *Techniques and Publication*. New York: Harvest Books, 1963. Print.

"Mummies and Mummification." Digital Egypt, 2003. Web. 30 Mar. 2009. <http://www.digitalegypt.ucl.ac.uk/mummy/ok.html>

Museum, B. Mesopotamia.co.uk. Web. 27 Mar. 2009. <http://www.mesopotamia.co.uk/menu.html>

Nemat-Nejat, Karen Rhea. *Daily Life in Ancient Mesopotamia*. Westport, CT: Greenwood Press, 1998. Print.

Neumann, I. "Sublime Diplomacy: Byzantine, Early Modern, Contemporary." Clingendal.ni, 2005. Web. 29 Mar. 2009. <http://www.clingendael.nl/publications/2005/20051200_cli_paper_dip_issue102.pdf>

Newton, Isaac. *Philosophiae Naturalis Principia Mathematica*. Trans. I. Bernard Cohen and Anne Whitman, 3rd ed. San Francisco: U of California Press, 1999. Print.

Nicholas, John M. *Project Management for Business and Engineering: Principles and Practice*. Oxford: Butterworth-Heinemann, 2004. Print.

Nicole, David. *The Crusades*. New York: Osprey Publishing, 2001. Print.

Noll, Mark A. *Elwell Evangelical Dictionary of Theology*. Ada, MI: Revell, 1984. Print.

Norwich, John Julius. *Great Architecture of the World*. London: Mitchell Beazley, 1975. Print.

Numbers, Ronald. "Science without God: Natural Laws and Christian Beliefs." *When Science and Christianity Meet*. Eds. David C. Lindberg and Ronald L. Numbers. Chicago: U of Chicago Press, 2003. Print.

Nuttgens, Patrick. *The Story of Architecture*, 2nd ed. London: Phaidon Press, 1997. Print.

O'Connor, Colin. *Roman Bridges*. Cambridge: Cambridge UP, 1993. Print.

O'Leary, D. L. *How Greek Science Passed to the Arabs*. 1929. Web. 1 Apr. 2009. <http://www.aina.org/books/hgsptta.htm>

Onians, John. "Architecture, Metaphor and the Mind." *Architectural History*, 1992. Print.

Orlandi, Stefano. *S. Maria Novella and the Monumental Cloisters*. Rev. ed., trans. A. M. Greathed, rev. P. Isnardo and P. Grossi. Florence: Edition S. Becocci, 1980. Print.

Osborne, R. *Civilization: A New History of the Western World*. New York: Pegasus Books, 2006. Print.

Osigweh, C.A.B. *Professional Management: An Evolutionary Perspective*. Dubuque, IA: Kendall/Hunt, 1985. Print.

Osler, W. *The Evolution of Modern Medicine*, Kessinger Publishing, 2004. Print

Ostdiek, Vern and Bord, Donald. *Inquiry into Physics*. Belmont, CA: Thompson Brooks/Cole. Web. 22 Dec. 2009. <http://books.google.com/books?id=7kz2pd14hPUC&pg=PA123&sig=zOszHawWGqjbLs39NT9h_RidUGI>

Ousterhout, R. *The East, the West, and the Appropriation of the Past in Early Ottoman Architecture*. Gesta (2004): 165–76. Print.

Ousterhout, Robert. *Master Builders of Byzantium*. Philadelphia: U of Pennsylvania Museum of Archeology and Anthropology, 2008. Print.

*Oxford English Dictionary*. Oxford University Press, 1989. Print

Palagia, Olga. *The Pediments of the Parthenon*. Leiden: E. J. Brill, 1993. Print.

Partridge, Loren. *The Art of Renaissance Rome 1400–1600*. New York: Harry N.Abrams, 1996. Print.

Patel, Samir. "Ghost Particles and Pyramids: How Physicists and Archaeologists 'See' Inside Ancient Monuments." *Archeology* (2008). Print.

Peirce, Charles S. "How to Make Our Ideas Clear." *Popular Science Monthly* 12, 1878. Print.

Penrose, F.C. The Orientation of Geek Temples. *Nature*, 48.1228, 1893. Print.

Petersen, Andrew. *Dictionary of Islamic Architecture*. London: Routledge, 1996. Print.

Petruccioli, Attilio, and Pirani, Khalil. *Understanding Islamic Architecture*. London: RoutledgeCurzon, 2002. Print.

Phillips, Joseph. *PMP Project Management Professional Study Guide*. New York: McGraw-Hill Professional, 2003. Print.

"Philosophy – Series of Footnotes to Plato." Age-Of-The-Sage.org, 2009. Web. 31 Mar. 2009. <http://www.age-of-the-sage.org/philosophy/footnotes_plato.html>

Pierotti, Piero. *Deotisalvi: L'architetto pisano del secolo d'oro*. Pisa: Pacini Editore, 2001. Print.

Pindur, W. and S.E. Rogers *"The History of Management: A Global Perspective."* Journal of Management History Vol.1, No.1, 1995. Web. 31 Mar. 2009. <http://www.drmanage.com/images/1202965572/History%20of%20Management. pdf>

Plutarch. *Life of Pericles*. Web. 29 June. 2009.
< http://www.bostonleadershipbuilders.com/plutarch/pericles.htm>

Polastron, L. *Books on Fire: The Tumultuous Story of the World's Great Libraries*. London: Thames and Hudson, 2007. Print.

Pollock, S. *Ancient Mesopotamia: The Eden that Never Was*. Cambridge: Cambridge UP, 1999. Print.

Pomeroy, Sarah B., Stanley M. Burstein, Walter Donlan, and Jennifer Tolbert Roberts. *Ancient Greece: A Political, Social, and Cultural History*. New York: Oxford UP, 1999. Print.

*A Brief History of Ancient Greece: Politics, Society, and Culture*. New York: Oxford UP, 2004. Print.

"Project" *Wikipedia*. Web. 26 Nov. 2009. <http://en.wikipedia.org/wiki/Project# Overview>

"PMBOK Guide." *A Guide to the Project Management Body of Knowledge*, 4th ed. Newtown Square, PA: Project Management Institute, 2008. Print.

"PMBOK Guide." *A Guide to the Project Management Body of Knowledge*. 3rd ed. Newtown Square, PA: Project Management Institute, 2004. Print.

Punter, D. E. *A Companion to the Gothic*. New York: Wiley-Blackwell, 2001. Print.

Ramroth, William. *Project Management for Design Professionals.* Chicago: Kaplan, 2006. Print.
Rhodes, P. (ed.) *Athenian Democracy.* New York: Oxford UP, 2004. Print.
Rhodes, Robin Francis. *Architecture and Meaning on the Athenian Acropolis.* Cambridge: Cambridge UP, 1995. Print.
Rice Jr., Eugene F. *The Foundations of Early Modern Europe.* New York: W.W. Norton, 1970. Print.
Riley-Smith, J. *The Atlas of the Crusades.* New York: Facts on File, 1990. Print.
Robertson, D.S. *Greek and Roman Architecture,* Cambridge: Cambridge UP 1969. Print.
Robinson, O.F. *Ancient Rome: City Planning and Administration.* London: Routledge, 1922. Print.
Rodley, Lyn. *Byzantine Art and Architecture: An Introduction.* Cambridge: Cambridge UP, 1994. Print.
Rolbiecki, J. *The Political Philsophy of Dante Alighieri.* New York: General Books, 2009. Print.
"The Roman Empire." *UNRV History – Roman Empire.* Web. 11 Aug. 2009. <http://www.unrv.com/>
"Rome.info Fall of the Roman Empire, Decline of Ancient Rome." Rome Info. Web. 10 Aug. 2009. <http://www.rome.info/history/empire/fall/>
"Roman Catholicism: The Renaissance of the 12th Century." *Encyclopedia – Britannica Online Encyclopedia.* Web. 11 Aug. 2009. <http://www.britannica.com/EBchecked/topic/507284/Roman-Catholicism/257683/The-renaissance-of-the-12th-century>
Root, Mary M. "Egyptian Surveying Tools." *Surveyor History* Jan (1990). Web. Mar. 2009. <http://www.surveyhistory.org/egyptian_surveying_tools1.htm>
Roth, Leland M. *Understanding Architecture: Its Elements History and Meaning.* Oxford: Westview Press, 1993. Print.
Ruiz, Ana. *The Spirit of Ancient Egypt.* New York: Algora Publishing, 2001. Print.
Saalman, Howard. *Filippo Brunelleschi: The Cupola of Santa Maria del Fiore.* London: A. Zwemmer, 1980. Print.
Sacred Destinations. "Romanesque Architecture." Web. 22 Mar. 2009 <http://www.sacred-destinations.com/reference/romanesque-architecture>
Saggs, W.F. *Civilization before Greece and Rome.* New Haven, CT: Yale UP, 1989. Print.
Saliba, George. "Islamic Science and the Making of Renaissance Europe." Library of Congress, 27 Aug 2006. Speech. 30 Mar 2009. <http://www.loc.gov/today/cyberlc/feature_wdesc.php?rec=3883>
Saliba, George. *A History of Arabic Astronomy: Planetary Theories During the Golden Age of Islam.* New York: NYU Press, 1994. Print.
Sasson, Jack. *The Civilizations of the Ancient Near East.* New York: Charles Scribner's Sons, 1995. Print.

Sax, Margaret, Nigel D. Meeks, and Dominique Collon. "The Early Development of the Lapidary Engraving Wheel in Mesopotamia." *Iraq*, 2000. Print.

Scarre, C. *The Penguin Historical Atlas of Ancient Rome.* London: Penguin Books, 1995. Print.

Schivelbusch, Wolfgang. *The Railway Journey: The Industrialization of Time and Space in the 19th Century.* New York: Urizen Books, 1977. Print.

"The Scientific Revolution." Web. 10 Jan. 2009. <http://en.wikipedia.org/wiki/The_Scientific_Revolution>

Scofield, Bruce. "The Nature of Mesopotamian and Non-Western Astrology." Web. 28 Mar. 2009. <http://www.onereed.com/articles/nonwesternast.html>

Scott, Robert. *The Gothic Enterprise: A Guide to Understanding the Medieval Cathedral.* Berkeley: U of California Press, 2006. Print.

Sears, Frank. *Roman Architecture.* Ithaca, NY: Cornell UP, 1982. Print.

"See Strasbourg Cathedrals in France." *Suite 101.* Web. 26 Nov. 2009. <http://france-travel.suite101.com/article.cfm/see_strasbourg_cathedral_in_france>

Sharma, S., F. Casanova, W. Wache, A. Segre, and B. Blumich. "Analysis of historical porous building materials by the NMR-MOUSE®." *Magnetic Resonance Imaging* (2003): 249–55. Print.

Shaw, Ian. "Building the Great Pyramid." BBC Ancient History In Depth, 5 Nov. 2009. Web. 21 Mar. 2009. <http://www.bbc.co.uk/history/ancient/egyptians/great_pyramid_01.shtml>

"The Sienese Engineers." *Institute and Museum of the History of Science,* 2004. Web. 20 Mar. 2009. <http://brunelleschi.imss.fi.it/genindice.asp?appl=LIR&indice=63&lingua=ENG&chiave=800257&xsl=listagenerale>

Siliotto, A. *The Discovery of Ancient Egypt.* Edison, NJ: Book Sales, 1998. Print.

Singer, Charles, E.J. Holmyard, A.R. Hall, and T. I. Williams. "History of Technology." *Technology and Culture,* 1960. Print.

Singer, Charles. *A Short History of Science to the Nineteenth Century.* Oxford: Clarendon Press, 1941. Print.

Skinner, Quentin. *The Foundations of Modern Political Thought. Vol. I: The Renaissance.* London: Cambridge UP, 1978. Print.

Skinner, Quentin. *The Foundations of Modern Political Thought. Vol. II: The Age of Reformation.* London: Cambridge UP, 1978. Print.

Smail, R.C. "Crusaders' Castles of the Twelfth Century." *Cambridge Historical Journal,* 1951. Print.

Snell, Daniel C. *Life in the Ancient Near East: 3100–332 BCE.* New Haven: Yale UP, 1997. Print.

Sommerville, J.P. "The Twelfth Century Rennaissance." Web. 11 Aug. 2009.

Soo, Lydia M. "St. Paul's Cathedral." In *International Dictionary of Architects and Architecture,* ed. Randall J. Van Vynckt. 2 Vols. Volume 2: *Architecture,* 459–462. Detroit: St. James Press, 1993. Print.

Spengler, Joseph J. *Origins of Economic Thought and Justice.* Carbondale, IL: Southern Illinois UP, 1980. Print.

Stamper, John W. *The Architecture of Roman Temples: The Republic to the Middle Empire.* Cambridge: Cambridge UP, 2005. Print.

Stark, R. *God's Battalions: The Case for the Crusades.* New York: Harper One, 2009. Print.

Starn, R. Renaissance Redux. *The American Historical Review,* 103.1, 1998. Print.

Steffens, Bradley. *Ibn al-Haythan: First Scientist.* NC: Morgan Reynolds Publishing, 2006. Print.

Steiner, Frances H. *French Iron Architecture.* Ann Arbor, MI: UMI Research Press, 1984. Print.

Sterns, P. *The Industrial Revolution in World History.* New York: Westview Press, 2007. Print.

Stevens, Martin. *Project Management Pathways.* Princes Risborough: APM Publishing, 2002. Print.

Stewart, Matthew. "The Management Myth: Most of Management Theory Is Inane, Writes Our Correspondent, the Founder of a Consulting Firm. If You Want to Succeed in Business, Don't Get an M.B.A. Study Philosophy Instead." *The Atlantic Monthly* June 2006. *Questia.* Web. 12 Aug. 2009.

Stiebing Jr., William H. *Ancient Near Eastern History and Culture.* New York: Longman, 2003. Print.

Stierlin, Henri. *Unfolding History: Castles, Fortresses and Citadels.* London: Thames & Hudson, 2006. Print.

Stone, E.C., D.H. Lindsley, V.V. Pigott, G. Harbottle, and M.T. Ford. "From Shifting Silt to Solid Stone: The Manufacture of Synthetic Basalt in Ancient Mesopotamia." *Science* (1998): 2091–4. Print.

Striphas, T. *The Late Age of Print: Everyday Book Culture from Consumerism to Control.* New York: Columbia UP, 2009. Print.

Strizhak, Viktor, Igor Penkov, and Toivo Pappel. "Evolution of Design, Use, and Strength Calculations of Screw Threads and Threaded Joints."

*HMM2004 International Symposium on History of Machines and Mechanisms.* Amsterdam: Kluwer Academic Publishers, 2004. Web. 21 Dec. 2009. <http://books.google.com/books?id=FqZvlMnjqYoC&printsec=frontcover&dq=%22archimedean+simple+machine%22&source=gbs_summary_r&cad=0>

Sutcliffe, Anthony. *London: An Architectural History.* New Haven: Yale UP, 2006. Print.

Sweeney, James Ross. "Chivalry." *Dictionary of the Middle Ages Vol. III.* Ed. Joseph R. Strayer. New York: Charles Scribner's Sons, 1983. Print.

Tatakes, Vasileios N. and Moutafakis, Nicholas J. *Byzantine Philosophy.* Indianopolis: Hackett Publishing, 2003. Print.

Tavernor, Robert. *On Alberti and the Art of Building.* New Haven: Yale UP, 1998. Print.

Taylor, Rabun. *Roman Builders: A Study in Architectural Process.* Cambridge: Cambridge UP, 2003. Print.

Taylor, Frederick W. *The Principles of Scientific Management.* New York: Harper Bros., 1911. Print.

Temko, Allan. *Notre-Dame of Paris.* New York: Time, 1962. Print.

Terenzio, Alberto. "La Restauration du Pantheon de Rome." *Institut de Cooperation Intellectuelle* (1933): 280–285. Print.

"Theopedia, John Calvin." *Theopedia.* Web. 11 Nov. 2009. <http://www.theopedia.com/John_Calvin#The_Protestant_work_ethic>

*Thinkquest.Org,* 1999. Web. 27 Mar. 2009. <http://library.thinkquest.org/26602/government.htm>

"Third Industrial Revolution 1940's–today." *Wikipedia.* Web. 26 Nov. 2009. <http://lessons-from-history/node/56>

Thompson, Peter, Georgia Papadopoulou, and Eleni Vassiliou. "The Origins of *Entasis*: Illusion, Aesthetics or Engineering?" *Spatial Vision* (2007). Print.

Thurston, Hugh. *Early Astronomy.* New York: Springer, 1994. Print.

Toman, R. A. *Romanesque: Architecture, Sculpture, Painting.* Duncan, SC: H.F. Ullman, 2008. Print.

Trafton, S. *Egypt Land.* Duke UP, 2007. Print.

Turnbull, D. "The ad hoc Collective Work of Building Gothic Cathedrals with Templates, String, and Geometry." *Science, Technology, and Human Values,* 1993. Print.

Turner, Howard. *Science in Medieval Islam.* Austin: U of Texas Press, 1997. Print.

Tyerman, Christopher. *God's War, A New History of the Crusades.* Cambridge, MA: Harvard UP, 2006. Print.

Van De Mieroop, M. *King Hammurabi of Babylon.* New York: Blackwell, 2005. Print.

Van Doren, Charles. *A History of Knowledge.* New York: Ballantine, 1991. Print.

Vanderpool, James Groat. "A Comparison of Byzantine Planning at Constantinople and in Greece." *The Art Bulletin,* 1936. Print.

VanMilligan, Alexander. *Byzantine Churches in Constantinople.* London: Macmillan, 1912. Print.

Vitruvius. *Wikipedia.* Web. 12 Nov. 2000. <http://en.wikipedia.org/wiki/Vitruvius>

Vitruvius, Marcus. *The Ten Books of Architecture Online.* Web. <http://penelope.uchicago.edu/Thayer/E/Roman/Texts/Vitruvius/home.html>

Walker, Frank. *The Italian Renaissance.* New York: Facts on File, 1995. Print.

Walker, Paul Robert. *The Feud that Sparked the Renaissance: How Brunelleschi and Ghiberti Changed the Art World.* New York: William Morrow, 2002. Print.

Ward-Perkins, John B. *Roman Architecture.* Milan: Electra, 2003. Print.

*Roman Imperial Architecture.* 2nd ed. New York: Penguin, 1981. Print.

Warner, M. and Witzel, M. "General Management: Back to the Future. *Human Systems Management* 16.4, 1997. Print.

Warner, Rex. *Thucydides: The History of the Peloponnesian War.* Rev. and trans. London: Penguin Group, 1972. Print.

Warren, John. "Creswell's Use of the Theory of Dating by the Acuteness of the Pointed Arches in Early Muslim Architecture." *Muqarnas* 8, 1991. Print.

Weaver, Patrick. "The Origins of Modern Project Management." *PM World Today*. Mar. 2008. Web. 23 March 2009. <http://www.pmforum.org/library/second-edition/2008/PDFs/Weaver-3-08.pdf>

Weaver, Patrick. "A Brief History of Project Management." *APM Project* 19.11, 2007. Web. 23 March 2009 <http://www.mosaicprojects.com.au/PDF_Papers/P061a_A_Brief_History_of_Project_Management.pdf>

Weber, Max. *The Protestant Ethic and the Spirit of Capitalism*. Trans. Peter Baehr and Gordon C. Wells. London: Penguin Books, 2002. Print.

Weightman, G. *Industrial Revolutionaries: The Making of the Modern World*. New York: Grove Press, 2009. Print.

Westfall, Richard S. Preface to *Opticks* (1704), quoted in *Never at Rest: A Biography of Isaac Newton*, Richard S. Westfall. Cambridge, Cambridge Paperback Library, 1983. Print.

West, Martin. *The Oxford History of Greece and the Hellenistic World, Chapter 5: The Early Greek Philosophy*. Oxford UP, 2001. Print.

*What is Civil Engineering?* "History of Engineering." Web. 22 Mar. 2009. <http://whatiscivilengineering.csce.ca/history_engineering.htm>

Wiet, Gaston. *"Golden Age of Arab and Islamic Culture: Chapter 5."* Bagdhad: Metropolis of the Abbasid Caliphat. Web. 20 Mar. 2009. <http://www.khamush.com/sufism/golden.htm>

Wikander, Orjan. "Archaic Roof Tiles the First Generations." *Hesperia*, 59.1, 1990. Print.

Wildford, John. "Discovery of Egyptian Inscriptions Indicates an Earlier Date for Origin of Alphabet." *New York Times* 13 Nov (1999). Web. 29 Mar. 2009. <http://www.nytimes.com/library/national/science/111499sci-alphabet-origin.html>

Wilkins, Robert. "Neurosurgical Classic-XVII Edwin Smith Surgical Papyrus." *Journal of Neurosurgery* March (1964). Print.

Williams, B. *The Age of Knights and Castles*. Chicago: World Books, 1996. Print.

"William Whewell." *Encyclopedia Britannica*. Web. 29 April 2009. <http://www.britannica.com/EBchecked/topic/641764/William-Whewell>

Wilson, Andrew. "Machines, Power, and the Ancient Economy." *The Journal of Roman Studies*, 2002. Print.

Wilson, Arthur. *The Living Rock: The Story of Metals since Earliest Times and Their Impact on Civilization*. Cambridge: Woodhead Publishing, 1994. Print.

Wittkower, R. "Brunelleschi and 'Proportion in Perspective'." *Journal of the Warburg and Courtauld Institutes*, 1953. Print.

Witzel, Morgen. *Fifty Key Figures in Management*. Kentucky: Routledge, 2003. Print.

Woods, C. Bilingualism, "Scribal Learning, and the Death of Sumerian." *Margins of Writing, Origins of Culture*, ed. S. Sanders, 91–210. Chicago: U of Chicago Press, 2006. Print.

Wrege, C.D. and R.M. Hodgetts "Frederick W. Taylor's 1899 Pig Iron Observations: Examining Fact, Fiction, and Lessons for the New Millennium." *Academy of Management Journal*, 43.6, 2000. Print.

Wren, Daniel A. *The Evolution of Management Thought.* 4th ed. San Francisco: John Wiley & Sons, 1994. Print.

*The History of Management Thought.* 5th ed. San Francisco: John Wiley & Sons, 2004. Print.

Yenne, Bill and Martin Grosser. *100 Inventions That Shaped World History.* San Mateo: Bluewood Books, 1993. Print.

Yeomans, Richard. *The Story of Islamic Architecture.* New York: New York UP, 2000. Print.

# Index

**D**



**E**

**Q**



**R**

Printed in Great Britain
by Amazon

40033777R00146